The Soil

THE NISSAN INSTITUTE/ROUTLEDGE JAPANESE STUDIES

Editorial Board:

The Soil

Nagatsuka Takashi

A Portrait of Rural Life in Meiji Japan

translated and with an introduction by

Ann Waswo

R

ROUTLEDGE
London and New York

First published 1989 by Routledge
11 New Fetter Lane, London EC4P 4EE
29 West 35th Street, New York NY 10001

Typeset by Pat and Anne Murphy, Highcliffe-on-Sea, Dorset
Printed in Great Britain by
Billing & Sons Ltd, Worcester

British Library Cataloguing in Publication Data

Nagatsuka, Takashi
    The Soil: a portrait of rural life in Meiji Japan —
    (The Nissan Institute Routledge Japanese studies series)
    1. Fiction in Japanese, 1868–1945 —
    English texts
    I. Title   II. Tsuchi. *English*
    895.6'34 [F]

    ISBN 0-415-03074-9

Library of Congress Cataloging-in-Publication Data

Nagatsuka, Takashi, 1879–1915.
    [Tsuchi. English]
    The Soil / by Nagatsuka Takashi: a portrait of rural life in
Meiji Japan, translated and with an introduction by Ann Waswo.
    p.   cm. — (The Nissan Institute/Routledge Japanese studies series)
    Translation of: Tsuchi.
    1. Nagatsuka, Takashi, 1879–1915 — Translations, English.
    I. Waswo, Ann.   II. Title.   III. Series.
    PL812.A46T713   1989
    895.6'34 — dc 19   88-34308 CIP

    ISBN 0-415-03074-9

Contents

Acknowledgments

I first learned of the existence of *Tsuchi (The Soil)* some twenty years ago when I was a graduate student in Tokyo collecting material for what later became a book about Japanese landlords. During one of my infrequent but always useful visits to my unofficial mentor, Professor Furushima Toshio, then Dean of the Faculty of Agriculture at Tokyo University, I had somehow felt emboldened to complain that after several months' work in libraries I was saturated with information about crop yields, rent levels and the concentration of land ownership in the Meiji era (1868–1912). 'Couldn't you suggest some books about the texture of rural life at the time?', I asked. Professor Furushima smiled, ruefully I thought, and replied that since he and many other Japanese scholars of his generation had grown up in villages or small towns and knew what the texture of rural life was like, they had not dealt with that facet of the country's agrarian history in their work. 'You ought to read *Tsuchi*', he advised, and so, eventually, I did.

At the outset my intention was simply to mine the novel, as other historians have mined other novels, for anecdotal information about rural values, customs and social relations. That I subsequently took the more radical decision to translate it in its entirety stemmed primarily from my realization that although *Tsuchi* was undeniably a novel it was simultaneously an informal ethnography of a rural community and its inhabitants in the early 1900s and, as such, a valuable historical document.

Except for the dialect the characters speak, which I have found no viable way of capturing in English, and a relatively small number of Japanese terms that are defined in an appended glossary, I have tried to provide as accurate and as complete a translation as I could. I should emphasize, however, that it has been as an historian and not as a specialist in literature that I have approached the task. To be frank, the ethnographic features of the novel have always interested me more than its equally careful observations about natural phenomena, and I am quite sure that this bias, despite my efforts to control it, is still reflected in my rendering of the text. I am also quite sure that I have failed to notice, much less to correct, what others more skilled in Japanese than I will detect as blatant errors of translation. For the latter, especially if they result in misconstruction of the narrative, I apologize.

Without in any way tainting them with responsibility for such errors, or for other shortcomings in what follows, I would like to thank Gail Bernstein, Karin Blair, Sarah Metzger-Court, Eiichi Motono, Arthur Stockwin, Richard Waswo, and in Japan Watanabe Yoshio, Shirai Atsushi, Shirai Takako, Noguchi Mitsuo, Nagase Jun'ichi and Kawamura Yoshio (whose own translation of the novel was privately published in Japan in 1986) for the special help they have given me at one time or another during the rather long time it has taken me to get this translation finished. I would also like to thank the University of Virginia and the Inter-Faculty Committee for Japanese studies, University of Oxford, for financial support at the beginning and end of the project.

A.W.
Oxford, 1988

Translator's introduction

The hamlet of Kossho, now part of the town of Ishige, lies on the western bank of the Kinu River in Ibaraki Prefecture, some 44 miles as the crow flies to the northwest of Tokyo. There on the 3rd of April 1879 Nagatsuka Takashi was born, the first son of a substantial landowning family, and there, at his family home and at a desk in the library of the village school during the spring and summer of 1910, he wrote *Tsuchi (The Soil)*, his only novel. Serialized in the *Tokyo Asahi Newspaper* in 151 installments between June and November of that same year, the complete novel was published in book form in 1912. Three years later, on the 8th of February 1915, its author, not quite 37 years old, died of laryngeal tuberculosis.

The community depicted in *The Soil* is Kossho, the author's native place, and the characters whose lives are examined in minute detail over a period of some six or seven years are all drawn from life, so unambiguously and vividly at times that a few local residents — notably 'Otsugi' (about whom, more later) — are said to have been embarrassed by the special attention the novel focused upon them. Their discomfort, itself indicative of a belief that is still widespread in the Japanese countryside (and perhaps in all small communities everywhere) that not being talked about is proof that one is behaving properly, is also testimony to Nagatsuka's powers of observation and to his determination to provide a realistic portrait of village life.

I do not have the sense that Nagatsuka meant to embarrass anyone in Kossho, least of all 'Otsugi', who emerges in the novel as a warm and sympathetic figure. Nor, on those occasions when he as author/narrator adopts a somewhat didactic tone, is he trying to instruct or uplift his fellow villagers. On the contrary he is seeking to explain the 'old', agrarian Japan and its problems to the denizens of the 'new', urbanized and industrializing Japan, who were in a position to read the *Tokyo Asahi Newspaper* and who

viii

usually gave no thought to those, still the overwhelming majority of the Japanese population, who were not full participants in the nation's modern transformation. (See, for example, the opening paragraphs of Chapter 7.)

I use the term 'fellow villagers' advisedly, for Nagatsuka, despite being born a wealthy farmer's son and despite having had access to education and experience in the wider world beyond the hamlet of his birth, was none the less a man of Kossho, and albeit in a somewhat attenuated form, a man of the soil. Not long after ill health forced him to withdraw from middle school in Mito in 1896 at the end of his third year of study, his duty as an eldest son required him to begin assisting his mother Taka (the model for Okamisan, the mistress, in the novel) in the day-to-day management of the family's substantial but dwindling acreage of forest and arable land, a task that had been left to her since the late 1880s when her husband Genjirō had first been elected to the prefectural assembly.

Although Nagatsuka was still able to pursue the literary interests he had developed while in school, and for a brief but crucially important period between 1900 and 1902 to study poetry in Tokyo with Masaoka Shiki, an advocate of *shasei* (or 'sketches from life'), more and more of his time was spent in farming the six acres the family cultivated itself with the help of hired labor. From about 1905 he began experimenting with fertilizers, crop rotation, charcoal making, raising bamboo for commercial sale, and other measures he hoped would rescue the family from a financial crisis caused by his father's political career and, it would appear, by his father's sometimes rash willingness to stand as guarantor for the debts of others.

As a result, by the time he wrote *The Soil* Nagatsuka was well aware of the difficulties local farmers faced in wresting a livelihood from the none-too-rich loamy soil of the district and of the disadvantages they experienced now that their community, once well situated for water transport to the capital, had been bypassed by the railroad and become a hinterland of sorts. To these insights were added many details of everyday life in the community he had recorded in one of the notebooks he carried with him at all times, the literary skills he had honed since leaving school in writing poems, essays, and short stories, and a keen ear for status distinctions in speech and for *Ibaraki-ben*, the local dialect.

Like most Japanese novels of the early twentieth century, *The Soil* is slowly paced, more concerned with mood and the minutiae of daily life than with dramatic events. It is filled with descriptions of nature. Indeed, natural phenomena and the experiences of human beings are closely intertwined in the narrative. (See, for example, the opening paragraphs of Chapters 6 and 14.)

The Soil differs from most other novels of its time in that it focuses not on political or intellectual elites, or upwardly mobile young men seized by identity crises, but on ordinary people. The main characters are members of a tenant farming family. At the outset, the wife, Oshina, dies from a self-induced abortion. Despite her grisly death, Oshina remains a presence in the book thereafter, both by means of a series of flashbacks in which her husband, Kanji, remembers their life together, and by means of Otsugi, their daughter, who was 15 when her mother died and who becomes more and more like her — dutiful, to be sure, but also resourceful, determined and resilient — as she assumes the adult roles of farm laborer, housekeeper, and surrogate mother to her younger brother, Yokichi. Kanji, who is physically strong but more than a little weak-willed, provides Otsugi with ample opportunities to demonstrate her mettle (as did her mother before her) by rescuing him from the trouble he gets into — principally, but not exclusively, by stealing food. It is by means of this trouble and by means of Kanji's strained relationship with Uhei, his dead wife's stepfather, that the reader encounters the larger community in which Kanji and his children live.

What emerges is a very sensitive and, in my view, psychologically sophisticated portrait of its central characters and of the community as a whole. In addition, the novel provides a wealth of information about farming, courtship, marriage, child-rearing, health care, the lives and problems of the elderly (such as Uhei), folk religion, and funeral customs in the late Meiji era. What I consider its greatest strength is its portrayal of covert and overt tensions within the community: the persistent and sometimes vicious gossip, the petty and not so petty rivalries, and the ways in which conflict was contained.

At only one point in the novel, toward the end of Chapter 19, does Nagatsuka specify the acreage that Kanji has planted to a particular crop. Nor are we told precisely how land ownership and cultivating rights were distributed among the inhabitants of the village. It becomes clear, however, that Kanji is one of a number of poor farmers at the bottom of an economic and social hierarchy that culminates in the master, East Neighbor (so referred to by Kanji because the master's house lies to the east of his own).

Kanji possesses no land and must pay rent in kind to the owners of the fields he cultivates. Again, we are not told precisely how much rent he pays, but we discover that, having paid it, he lacks enough food to tide himself and his family over until the next harvest. Hence his need to seek paid employment during the winter months and his dependence on, and consequent deference toward, East Neighbor.

While she lived, Oshina added to the family's cash income by peddling foodstuffs in the surrounding countryside and by selling eggs to the other peddlers who came to her door, but their primary activity was, and remains, farming. Kanji's fields are scattered throughout the village — a paddy field directly below the house; two (or more) upland, or dry fields some distance away on which he grows barley, millet, soybeans, winter wheat, and vegetables; and, eventually, some newly reclaimed fields in the forest for growing upland rice. In all probability he cultivated no more than about 2 acres of land in all.

Others in the community, such as Kanji's South Neighbor, had larger holdings (whether owned, tenanted, or a combination of both) and were able to devote some of their land to such potentially lucrative crops as mulberry, whose leaves were fed to silkworms, or to vegetables, which they then took to market to sell. Some owned a horse for use in plowing fields and transporting produce, but most relied on the labor of able-bodied members of their families in the day-to-day chores of farming. For such major tasks as the transplanting of rice seedlings into paddy fields or maintaining the irrigation system so essential to wet rice culture, however, villagers pooled their labor. In addition, more informal labor exchanges (or the exchange of labor for the use of special tools or implements) such as that between Kanji and South Neighbor took place from time to time.

There are two 'outsiders' resident in the village: the policeman and the schoolteacher. In accordance with prevailing administrative practice, these representatives of the Meiji state had been posted to a community other than that of their birth in order to ensure their impartiality and their responsiveness to directives from Tokyo. While the teacher remains a shadowy figure who is referred to in passing but never seen, the policeman is portrayed as a rather arrogant posturer. Neither of these outsiders can be considered a farmer, although both may have raised a few vegetables or some rice on the side, but everyone else in the village, with the possible but unlikely exception of the proprietor of the village shop, depended on farming to an important extent.

In these respects, as a place where labor-intensive, small-scale family farming prevailed, the community depicted in the novel was fairly typical of rural Japan in the early 1900s. That said, it was certainly better off than some of the villages across the Kinu River, where firewood was scarce and floods an almost annual occurrence, and better off still than communities deep in the mountains, where the soil was poorer, the growing season shorter, and markets even further away. Yet, as noted previously, Kossho had been bypassed by the new railroad and had become a hinterland of sorts. Changes there were — less unsettling, perhaps, but also less remunerative than changes in more favored locations. Only the more affluent local farmers can afford the new biological fertilizers; only East Neighbor regularly travels outside the community and has the literacy and *savoir faire* to deal with such 'alien' forces as the police; only his wife knows of, and is regularly able to take advantage of, the lower prices and higher quality of consumer goods on sale in town.

To be sure, the master and mistress have no worries about getting enough to eat, as Oshina observes in a flashback, and unlike other villagers they do not lace their rice with large quantities of barley to stretch the supply. Moreover, they have employees to do much if not all of the physical labor in producing the food they consume. Yet even allowing for the sentimental bias in Nagatsuka's portrayal of the mistress — he was, after all, writing about his own mother — it is clear that East Neighbor's family remains 'of the village' and involved, directly and indirectly, in its affairs. Precisely because they are relatively affluent and possess knowledge of the wider world, they are part of the cement that holds the community together. They are probably the donors of the good-quality sake and sushi to the participants in the sun-chanting ceremony described in Chapters 22 and 23; they provide advice and casual employment to others; and the mistress, in particular, plays an active role in settling local quarrels. The other villagers respect them and value the services they provide.

If East Neighbor's family was the apex of the community, Kanji's was the nadir, as symbolized by the marginal position of his decrepit house on the westernmost edge of the village. That house was Oshina's natal place, and Kanji, like Uhei before him, had married into her family as an adopted son-in-law. This was a fairly common practice in both rural and urban Japan, resorted to as a means of maintaining the family line when there was no son. The adopted son-in-law, like an inheriting (usually first-born) son, became househead upon the retirement of his wife's father and assumed responsibility for managing the family property (however exiguous), carrying on the family occupation and officiating at memorial rites for deceased members of the family.

Having entered the family by means of marriage, neither Uhei nor Kanji has the full authority of an inheriting son. Thus Uhei defers to Oshina's other relatives when her elopement with Kanji is discussed, and although there were additional reasons for it Kanji defers to Oshina throughout their life together. In other respects, however, the situation of both men is fairly typical for the time and place. They had both married women of their own choosing, with whom they had had premarital sexual relations and for whom they had a strong attachment. Not until later did the practice of arranged marriage between individuals who had little or no previous acquaintance with one another — essentially the practice of Japan's warrior class during the preceding Tokugawa period — penetrate to ordinary residents of the countryside.

An element of the warrior ethos that *had* penetrated the countryside was the Confucian ethic of filial piety. A child was held to be indebted to his or her parents for the gift of life and for the nurture received in infancy. That debt must be repaid by respect and obedience and by support of the parents in their old age.

Having come to dislike Uhei, Kanji is less than assiduous in the performance of filial piety toward him. Indeed, the conflict between the two men is one of the major themes of the novel. With his own children, however, Kanji is somewhat more caring, although he is constrained by poverty in demonstrating his affection for them. One senses, too, that he has been psychologically wounded by the loss of his wife. Oshina was more to him than the energetic co-worker necessary to the family's survival; she also supplied the warmth and compassion that he somehow lacked himself. Without her to guide him, he steadily degenerates into a lesser, purely physical being who is gruffer than he intends to be with Otsugi and who ignores many of the norms and values of the community.

The modern reader cannot help wondering if the pampered, unrelentingly self-centered Yokichi is another Kanji in the making. To be sure, it is the major female figures in the novel — first Oshina and then Otsugi — who pamper him the most and who deny themselves food or much-needed rest in the process. Although the terminology would have been unknown to its author, *The Soil* also sheds light on gender-role socialization in the home and the resultant emotional dependence of males on females in late Meiji Japan.

Although the women portrayed in the novel do not conform to the prevailing (and highly problematic) stereotype of the weak and submissive Japanese female, they clearly do occupy a distinct social niche in their families and within the community as a whole. Their speech is generally more polite than that of males; they linger in the kitchen at celebratory meals while their menfolk eat and drink their fill; while Yokichi goes off to the village school, his older sister's formal education consists of sewing lessons. As Kanji's own older sister, Otsuta, reveals in extreme form, however, they are not incapable of highly manipulative and even self-serving behavior. Perhaps because, as daughters, they were coddled only briefly as infants before being introduced to responsibility, they are strong in a deeper way than the men who perform the heaviest manual labor in farming and who nominally exercise authority over them.

Both men and women take part in the gossip that is a staple of village life. The village is, after all, the center of their world, and they are keenly interested in what occurs or appears to be occurring within it. Like gossips everywhere, they are prone to put the worst possible construction on events until, as in the case of Kanji's relationship with Otsugi, they perceive evidence to the contrary. At the same time, they will rally to the support of those who are in difficulty, as they do in providing condolence money to Kanji after Oshina's death or in aiding (the one more, the other less as befits their respective statuses) both the master and Kanji during the catastrophe that moves the novel toward its conclusion.

Kanji, who is at first too poor to engage in 'simple acts of friendship' and then too stingy to do so, is not really a full-fledged member of the community. Just as he looks down on the women he encounters on his trip across the river to the blacksmith's in Chapter 7 and gains satisfaction from discovering people worse off than himself, so too his neighbors tend to look down on him. We learn in Chapter 14 that he was teased and ridiculed as a child, and in Chapter 8 we see Yokichi being subjected to similar treatment by his playmates. In both cases it is their inferior status that makes them vulnerable.

It is chiefly Kanji's violation of community norms and values as an adult, however, that accounts for the low opinion that others have of him. He will not do the 'proper' thing and marry Otsugi off (or adopt a husband for her) when she reaches 20; he begrudges Uhei the food and shelter to which he is entitled; when he craves fresh vegetables he steals them from within the community instead of from fields in an adjacent village. Immune to the indirect warning he receives from the master, he runs afoul of the law for stealing oak stumps and is only saved from prison by the timely, if somewhat convoluted, intervention of the mistress. What appears to make a good citizen of him at last, in the final pages of the novel, is not pressure from the community to conform — although those pressures are great — but his fear of further loss, further punishment at the hands of the gods, and more trouble with the police.

The ethnographic reading I have just given represents only one of a number of readings of the novel. Over time, *The Soil* has created a series of images of rural life in the late Meiji era. To be more accurate, readers of the novel have responded to its content — which, in a narrow sense, is fixed — in differing ways at different times. As I see it, roughly the following (sometimes overlapping) sequence of readings has occurred: (1) the novel as bestiality; (2) the novel as false consciousness; (3) the novel as exemplar of the healing powers of community; (4) the novel as ethnography (or social history); (5) the novel as paradise lost; and (6) the novel as entrance examination fodder.

I have already discussed the fourth reading, which flourished in the 1960s and early 1970s and to which many specialists in rural social history still adhere. Let me now describe each of the others.

Natsume Sōseki, who was responsible for the literary pages of the *Tokyo Asahi* in late Meiji, had formed a favorable opinion of one of Nagatsuka's short stories and had invited him to write a novel for serialization in the paper. *The Soil* was the result, and, at first, response to its appearance was good: the critics were impressed, and copies of the paper continued to sell as well as in the past. By September of 1910, however, when eighty installments had been carried, Nagatsuka was contacted by a member of the editorial staff and told, decorously but definitely, that it would be appreciated if he would wrap the story up as soon as possible; it was not a novel for 'the common reader', and female students in particular did not appear to like it.

The discomfort conveyed in this demarche, which Nagatsuka ignored, was more clearly expressed in Sōseki's introduction to the 1912 publication of the novel by Shunyōdō. The introduction is said to have been written in Sōseki's typically candid style. I think there was more to it than that: Sōseki did not like the novel, there is a begrudging tone to what he wrote — something more than candor — and one suspects he would have distanced himself from the project entirely had Nagatsuka not come to him personally to solicit his participation and been ailing from the disease that would kill him in a few years' time. Consider the following excerpts from Sōseki's introduction:

The characters in *The Soil* are the poorest of farmers. They have no education, no dignity. Their lives are like those of maggots hatched out of the soil. Nagatsuka . . . portrays every detail of their almost beastly, impoverished lives. He describes their vulgarity, shallowness, superstitiousness, simple-mindedness, cunning. . . .

Those who read *The Soil* will feel themselves dragged into the mud. That is certainly how I felt. Some may wonder why Nagatsuka wrote a book that is so painful to read. To them I would reply: might it not be beneficial . . . to recognize the tragic fact that in this very era such [wretched] people are living in the countryside, and not very far from the capital? For my part, I hope that young men and women who yearn for pleasure will find the courage to read *The Soil*, even though it is painful. When my daughters are older and talk of going to concerts and plays . . . I will give them *The Soil* to read. No doubt they will complain and ask for some more entertaining romantic novels instead. But I will tell them to read it . . . [precisely] because it is painful to do so. I will advise them to persevere in reading it . . . to learn about the world, so that something of the dark, dreadful shadows of life will be [impressed] upon their character. I firmly believe that among young women (and young men as well) who have grown up in comfort without any cares whatsoever, a devout and pious disposition can only arise from deep within these dark shadows.

In essence, Sōseki is repelled by the image of rural life he discovers: farmers are the repository of all the 'evil customs of the past' that Meiji Japan had renounced, an affront to the Meiji dream of Japan's economic, political, and social transformation into a 'first-rate' country. Nothing can be done for them, but 'the dark, dreadful shadows' they cast can be put to use as a character-building exercise for the privileged young.

During the 1920s and early 1930s a new reading of the novel surfaced, that which I have termed 'the novel as false consciousness'. To Marxist-Leninists and the left in general, farmers were, objectively, an oppressed proletariat. Nagatsuka's treatment of them and of the community in which they lived was too loving, too subjective. Given his class origins, as a landlord's son, it was not surprising, in their view, that he had nothing to say about the causes of Kanji's poverty or about its cure. The novel was, at best, irrelevant; if believed, especially if believed by farmers, it was counter-revolutionary.

In the mid to late 1930s, yet another new reading appeared, as Japan mobilized for war. First in a stage play and then in a film by Uchida Tomu in 1939, *The Soil* became a celebration of community. Kanji, the loner, was brought back to normality and his proper sense of parental and filial duty by the agency of others — the mistress in particular; the slightly built old man who cares for Uhei, his friend from childhood days; and the villagers' collective wish to preserve harmony. I saw the film, except for its missing first reel, in Tokyo in 1979. I confess that I could not understand all the dialogue — reading *Ibaraki-ben* is difficult enough — but I detected little of the communal malice that I find in the novel. Instead, the emphasis was upbeat; the message — that by working together everything, even the New Order, was possible.

Skipping over the fourth reading, we arrive at the fifth, the novel as paradise lost. This I would date from the late 1970s, when country restaurants (*inaka-ryōriya*) sprang up in Tokyo (and perhaps elsewhere in urban Japan); when a bar serving 'famine food' as snacks opened in the Tokyo district of Ikebukuro; when farmers in villages not too far from metropolitan centers began redecorating their homes with sunken hearths (*irori*) and other features of a vaguely remembered rural life so as to attract urban tourists. *The Soil* began to be read again in these years. No doubt a contributing factor was that, as of the mid-1960s, it had entered the public domain: there were no copyrights to pay for, and so a series of easily affordable paperback editions appeared. While the book became a cult novel for literati, who admired its imagery, it became a different kind of cult novel for general readers who admired the simplicity and purity of the rural life it portrayed.

One such general reader was Yamashita Sōichi, a farmer (and writer) from Saga Prefecture, who reported in the pages of the *Asahi Newspaper* that he had been reading *The Soil* once a decade since his youth. The previous time he had done so he had found it rather 'boring', but this time the 'richness' of the life it portrayed had become clear to him. The villagers lived in harmony with a bountiful nature; they ate safe, uncontaminated food; old people were well-cared for by the community, in contrast to rural Japan today, where the suicide rate among the elderly surpasses that of urban Japan.

Finally we come to the present, and the appearance of *The Soil* in the Japanese-language (*kokugo*) section of the 1986 university common preliminary entrance examination. The opening pages of the novel are quoted, followed by eight multiple-choice questions. Three of the latter test reading comprehension skills in a narrow sense: e.g. the precise sequence of events in Oshina's descent from the forest to the paddy field and on to her own house. One tests understanding of a literary device, and the remaining four concern interpretation of the passage. The last of these is about the 'meaning' of the passage as a whole. Two of the five choices offered are clearly inappropriate; two of the others are plausible enough, especially if one had read the entire novel; the 'right' answer deals strictly with the opening pages and is rather blandly descriptive.

The Soil, a vibrant and richly nuanced novel, is thus reduced to a tightly constrained linguistic/literary exercise. As with Sōseki's introduction, here again the young are targets of the exercise, but now it is not their character that is at issue. They are reading for a good score, not for edification. In making a testable 'object' of *The Soil* the examiners have demonstrated, no doubt unwittingly, just how remote and marginal village life has become in today's highly urbanized and affluent Japan.

1

The powerful west wind had tormented the forest all day, striking the trees with invisible blows until the leafless branches moaned in pain. Now the winter sun, emanating a yellow glow, was about to set. Abruptly the wind ceased, although dust-laden clouds hung uneasily above the treetops threatening another assault. As if remembering their suffering, the branches trembled from time to time, their rustling breaking the eerie silence.

Once again Oshina put down her shoulder pole and buckets. It was her custom in her spare time to go about from village to village peddling bean curd. Since she took only what she could carry in her buckets, little capital was required. Of course her earnings were also meager, but it was better than relying on farming alone. If she went her usual route through the countryside she would sell all she carried. On the return trip, after she emptied out the water and broken bits of bean curd, her pole would be lighter, and in her purse would be a little cash for everyday expenses. At all hours of the day, as long as there was light, Oshina kept busy at one task or another; soaking straw for rope-making, sweeping up leaves, her hands were never idle. She had always been strong and healthy, though, and did not mind incessant work.

On this particular day she had not wanted to leave home, but the winter solstice was coming and she had felt she must go out to get some *konnyaku* to sell. If she did not hurry the other peddlers who appeared at this time of year would cover her territory before her. Since there was no *konnyaku* in her own village she had to go some distance for it across the fields and through the forests. Thinking that she might do a little business on the way, she had carried some bean curd along. The strong wind that had arisen the night before slowed her progress. Her whole body shivered from the cold, and her hands, red from reaching into the icy water to scoop out bean curd, burned painfully. At some of her stops she had been able to warm herself briefly by a fire, but now it was late, her errand having taken far longer than she had anticipated. She hurried back towards her own village, through seemingly endless forest, fighting the wind all the way. She had felt tired and strangely listless, and several times she had stopped at the edge of the path to rest.

Now she stopped again, collapsing to her knees and leaning wearily against her shoulder pole. She looked miserable and disheveled. What was left of the wind blew from behind her and caught the edge of the dirty scarf she had tied about her head. It lifted her oily, red-tinged hair and revealed the soiled nape of her neck. As she sat there the trees continued their restless movement. Again and again the treetops by the side of the road bent forward as if to peek at Oshina below. After a time they moved back in unison. Shaking from side to side, they creaked and rustled noisily.

Sitting there, Oshina became aware of a growing numbness inside her, and for a moment she panicked. 'It's been a few days,' she thought to herself, 'It must be all right.' But she felt as if she were sinking. 'I'm just a little dizzy,' she thought again. Then there was a ringing in her ears, so loud that she could hear nothing else. Suddenly she came to and briskly shouldered her pole. She moved on through the forest until finally she could see the rice paddies. Just beyong them was the village, and right at the edge of the paddies, her own house. Blue smoke was rising up into the sky from the roof. Oshina thought anxiously of her two children. It was only about 30 or 40 feet down from the edge of the forest to the paddy fields, but rainfall had gouged out deep depressions in the slope. Oshina turned sideways and climbed down carefully, her right hand steadying the front bucket on her pole and her left hand on the rear. The weight of the *konnyaku* inside the buckets made it hard for her to retain her balance, but at last she made it down, her straw sandals covered with slush. There was an irrigation ditch along the length of the tiny paddy fields. Where a few large black alders stood was a narrow bridge. Oshina paused a moment at the ditch and looked ahead to her house. The village was on a rise, and behind her house were more trees. Some of them grew on the hillside and partially blocked her view, but through the empty branches of one particularly fine oak tree she saw the dented roof. Five or six chickens were making their way up from the paddy fields, scratching at the ground in search of food. Oshina carefully crossed the bridge. Although the sun had set it was still light, and for as far as she could see everything was bathed in a yellowish brown glow. Before climbing up from the fields Oshina put down her pole and made her way to a silverberry bush that stood at the base of the hillside. The chickens had been there, clawing the newly dug soil. She pressed it firm again with her foot. By now the wind had stopped completely. Not even the leaves of the radishes hung up to dry in the chestnut tree in her yard were moving. The chickens ran up and darted hopefully around Oshina's ankles, but today she paid no attention to them. Putting down her pole in the doorway, she called abruptly, 'Otsū?'

'Mother?' Otsugi replied immediately. Since the rain doors had been left closed that day the inside of the house was quite dark. Oshina had been unable to make out her daughter's form at first, but now Otsugi turned, and Oshina could see the red flames in the stove by which Otsugi sat.

'Mama! Mama!' Yokichi, strapped to his sister's back, waved his arms impatiently. While Otsugi untied him Oshina put down the buckets of *konnyaku* next to some straw bales in the corner of the dirt-floored kitchen. Then she picked up Yokichi, who began searching for her nipple, and sat down by the fire. Nearby a chicken was climbing awkwardly up to the roost, digging its claws into the makeshift rope ladder, both wings flapping. Up amid the blue smoke it quietly shut its eyes.

Since returning home Oshina had become a little warmer, but still she could not stop shivering. 'After a while,' she thought, 'we'll go out and have a bath at one of the neighbors. If I can just get warm again, I'll be fine.' A small pot sat on the stove, the soup inside it boiling. Outside it was completely dark. Otsugi took a burning faggot from the fire and lit the lantern. Then Oshina could see that her daughter wore only an unlined kimono and a short jacket. Normally she would have said nothing, but since she herself was so cold she felt irritated.

'Aren't you cold, dressed like that?' she asked sharply.

'Oh, no,' Otsugi replied nonchantly. Yokichi suckled intently at his mother's breast, and Oshina suddenly remembered that she had forgotten to bring him a treat.

'Isn't there some sugar over there, Otsū?' she asked. Without a word Otsugi kicked off her sandals and stepped up into the main room. From the cupboard she took out a small envelope made from old newspaper and sprinkled some sugar into the palm of her hand.

'Here you are,' she said as she put the sugar in Yokichi's out-stretched hand. What remained in her palm she herself licked off. Yokichi held his treat between his fingers and still suckling squeezed it clumsily into his mouth. Then he thrust his sticky hand up to his mother, who licked it clean.

Oshina uncovered the pot and peered inside. 'What's this? Potatoes?'

'Uh-huh. I added a few to the pot.'

'And the rice? That'll be cold, won't it?'

'Well, I was going to add that, too, and make gruel.'

Oshina thought that was a good idea. If she ate something hot and steamy she would surely get warm. Since she was so tired she left the preparations to Otsugi, who put a handful of cooked barley mixed with a little rice into the pot. Oshina poked at the fire while Otsugi removed the pot and hung a kettle in its place. She stirred the gruel a few times and then set out a tray on the ledge between the kitchen and the main room. Oshina sat down and began to eat, giving a little bit every now and then to Yokichi whom she held in her lap. When she put a piece of potato in his mouth, however, he immediately spat it out and began to cry. 'Too hot?' she asked, blowing against his cheeks. She chewed the potato a little herself and gave it back to him. In all she consumed three bowls of gruel even though she did not like it much. Then she drank a little hot water. At last she began to feel warm inside.

Otsugi went out to the well and poured a bucket of water over the empty cooking pot. 'You don't have to do anymore tonight,' Oshina told her when she returned, but Otsugi went over to the buckets in the corner.

'These need water.'

'That'd be nice, but really, you don't have to do so much . . .'

Before Oshina had finished speaking Otsugi was out in the yard again. When she reappeared in the doorway she was carrying the clean pot and the well-bucket. Soon the *konnyaku* were soaking in water.

Oshina and her children then went off for a bath at East Neighbor's house, a large compound surrounded by a forest.

It was dark outside. The cedars in the forest thrust up boldly into the cold night air. In the past this forest, which belonged to East Neighbor, had kept the sun from shining into Oshina's yard until fairly late in the day. Her family had truly lived in the shadows then. But one day the men from the land survey department had arrived in the area, setting up their tripods with the little flags on top. Because they could not see through the forest to complete their measurements they had cut down several trees. A big cedar had fallen to the west with a great thud right across Oshina's yard. Its branches had broken off, and their tips had dug into the soil. When the neighbors had come to dispose of the tree they had given Oshina all the branches and debris on her property, providing her with a huge supply of firewood. And although the neighbors had lamented the loss of their fine trees Oshina and her family had secretly rejoiced. Now there was an opening through the forest, and thereafter the sun shone on them from morning on. But even with some trees gone the forest still dominated its surroundings. At night it was especially awesome. Oshina's tiny house, perched on its narrow ledge, looked insignificant indeed.

Oshina disappeared into the darkness and emerged again in the neighbor's doorway. Several employees were inside making rope as night-work. Sitting cross-legged on the raised wooden floor, each man secured the piece he was working on beneath his feet and added more straw to it until his hands were high above his head. Then he reached down and pulled the completed portion behind him. So much rope had been made already that it piled up on the earthen floor of the entryway. Oshina knelt humbly on the wooden floor, waiting. Soon the men used up all the straw and began hauling in their ropes, measuring them expertly between their feet and hands and bundling them up as they went. Then they swept the leftover bits of straw off onto the dirt below. At last they were ready to bathe. Oshina watched and waited silently. She always had to wait when she came here, and sometimes she had gone elsewhere instead. But on this particular evening there were no other baths to be had. She had checked at two or three other houses first but finally had come here. The employees clustered by the roaring fire under the metal cauldron, waiting thier turns. Once bathed they stood by the fire again, their naked thighs red from the hot water.

'Come on over and get warm,' one of the men called out, 'It'll be your turn soon.' But Oshina sat still, trying to ignore the cold draft behind her. Very slightly, so as not to wake Yokichi, who was asleep in her arms, she shifted her weight to relieve her numb feet. When finally the men were finished Oshina hurriedly took off her clothes, thinking of nothing else but getting into the hot water. Otsugi held Yokichi, who was so exhausted that he did not know he had been taken from his mother's bosom. As Oshina felt warmth returning gradually to her body she began to feel revived. She wanted to stay in the soothing water forever. But then she began to worry that Yokichi would start fussing. Reluctantly she got out of the tub. Her face was flushed, and no matter how often she wiped her forehead she kept sweating. She felt fine at last. Quickly putting on her kimono she took Yokichi in her arms again so Otsugi could bathe. But at that moment a maid came in for a bath, and Otsugi had to wait. By the time Otsugi finally got out of the tub Oshina had begun feeling cold again. She regretted that she had not waited and gone last herself.

When they returned home the moon was shining brightly, revealing the forest around them. The gap where the trees had been cut down was especially well lit. It was very cold. When Oshina lay down under her thin, stained quilt at home she was shivering again, and her knees felt stiff and frozen.

2

Oshina woke up the next morning just as the faint light of dawn began shining through the cracks in the rain doors. She tried to raise her head from the pillow, but it throbbed too severely with pain. The sound of the chickens clucking noisily and flapping their wings up in the roost overhead grated on her ears. Otsugi was still sound asleep. When the cracks in the doors grew bright with light, like eyelids fully opened, the chickens began to squawk shrilly. Oshina had wanted to let Otsugi sleep late that morning, but when the chickens began their rumpus Otsugi suddenly awoke and looked around as if bewildered. Then she saw that her mother still lay beneath her bedding on the floor beside her.

'There's no rush,' Oshina said, 'I don't feel so good this morning, so let's take it easy.' Otsugi hesitated for a moment and then got up, slid open one of the doors with a clatter, and stepped out into the yard, rubbing her eyes sleepily. In the bucket by the well some potatoes she had left to soak were now locked in by a sheet of ice. Otsugi broke the ice with a fragment of whetstone. Then she realized that she had left the door of the house open and that all this morning cold was creeping inside.

'Mother, are you okay? I didn't think,' she said as she hurriedly slid the door shut again. Inside the darkened house one could see only the fire in the stove. 'It is really cold out there.' Otsugi shivered as she held her hands up near the flames. 'The potato water froze,' she continued, turning to face her mother.

'Hmm, looks like a lot of frost, too,' replied Oshina faintly. With her back to the doors she lay watching the flames.

'Everywhere it's all white,' said Otsugi as she stirred up the dried leaves in the stove with bamboo tongs.

'The cold at dawn woke me up,' said Oshina, lifting her head slightly. 'I don't feel like eating, but you go ahead and fix yourself something.'

Otsugi made another pot of gruel.

'Have a little, Mother,' she said as she put a bowl by Oshina's pillow. Smelling it Oshina thought she might as well try some, but when she turned over onto her stomach she again lost interest. Her movement, though, woke Yokichi, who had been sleeping beside her. Still lying down she gave him her breast, and once again she speared a few potatoes from the gruel for him.

When the doors were opened again a little later the sun had just risen above East Neighbor's forest and was shining directly into the yard. The frost that had lain in the shadows now glistened brightly. On the brittle leaves of the chestnut trees in a corner of the yard and on the radishes hung up to dry on its branches were drops of melting frost. The waste straw strewn over the yard as a ground cover during winter was wet, and icicles dripped everywhere, in the yard itself and in the mulberry field beyond.

Oshina felt very warm under her quilt. Every once in a while she would raise her head a little and look outside. Then she would gaze idly at the two buckets of *konnyaku*. The twigs of East Neighbor's trees looked strange indeed viewed lying down. When her eyes tired from staring at them she would shift to the buckets again. She had to do something about the *konnyaku*, she would think. But every time she thought about getting up she would become very drowsy.

'I'll make some *kiriboshi*,' Otsugi shouted loudly from the yard, but Oshina could hear her only faintly and did not understand what she had said.

After a while Oshina heard a splash of water, then a pause, and another splash. Otsugi was washing the radishes. Sitting on a straw mat laid out over the straw she began chopping. First she sliced the radishes sideways, then she cut the slices lengthwise into thin strips, like poem cards. She moved the knife a little awkwardly up and down on the cutting board and swept the white pieces of radish off into the bowl below it. When Oshina heard the sound of the knife she realized what the splashing sound a while before had been. Just a few days earlier she had mentioned that it was time to make *kiriboshi*, and it pleased her that Otsugi had remembered. The sound of the chopping seemed close by. Oshina pulled herself halfway out of the covers and looked out. Otsugi was kneeling with her back to the house, slightly bent forward, with her hair tucked up in a scarf.

'Everything okay?' Oshina called out.

'Uh-huh.' Otsugi turned to the side as she answered, her knife poised in mid-air. Oshina nestled back down under the covers. And once again she heard the sound of her daughter's inexperienced chopping. Then Yokichi, tired of being in bed so long, began to fuss.

Hearing him Otsugi called out, 'There now, want to come out

8

and see what I'm doing?' She came back into the house, warmed his clothes by the fire, and got him dressed.

'Yoki is a good little boy, so he'll stay close to his big sister,' Oshina told him. Then Otsugi put him on the mat beside her. Her fingers were dirty from putting more leaves on the fire, and when she began chopping again she left fingerprints on the radishes. Quickly she wiped her hands on her jacket. Yokichi reached out toward the cutting board.

'No, no! That's very dangerous,' warned Otsugi. 'Here, you can have this.' She gave him a slice of radish which he immediately put in his mouth.

'Poor little Yoki, it's too salty, isn't it?' Otsugi murmured indulgently. Oshina could hear all this clearly and knew just what was happening.

'Did you drop it? Here it is, over here. Don't drop it again, now.'

'Don't you do that! If you're a bad boy, I'll cut you up with this. You'll be all bloody, and you'll hurt all over.' Oshina kept on listening. The sound of the chopping stopped. Even without looking Oshina knew that Yokichi was into some kind of mischief and so Otsugi had grabbed his finger and bitten it to warn him. Now Yokichi no doubt had his finger in his own mouth, mimicking his sister. Oshina had been fairly strict in raising Otsugi and thought her more responsible than other children of her age. But now, hearing her playing with Yokichi, she realized that Otsugi was still a child. Oshina herself had been 16 when she had met Kanji. Would Otsugi, too, grow up quickly like that, she wondered. Otsugi was now 15.

Oshina still was not interested in food at noon. She resigned herself to staying in bed all day, but she thought she might be up to a little peddling the next day. That, however, was not to be. As before, Oshina could not leave her pillow. And she began to worry. More and more she thought about Kanji, who had left home not long before. He had done that sort of work around the village, she mused, but could he keep it up day after day? She pictured him out in the cold, working in just a shirt. And then the shirt would ride up, and his belly would be exposed. At night he would ache all over. She could see it all clearly as if he were really right there in front of her, so intensely did she miss him.

Kanji had gone off to a construction project on the Tone River. Some five or six other men from the area had signed on, too, after hearing the glowing reports of the recruiters who had come through early in the fall. Kanji did not know much about the project itself, but he had heard that a day's wages were 50 *sen* or more. That was unheard of for work in the off-season, and he had been delighted.

The project site was on lowland near Kasumigaura at a dike that had been built to separate the river from a lake made earlier by floods. Kanji was overcome by the great expanse of land there compared to his own village.

When Kanji had finally secured a job on the crew he had hurried to finish up his farming chores at home. With the winter solstice at hand there had been a great deal to do. The paddy fields needed tending, then there were the potatoes in the dry field, and the radishes. While Oshina was getting the fire going in the morning he had been out in the yard drying the rice. Then he had started to hull it. After that he had put the radishes up in the tree to dry. He had worked from before dawn to after dusk. Even so he had not finished all the rice, and there was still a bit of dry field to tend. But Oshina had said she would manage it all somehow, and he had set off.

It was almost 50 miles to the project site. Kanji had taken about one yen with him for expenses, but since he took his own food all he needed was money for the ferry. Arriving late at night he had gone to work the very next morning. After only a few hours of digging and hauling he had begun to regret his decision to come. The next day his hands ached so much he could not work, and he had stayed inside in the bunkhouse for a few days. About a week later a fierce wind had come up. All night long Kanji had tossed and turned sleeplessly under his thin quilt, his feet cold and his body shivering.

The next day he was back out in the mud, his stiff hands on the cold handle of his shovel. Then, all of a sudden, someone from his village appeared, delighted to have finally located him among the horde of mud-covered laborers. The man went on to tell Kanji that he had stopped overnight en route, but still Kanji had no idea why he had come. Finally he learned that Oshina had sent for him. He was alarmed to hear that she was sick. Over and over he asked about her condition, and from what the man told him he gathered it was not that serious. But he could not help worrying.

They left for home that night. Kanji himself wanted to hurry, and besides, he could not expect the weary messenger to return by foot, so they took a boat from Kasumigaura to Tsuchiura. The boat broke down during the night and arrived in Tsuchiura long overdue. It was after sunrise. Kanji hurriedly bought a package of sardines in one of the shops and set off on foot, walking as fast as he could. Even so it was dark by the time he arrived at the door of his house. A lantern was burning inside. He could see Oshina lying under her quilt. Then he saw Otsugi sitting at her feet. Kanji slid the door open and stepped inside. 'What's happened?' he asked from the dirt-floored kitchen.

'Kanji-san? Is that you?' Oshina turned towards the sound of his voice. 'I though maybe South Neighbor hadn't found you.'

'He found me all right. But what's wrong here?'

'I didn't think it was much at first. But I've been stuck here in bed for four days now. I'm feeling a little better today. I'm sure I'll be all right.'

'That's a relief.' Kanji sat down on the ledge and removed his sandals. 'It'd have been better if I'd come all the way on foot. But I couldn't ask South to walk back, so we took a boat. Then it broke down. I left South in Tsuchiura and came on by myself. He's really tired, so he won't make it back for some time yet.' As he spoke he placed the package of sardines close to Oshina's bedding and threw his knapsack on the floor. He went out into the yard to wash and returned to Oshina's bedside.

'I'm glad it's nothing serious. I didn't know what to think. You had anything to eat?'

'Otsū made me some gruel a while back, and I managed to put some of it away.'

'Well, here, try a little piece of this. I bought it on the way.' Kanji drew the lantern closer and unwrapped the fish. In the light the sardines looked bright blue.

'Oh, my . . .,' Oshina murmured as she rolled over onto her stomach.

'Bring us a fire,' Kanji said to Otsugi.

'You didn't have to do this, Kanji-san. I don't need that kind of thing.'

'Well, they'll keep a long time at this time of year. Besides, you need to get strong again.'

'But it must've cost a lot to come by boat.'

'Uh-huh, it was sixty *sen* for the two of us. I couldn't ask South to pay, so I paid for both.'

'Then, all the money you've earned so far is gone . . .'

'Oh, I got some left. Only worked a week, but I have about two yen left over. I'm going back there, after all, so I asked for an advance. Fellows from around here vouched for me,' Kanji announced proudly.

'It's so good to see you. I missed you.' Oshina put her head down on the pillow.

'Well, I was planning to come back once anyway. I have some work to finish up here, so it's all the same,' said Kanji, peering down at her.

'I see you got the rice bagged up,' he continued, looking over at the stack in the corner. Oshina just lay still. 'Over at the project you don't need any money, you know. I don't smoke, and they provide everything else you need on credit. Rice, firewood, whatever. Pay day's the fifteenth, and that's when we settle up.' Kanji went on, telling Oshina more about his job. 'They give you pure rice to eat, too. Every day, almost two quarts. The work's so hard you need almost that much. But I'm saving some of it and when I come back next time I'll be able to sell it and buy some really fine fish. Maybe even some salmon.'

'I'm glad it's working out,' Oshina said, turning her head. 'They say those construction bosses are no good, so I didn't know what to think.'

'Oh, they're a rough bunch, all right, but I keep out of their way.' While Kanji spoke Otsugi broke up some faggots and started a fire in the hibachi. Kanji put three of the sardines on the grill. Oil dripped from them as they cooked, turning the flames blue. The smell of fish and smoke filled the room and made Oshina hungry. Still lying on her stomach she picked up one of the sardines and began to eat it.

'Not too salty?' Kanji asked.

'Oh no, delicious.'

'The tradesmen around here don't have anything like 'em,' Kanji said, watching her intently. She ate two of the fish and looked down at Yokichi.

'He'll really fuss if he wakes up,' she said.

'Go on and have the other one,' Kanji urged her.

'I've had plenty, really. Maybe Otsugi will eat it.'

'I'll have a little rice myself,' Kanji said, taking out his lunchbox and starting on the cold leftovers.

'Otsū,' Oshina called out. 'Bring some hot tea.'

'Don't need any. On the job we make do without it.' Kanji ate a few *umeboshi*. Then he gave Otsugi a piece of the remaining sardine and took a bite himself.

'You say these are good, but they're too sweet for me,' he said, and drank a few cupfuls of cool water. Finally he reached into his knapsack and took out a package.

'This is the rice I saved up so far. If I'd come back without it someone might've stole it.' He handed the package to Otsugi.

'I wondered what you had in that huge knapsack,' Oshina said teasingly.

'Well, the firewood was too much so I left it behind,' Kanji replied, looking a bit insulted. 'How about a little massage to make you feel better?'

Oshina smiled. 'That's all right. I've been feeling better all day. Otsugi rubbed my feet just a while ago. You ought to be able to go back to work in a few days.

'I feel really good tonight,' she continued, 'Really, Kanji-san. And you must be tired.'

It was late, and very still, as if everything in the darkness outside had frozen. Even in the buckets of *konnyaku* by the wall thin sheets of ice had formed.

3

Frost lay white on the straw in the yard the following morning. Three mats of radish strips were spread out on top of the straw, each strip frosted with tiny specks of ice that glistened in the morning sun. The white strips had been set out to dry without any preliminary steaming. Day and night they would remain there and unless it rained they would become covered with dust and grit.

Kanji headed off along a path lined with icicles for South Neighbor's house on the other side of the mulberry field. When he returned some time later, carrying a loom, the frost had melted a little in the sunshine and lay stickily on the ground. Oshina had been very lonely during the short time he was away. She felt a little better that morning, much to his relief. He spread out another mat on the straw and began weaving bales, his body warmed by the distant winter sun. The loom he used was a simple tool with legs at both ends, like the frame of a pack saddle. He wove by putting a handful of straw on the pole between the legs and moving the shuttle back and forth while feeding in rope. Kanji needed five of these bales, smaller and stronger than the ones inside the house, to hold his rent rice, but all he had been able to do before leaving for the construction project had been to gather the straw and rope. He had worried about this unfinished task ever since.

Oshina opened one of the rain doors. She could see the bright blue sky and the light reached almost to her bed. Until today she had felt too depressed to look out-of-doors. Now she saw that the radishes hanging on the oak tree had dried to a brown color. Otsugi was sitting near Kanji, cutting some of them up. Faintly Oshina could hear the sound of her knife alternating with the clatter of the loom. It reassured her to see both of them there. The day was very still, and not even the hanging radishes moved. She was certain that she would soon be well.

Kanji finished weaving a bale and spread apart the little bundle of straw attached to one corner to make a round opening. Then he opened up one of the coarse rice bales that Oshina had filled and poured in the correct measure of rice. There were a few red grains among the white, but what stood out were the crushed grains and bits of chaff mixed in with the rest.

'There's a bit too much waste stuff here,' he called out suddenly.

'I know,' Oshina replied apologetically from inside the house, 'but I really winnowed it a lot before wrapping it up. There's a lot of red, too, so I guess something's wrong with the grinder.'

'Well, there's no need to worry. This little the Master will overlook,' Kanji replied hastily, concerned that he had upset her. He piled the bales up one by one against the wall, and Oshina stared at them intently. It was one of the things that always made her feel cheerful. Kanji lifted the cover of one of the buckets by the pile and said, 'Ah, we have some *konnyaku*.'

'I went and got it just before I got sick,' Oshina replied. Kanji put the cover back on.

The sun that had been moving slowly across the calm sky suddenly began to sink, as if it had stumbled. Winter days were now at their shortest. Since there was still light Kanji took a hoe and went off to the barley field. Before he could do much work, however, the sun set, and it quickly became cold and gloomy. Oshina waited uneasily for him to return, her eyes closed in the darkness.

There were only two days left until the solstice. In the morning Kanji once again uncovered the *konnyaku*. 'Maybe I ought to go out and sell 'em. It's no good just having 'em sitting here.' He looked inquisitively at Oshina.

'That's so, but you know what I'd really like is for you to pickle some radishes. I've been looking at the tree, and I'm afraid they've gotten too dry,' she replied. 'If only I wasn't sick I could do 'em myself.' She wanted him to stay at home, but she could not bring herself to say so directly.

'Check on the salt, won't you?' she continued. 'I think there's enough. Then there's bran in this bucket here. Use that. The bran in the other bucket has some sand in it.'

'What's the difference?' Kanji asked. 'You don't eat the bran. Why not mix 'em together?'

'No, don't do that! They say that sand will poison pickles. That's why I kept it separate.'

'Well, okay,' he replied. Then he checked on the salt. 'Looks like there's just barely enough.' Oshina watched contentedly as he got up on the ladder to take the radishes down and spread out the bran and salt on a mat.

But the day before the solstice Kanji went off with the *konnyaku*. Oshina did not try to stop him this time. Since it was late and others

15

had been out before him he would not sell much, she was sure. When he came back that evening, though, he said, 'Here, you're in charge of the *konnyaku* business, so you get all the money.' He dropped some copper coins on the floor near her pillow. She picked them up and counted them one by one. Even deducting what she had had to pay for the *konnyaku* there was still quite a bit left over.

'I don't believe it!' she said. 'Do you have any of it left at all?'

'Just a bit. Not enough for another trip out,' he replied happily. Oshina put the coins away under her bedding. She had been lonely while he was out, but now that he had done so well, much better than she had imagined possible, she did not feel unhappy anymore.

'The rape's still out in the field, you know,' he told her.

Oshina was alarmed. 'What? Oh, I just forgot all about it. Is it all right?'

'I'm going out now to get in as much as I can.' Then Kanji left, taking Otsugi with him. No one else in the village had left their rape in this late. Kanji borrowed a cart, and before dusk they managed to bring in two loads. The lower leaves were all withered and yellow, but the plants were not ruined. Even though she was left alone in the house again Oshina did not feel sad. Instead she thought happily about the harvest Kanji and Otsugi were bringing in. In the busy summer season, before there were any fresh vegetables available, pickled rape greens were all they had to eat with their rice. It was vital that they have as large a supply as possible.

The day of the solstice was calm. As usually happened about this time of year the wind suddenly stopped blowing. For a time the sun shone brightly, warming the cold air. Oshina had felt cheerful since morning. Later in the day she even got out of bed. She felt weak and strangely weightless, but she made her way over to the doorway, enticed by the sunlight, and sat down. Yokichi was with her. She dangled him over the ledge and tickled him playfully.

Kanji and Otsugi were over by the well, preparing the greens. First they cut off their roots and washed them. Then they tied a layer to a ladder and set the ladder up in the sun. The greens with many dead leaves they boiled in a kettle and hung up on a rope to dry. Finally they boiled some greens for lunch. Oshina watched them at work. She was aware of the glaring sunlight, as if her eyes had weakened a bit in the days she had spent in bed. The plate of greens she ate made her thirsty, but they tasted delicious.

When the greens on the ladder were dry Kanji put them in a large basin, added some salt, and stomped them down with his feet. Then he added more salt and stomped on them again. All the while Oshina gave him advice on how much salt to use, and he followed her instructions carefully.

Since she did not feel especially tired, even though she had been up for some time, Oshina put on her sandals and slipped out the side door. After checking on the greens hanging on the rope, she walked down through the trees to the edge of the rice paddy. Once again she stood by the silverberry bush, quietly tamping down the earth with her foot. Suddenly she heard Kanji calling her, and she made her way back up the slope, grabbing onto tree trunks and bamboo stalks to ease the climb. Just as she came around the side of the house Kanji called out again. Standing beside him was a peddler, his carrying pole still slung over his shoulder.

'He wants eggs,' Kanji told her, returning to his bucket of greens. Oshina looked in the drawer of the cabinet and found twenty eggs.

She called out to Otsugi. 'Take a look up in the roost, will you? I haven't checked for almost a week, so there'll be some more.' Otsugi climbed up on top of the rice bales. When she opened the coop one hen came lurching out and headed for the forest. The others cackled noisily. Otsugi reached in and collected the eggs, putting them one by one into the sleeve of her jacket. Then with the sleeve dangling she descended unsteadily to the floor. She had found only six. The peddler took a scale and a brass plate from his basket.

'What's the price?' Oshina asked him.

'Eleven and a half *sen* a hundred *momme*. It's gone down a lot,' he replied as he put the eggs into a shallow basket. Holding the scale aloft, he adjusted the beam, pulled the weight, and read off the total.

'Altogether, 423 *momme*, 2 *bu*,' he said, showing the reading to Oshina. Then he picked up a tiny abacus and began calculating. 'First we deduct the weight of my basket. Then it's about 408 *momme*, 2 *bu*. Now let's see, we've got twenty-six eggs, here, so each one . . .'

Oshina interrupted, 'What are you figuring for this little basket?'

'Why, fifteen *momme*.'

'It looks more like ten to me.'

'Well, here, take a look at it.' He held the basket out towards Oshina. 'It's fifteen *momme* all right. I use a bigger one than most people.' Then he resumed his calculations.

'So they weigh 15 *momme* 7 *bu* each. They're a little small, aren't they?' He moved the beads of the abacus slowly. 'They'll bring you 46 *sen* 8 *rin* 6 *mo* 3 *shu*. Why don't we just round that off to 46 *sen* 8 *rin*?' He took out his purse and counted the coins.

'Oh come on now, Oshina,' Kanji called out. 'Keep a few and eat 'em yourself.'

'But we can use the money to buy other food,' she replied. 'Besides, he's figured it up and all. I'm really much better, so don't worry.'

Kanji stopped working and came over. His hands were covered with salt, and both his hands and feet were bright red from the cold water. 'No such thing! You keep a few for yourself. You still got to be careful.'

'Oh well, maybe so.' Oshina picked out two of the smallest eggs.

'Not those, these,' said Kanji, picking out three larger ones. Some of the salt on his fingers stuck to the shells.

'Well, then. I'll just weigh the ones you've taken back.' This time the peddler put the three eggs into the brass plate. 'You can always collect more for yourselves, you know,' he said as he lifted the scales. The beam moved wildly up and down.

'Don't you cheat us, now,' Oshina remarked, smiling faintly.

'What a silly thing to say,' the peddler replied indignantly. 'Why, these scales have just been inspected. The beam's supposed to work like that. There now, they weigh 50 *momme* 1 *bu*. That's 'cause they're pretty big.'

'They got salt on 'em,' Kanji laughed. 'That's what makes 'em weigh so much.'

The peddler did not smile. 'So they're worth 5 *sen* 5 *rin* 6 *mo* plus a little. Now what was the price I figured before, I wonder?'

'You said 46 *sen* 8 *rin*, plus a little,' Oshina answered quickly.

The peddler took up the abacus again. 'So the difference is 41 *sen* 3 *rin* plus. You do a little trading yourself, don't you, so you have a head for figures. Say, you have a cold or something? You look a little under the weather.'

'Uh-huh, just a bit,' Oshina replied. 'Isn't it a little more than 41 *sen* 3 *rin*?'

'No point figuring out the rest. Can't get any of those little old coins anymore.' He reached into his basket and took out some matches.

'Oh no, not matches again!' Oshina was smiling.

'They do just fine for little amounts,' he said, giving her a few along with the money he owed her. 'All the peddlers use 'em these days.'

'Seems to me the price is awful low,' Kanji remarked. 'The eggs will keep a long time in this cold weather, so you'd think they'd be worth more instead of less.'

'They're imported from Shanghai nowadays. That brings the price way down. Eggs are dirt cheap over there, you know.' The peddler put the eggs into his carrying basket and lifted his pole. 'We can't make any money off 'em either. You farmers have the best of it, growing rice. Price is always good. But collecting eggs! We lose a lot when the market drops. People get dysentery, they want to eat eggs, but still, peddlers lose their shirts.'

He started to leave. 'I'll stop by again. Please put some aside for me,' he said as he walked off, this time speaking more formally.

Oshina put the money in the purse she kept under her bedding. Then she took a *marume* box from the cabinet and put the eggs in it. Cotton had once been raised in this region, and as night-work all the women had made thread, winding it up on the spindles until it was as thick and round as a candle. Each spool was called a *marume*. Now, however, cotton was no longer grown, and only a few *marume* boxes were left, gathering soot in dark corners and used only to hold bits and scraps of cloth. Oshina noticed that her thick money purse was showing under the bedding. She smoothed out the lump and lay down. For some time now she had felt exhausted, but as soon as she was in bed again she relaxed and felt better.

That night, the night of the solstice, the whole family ate a little *konnyaku* to clean out the grit that had accumulated in their intestines during the previous year. Oshina was sure she would be up and around the next day. And since he had finished up his chores at home Kanji decided to go back to the Tone River.

4

That night Oshina's condition worsened. She woke Kanji not long after he had fallen asleep with her pitiful whisper:

'I can't open my mouth at all!'

Her jaws were locked shut, and no matter how much saliva she swallowed, her throat remained constricted. She was terrified, and so was Kanji.

'What? It's worse? Just try to hang on till morning, okay?' He tried to reassure her, but he himself had no idea what to do. He lay in bed uneasily until dawn. Then, even more concerned about her, he sent a neighbor for the doctor while he remained at her bedside. They did not usually summon a doctor, but this time Kanji was too alarmed to think of the money it would cost. The doctor lived to the east, across the Kinu River.

Thinking it might help relax her Kanji rubbed Oshina's feet, but her listlessness only frightened him more. All morning he flitted about nervously. Then one of the neighboring wives came by to sit with her, and he was able to dash off and see what was keeping the doctor. As he crossed the river by ferry he spied the messenger he had sent out earlier coming back across on the other boat. In midstream they shouted out to one another. Kanji, having promised Oshina that he would return with help, went on to the doctor's house, hoping that he could hurry him along. Finally the doctor, an old hat perched on his head, was ready to leave. Kanji carried his bag. The doctor moved along slowly in his clogs; unless it was a special emergency he never went by rickshaw. That was one reason poor farmers, who could not afford the fare, called on him for aid.

Kanji described Oshina's condition and invited the doctor's opinion as they went, but the doctor replied irritably that he was not about to venture a diagnosis sight unseen. When finally he did see Oshina, however, he nodded grimly. She had the symptoms of tetanus, just as he had thought. Apologizing that he was an old man and did not own one of those hypodermic syringes, he excused himself. Kanji in haste made for the other doctor in the area. This one wrote out a few words on a slip of paper and told him to hurry to the apothecary shop. He would come to their house later to administer the medicine. With that Kanji dashed off across the river again and asked for the two little vials of medicine the doctor had prescribed. When he learned that each one cost 75 *sen* he felt faint. But he bought them and made for home. Then, toward evening, after completing his other calls, the doctor arrived to administer the shot. He wiped Oshina's thigh with a damp piece of gauze, pinched up the flesh between his fingers, and drove in the needle. After a while he extracted it, pressed the puncture with his finger, and applied an adhesive plaster. All this took place by the dim light of the lantern which Kanji held close by as directed by the doctor.

The doctor came again the next morning and administered another shot. Then, saying that everything should be all right now, he left. But Oshina still showed no signs of recovery. Not only that, she began to grow noticeably weaker. That evening she suddenly went into convulsions. Her arms and legs stiffened, and her entire body trembled violently. These convulsions recurred from time to time, causing Oshina such suffering that it was painful even to watch. Her face would become weirdly contorted, her mouth drawn grotesquely to one side. Afraid to leave Otsugi there alone to look after things Kanji had to wait until dawn to go off again for the doctor. Once more he was sent off running to buy medicine. But the Number 2 blood serum the doctor had specified this time was not available anywhere. It doesn't keep long, he was told at the apothecary, so they didn't order much at a time. Besides, it was very expensive. 'What's it cost?' Kanji asked. 'Three yen a bottle.' He looked into his purse. Even if they had had some in stock he could not have paid for it.

Kanji returned home but was quickly sent back to the apothecary. He was out of breath, but he welcomed the opportunity to go on another errand, for only by doing as he was ordered by the doctor did he feel he had a chance to help. The doctor injected the Number 1 blood serum that Kanji had obtained. It was wasted effort, however. Oshina's convulsions came more rapidly now. It was hard for her to breathe. A few neighbors knelt sadly around her bed.

'Won't someone go to Noda?' Oshina suddenly asked. Both Kanji and the neighbors had been so distracted that they had forgotten to notify Uhei.

'I'll see to it he comes tomorrow,' Kanji whispered. Despite the hour one of the neighbors agreed to go fetch him.

A little after noon the next day Uhei arrived with the neighbor in tow. As he moved his large frame across the threshhold Oshina was screaming out in pain.

'Where's it hurt?' Kanji asked. 'How about a massage?'

'It's my back, my back!' was all she could reply.

One of the wives spoke up. 'Your father's here, Oshina-san! Get hold of yourself, now.' Oshina did manage to calm down a little.

'Shina, what is it? Bad?' Uhei was a man of few words.

'I've been waiting for you,' Oshina moaned. 'It's awful.'

Uhei frowned. 'Looks serious,' he muttered. After that he said nothing. Oshina grew steadily worse. The doctor gave her a shot of morphine to relieve the pain and let her sleep a little. But she woke up after a time and began convulsing violently again, her body bent back as if she were dangling from a rope.

'What's going to happen to me, Doctor?' she asked all of a sudden. The doctor just stroked his mustache and said nothing.

'How about it, Doctor?' Kanji asked.

'Best thing is to tell the patient everything's all right,' he whispered.

Kanji bent down close to Oshina. 'He says you'll be okay. Just be brave for a bit longer,' he repeated over and over.

'But I can't take much more,' Oshina moaned. 'I won't last till morning. I'm scared . . .' Her words, barely escaping between her clenched teeth, made everyone uncomfortable, but they knew she was right. The doctor gave her a large dose of morphine and left.

That night the convulsions came one right after another, and Oshina's temperature rose sharply. Even though she hadn't been able to drink anything her tangled hair was wet with beads of sweat. The damp bedding smelled foul.

'Come here, Kanji-san,' she moaned.

'I'm here, I'm not going anywhere.'

'Kanji-san!' she cried out again.

'What is it? I'm here,' he repeated. Hadn't she heard him?

'Papa, I'm sorry,' she murmured. Then she grabbed Kanji's hand.

'Otsū . . . ,' she stammered, and was seized by another convulsion.

'When I die, Kanji-san . . . in the casket . . .'

Kanji leaned closer to her, and after a pause she continued. 'On the path in the back paddy . . . there by the silverberry . . .' She spoke haltingly, fighting for breath, but Kanji understood.

She lapsed into convulsions and said no more. Then she suddenly cried out deliriously, *'Furoshiki, furoshiki!'* Kanji had no idea what she meant.

She began kicking furiously at the quilt, her whole body thrashing. The people seated around her grabbed her legs and held them down, restraining her in her death throes. When the convulsions stopped her breathing stopped too.

It was very quiet. One could hear the rain doors creaking faintly and the leaves rustling in the darkness outside. Oshina's body began to turn cold, her feet first and then her legs. When they realized that she was dead Kanji, Otsugi and the others who had gathered at her bedside could restrain themselves no longer. They began to cry uncontrollably. Everyone except for Yokichi, who was sleeping peacefully beside his mother's corpse. Uhei reached out and crossed Oshina's arms over her bosom. Then he put a weaving shuttle on top of the quilt. That would keep away the cats, who were said to walk on the dead and assume their forms.

The night grew colder and colder, but there was no fire inside the house. The neighbors could not leave until Kanji and Otsugi stopped crying, so they just sat there quietly, their cold hands pulled back inside their sleeves. Finally Otsugi lit some leaves in the stove and brewed some tea. Everyone sipped it in silence.

'You might've told me sooner, Kanji,' Uhei grumbled quietly, but everyone overheard. He had not known anything about Oshina's illness until the messenger had arrived early that morning. Hurriedly he had come to see what was the matter, and then it had all been over. He too had cried. But now he just sat there gripping his pipe between his lips and clicking his tongue. Kanji could do nothing but cry. From the time he had first learned Oshina was sick he had worried and thought of nothing else but caring for her. In his grief he did not even take notice of Uhei's complaint.

Oshina's death had affected the old man deeply. Now 71 years old, he had been working as a night watchman at a soy sauce brewery in Noda for the past year. He had married Oshina's mother and been adopted into her family when Oshina was already 3. After a short time he and Oshina had grown very fond of one another. All had gone smoothly as long as Oshina's mother had lived, but after her death Uhei had become more taciturn than ever. He and Kanji had never got on well. Gradually the gulf between them had deepened, despite all of Oshina's efforts to bring them together. Finally Uhei had obtained an introduction from one of the men in the village and gone off to Noda to work.

After they had drunk their tea one of the neighbors went off to notify Oshina's relatives in the village while the others made plans for the funeral. It was decided that everything would be taken care of the following day. As soon as it was light people went off to make arrangements at the temple, to buy death supplies, and to notify relatives in other villages. A few women came to the house to pay their respects, and then Kanji and Otsugi started to prepare the body. They rolled up one of the floor mats, filled a washbasin with water, and cleansed Oshina's emaciated face and limbs. Uhei sat by silently and watched. The body was then laid out on the soiled bedding on top of the slotted floor boards, and the dirty water poured off onto the soil below. The washing completed, the mat was put back in place. The rain doors had been thrust open that morning, and now all the mats inside the house were swept off. Four or five finely woven mats borrowed from East Neighbor were spread out over the old ones. Then, in accordance with the local custom, Kanji turned Oshina's purified body over to the neighbors.

The women cut a length of bleached cotton cloth in half and fashioned a simple shroud and a hood to cover the shadow of death on Oshina's face. Next they made some cloth socks for her feet and hung a cloth purse containing a few coins — just enough for the fare across the River of Death — around her neck. They tied up her hair with a flaxen ribbon and stuck in a white comb. Then Oshina's stiff body was bent into the fetal position and she was put into the casket. Since her head would have stuck up above its top, they had to push down on her neck until the bone broke. This awful task was always left to others, to spare the family. They tied a rope from her feet up around her neck to keep her in the proper position. The crude pine casket creaked under her weight. The pine boards for the casket stand were nailed together, and the casket was placed on top of it.

Early in the morning Kanji had slipped out of the house and walked down through the oak trees to the edge of the rice paddy. Soon he located the silverberry bush and detected the traces of digging. He scooped up the surface dirt with his sickle and then pushed aside the soft earth with his hands until he uncovered something wrapped up in a rag. Inside was a tiny corpse. Kanji picked it up carefully and looked around to make sure he was unobserved. Then he wrapped it up in a piece of old oil cloth and returned to the house. As Oshina was being put into the casket he slipped the little bundle into her arms. Her bony fingers held it tightly, and her sunken cheek touched against it. The funeral was being held on a day of the red-tongued god.

Although the burial itself and the simple feast that preceded it would be confined to neighbors and relatives, all the villagers stopped to pay their respects, each contributing 2 *sen* towards expenses. Later the priest and acolyte from the temple arrived, accompanied by a servant carrying a lacquered box. The acolyte lifted the lid of the casket, removed Oshina's hood, and stroked her cheeks with a razor. Now that this perfunctory shave was finished the lid was nailed in place. The leftover piece of bleached cotton cloth was wrapped around the casket and a funeral canopy, crudely made of crossed pine branches, was set on top. Finally an old mandala was laid over all. Only a few people were going to the burial, but even so there were two paper lanterns, and two large bamboo baskets decorated with paper flowers were held aloft during the procession. In the bottom of each basket a sheet of paper lay over the lattice-work, and on top of it were coins, one for each year the deceased had lived. During the procession the men carrying the baskets would shake them from time to time, and the village children would dash about to pick up the coins as they fell. The lanterns and baskets led the way. Next came the village prayer society, its members beating slowly on their drums and chanting the *nenbutsu*. The procession followed the main road through the village, and everyone came out to watch as it passed by. All the while the shoddily made casket pitched from side to side. Kanji followed behind it, in formal dress and carrying a memorial plaque. He had rented the clothes he wore, and they fit him poorly.

Around the grave dry red soil was piled up on all sides. The men had tried to find a spot where no one had been buried before, but the graveyard had long been in use. As usual they had unearthed a few bones — a hand here, a foot there — as they had dug. The priest's servant removed the piece of cloth from the casket and placed it in his lacquered box. Then the casket was lowered on ropes into the grave until it rested on the red soil below. The casket stand was placed over the grave, and the lanterns and baskets were set beside it. Hardly a day passed in Oshina's life when she had not felt the soil beneath her feet. Barefooted except in icy winter, she had been its creature. And now, in death, she was its creature still. Separated only by a thin layer of pine, her feet would rest on the soil forever.

After the funeral party left, a wind had come up, sweeping away the dust in Kanji's yard. The wives from the neighborhood who had come to help with the food and cleaning up had little to do, since there had been few guests at the feast. Now they were eating leftovers. Instead of barley mixed with rice, the farmers' usual fare, pure rice had been served. It was a rare treat, and the women ate all they could manage to stuff into their mouths. They were gathered by the back door gossiping.

'Did you hear how the casket rattled!' one of them remarked.

'It's supposed to,' another answered. 'The spirit inside is worried about those it's left behind.'

'She hated to leave Kanji, I'll tell you that.'

'That's right. But if she misses him too much her spirit will come back and fetch him.'

'I'd hate that, if someone came for me!'

'Well, even if you begged and begged, no one would come back for you.'

On and on they went, talking without reserve. Then there was a brief lull.

'It's sad about Oshina,' one woman said.

'Uh-huh,' another answered, 'Lots of people do it, after all.'

'They say she caught a cold, but I don't believe that story. You don't die from colds!'

'It's always the poorest who die from it.'

'You know, I heard she did it for others, too.'

'That's so. I wouldn't go around talking about it, but I heard sometimes she got 50 *sen*, 80 *sen* for it.'

'80 *sen*! That's a lot for woman's work. But this time it cost her her own life.'

'Uh-huh, it was a punishment for doing wrong.'

'You better watch out, saying things like that about the dead! Don't you know a spirit can come back and possess you if it gets angry?'

After a brief silence, one of the women picked up a piece of radish and stuck it in her mouth.

'Now how'd you like it if someone caught you doing that?' she was asked.

The woman peered out at the yard. 'Pretty private here.' Then she chuckled. 'An old bag like me, nobody's trying to marry me off so I don't have to worry about how I act any more. What a relief!'

All of them burst out laughing.

Until the people who had gone to the burial returned they would keep on talking. Constrained by the occasion they had remained quiet during the feast itself, but as soon as they were alone in the kitchen, their sleeves tied up to wash dishes, they had relaxed. It may have been a sad day for others, but for them it was a happy occasion, their only chance to visit, to eat decent food, to rest from work. While others grieved, they satisfied their hunger. The sorrows of others were of no concern to them. They went on laughing.

Oshina had once been a part of this group. But today she had put her laughter behind her and returned to the soil.

5

Oshina had killed herself with her own hands.

She had been nineteen when Otsugi was born, and the next year she had got pregnant again. They were barely surviving as it was, so another child was out of the question. Oshina's mother had done the abortion that time, when Oshina was seven months along. It had been in the autumn when the weather was still warm. After a few days Oshina had gone back to work cutting grass in the forest. Then, feeling she might have overdone it a bit, she stayed home until she had recovered fully. She had not become pregnant again for a long time. Yokichi was born when Otsuga was 13. Kanji and Oshina had both looked forward to his birth, for now with Otsugi old enough to help care for a baby they would still be able to keep up with all their work. When Yokichi turned 3 they decided to put Otsugi into service somewhere. A girl her age could earn about 10 yen a year. And in addition to the income they would have one less mouth to feed, an important consideration for such a poor household.

Just as the rice ears were growing heavy this plan was upset. Oshina noticed the change in her body. Whatever had kept her barren all those years had ended with Yokichi, and she was pregnant again. She and Kanji were alarmed. If they sent Otsugi into service as planned Oshina would be left with two infants to care for and would be unable to do as much work as before. The loss of even the small amount of income she brought in would be a major blow. By now it was time to harvest and dry the rice crop. Every day they worked busily beneath the clear sky, getting covered with dust and worrying guiltily about what to do. Only at night after they had lain down wearily on their bedding did they have a chance to talk about it. Kanji, who had never asserted himself in their relationship before, was unable to make a decision now.

'It's your belly,' he would say, 'so you just do what you want.' It was not that he was unconcerned. He simply could not bring himself to order Oshina to do anything.

'But I don't know!' Oshina would blurt out. Kanji would accept whatever she chose to do, but she could not decide such an important matter completely on her own. And so another opportunity to resolve the problem would slip away. The next day they would be back at work in the fields.

Meanwhile, a cold wind had swept suddenly across the sky, warning of winter. As if surprised at how late it was the branches of the zelkova trees abruptly scattered their dry, reddened leaves onto the ground below. Seeking the shelter of dark places, the little leaves flitted noisily across the farmyard and attached themselves to the racks of drying straw and to the mats covered with unhulled rice. Everything was confused and disorderly. It was time for Kanji to go off to the construction project he had signed up for earlier that fall.

'We can't keep putting it off, you know,' Oshina had said to him just before he left, hoping he would finally make a decision.

He had only replied, 'I still don't know what to say. You just do what you want.'

When Kanji had gone Oshina walked around amid the clutter of the yard, feeling alone and depressed. Finally she decided to go ahead and do it. She was then four months pregnant. It was said that this was the time when the risk to the mother was greatest, and indeed Oshina was to die. At four months the fetus is fully formed and one can easily tell its sex. When Oshina saw a small protuberance about the size of a grain of rice between its legs she felt a momentary wave of disappointment. But most of all she worried that people would find out what she had done. As many did at the time she first hid the tiny corpse under the floorboards of the house. Later she wrapped it up in a scrap of cloth and buried it by the silverberry bush at the edge of the rice paddy.

Perhaps things might have turned out differently if she had stayed in bed awhile to recover. But the mother who had done her chores for her the last time was now dead. With Kanji away, Oshina simply had to get back to work. Then, too, if she wanted to keep the neighbors from finding out, she had to act as if nothing were amiss. Still, how did she get the infection that killed her? No one else had been involved in the operation. Perhaps the bacillus had been on the winter cherry root she had used to break through into her uterus. Or perhaps it was in the dust that covered everything in sight. The only thing one will ever know for certain is that it came originally from the soil.

Some other neighbors dropped by the day after the funeral. Then Kanji donned his rented *haori* and *hakama* again and made the rounds of the village to express his thanks. Carrying an earthen teapot filled with water he paid a visit to the grave. Finally, after he had returned all the lacquered trays and bowls and after all the neighbors had gone away, he had nothing left to do but stare miserably at the white mortuary tablet propped up on the table. For two or three days the whole family remained indoors, sitting around listlessly and eating the leftovers from the funeral feast. With the rain doors shut it was gloomy inside the house.

There were four of them, including Uhei, who sat smoking in the dark, rapping his brass pipe occasionally against the hibachi. Neither Uhei nor Kanji said a word to one another. Kanji felt paralyzed, as if his heart had been torn from his body. Still, he could not keep from thinking about the rent rice he had to pay. That was something that always terrified poor tenant farmers. Not only did they fear their landlords, they also prized the land they tilled above all else and were loath to part with any of the crops they had secured after so much effort. They would never be free from this anxiety, for the soil held them prisoner. They were destined to suffer its torments forever.

It distressed Kanji to realize that, with the funeral over, he now had to give his landlord all those bales of rice he had filled just a few days ago. He knew he would have to do practically all the farming by himself in the future. He would be unable to go off any-more to do labor during the busy season. With two children to care for, too, he needed as much rice as possible just to get by. The idea of parting with even a single bale alarmed him. After several sleep-less nights he went and appealed to his landlord to let him borrow back half of the rice he owed until the following fall. The landlord, the former head of East Neighbor's house, consented. Then Kanji took some of the rice he had left and sold it, so hard-pressed was he for a little cash.

Kanji knew he had to return to the construction project. He must not let the boss think he had cheated him out of that advance, not with all the rough characters the boss employed to keep the crew in line. He had already received a postcard from the management asking when he would be back. That had scared him, but since he could not simply abandon the children he did not know what to do. While he wrestled with this problem the seventh day of mourning for Oshina came and went. Finally it occurred to him that if Uhei would postpone going back to Noda for a while he would be able to go off and earn some money. He could not bring himself to ask Uhei directly, so he persuaded South Neighbor to act as go-between. For the past week Kanji had made every effort to avoid looking in Uhei's direction. The very sight of that large hulk sitting by the hibachi had made him intensely nervous.

Kanji and Oshina had fallen in love with one another years ago. Kanji had gone to work for East Neighbor when he was 17. Since Oshina's family lived nearby he had gone there often on some errand or another. Increasingly he found himself dropping by just to see her. On evenings in the fall they would sit talking until late at night, munching on some of the soybeans he had set aside secretly while winnowing and baling East Neighbor's crop. He came even when he had lots of work to do. Their relationship grew out of these brief visits. That was when Oshina was 16. Kanji liked being in the master's service, and for close to three years he applied himself diligently. He was slight in build but muscular, and gradually he became skillful at his work.

Like the sunlight that manages to penetrate to the ground through even the thickest foliage, Kanji and Oshina found ways of seeing each other despite all obstacles. They were very happy.

Oshina became pregnant in the spring of her nineteenth year, although she herself remained unaware of it for some time. By summer, when she went about her chores in lightweight clothing, her condition should have been obvious to any discerning eye. Yet even her mother failed to notice, for she still thought of Oshina as a child. When finally she did notice it was far too late to do anything about it. Both sets of parents held a hasty conference. Kanji and Oshina were by then fiercely attached to one another. Afraid their parents might try to separate them, they ran off together one night, vowing to remain hidden until they were allowed to marry. Oshina in particular was determined to hold out until she had her way. Repeatedly she urged Kanji not to waver, and from that time on he always did as she said. The two of them had not been able to go far — they had hidden themselves at a friend's house in a nearby village. Meanwhile their parents were in an uproar trying to decide how to straighten out the mess the pair had made.

'It's a scandal!' Uhei had muttered angrily to himself, and so it was. But for that very reason the matter was settled fairly easily. Kanji was adopted into Oshina's family as a son-in-law, although he was to remain in East Neighbor's service until his time was up. There was a simple ceremony. A hastily appointed matchmaker brought Kanji to the house, where Uhei received him without a word. Kanji, who had always felt welcome there before, sat down awkwardly. Oshina, dressed only in ordinary clothes with her sleeves still tied up for work, remained standing at his side, her heavy belly swaying slightly. The matchmaker drank a cup of sake, and that was all there was to it. Shortly thereafter Oshina gave birth to a baby girl, Otsugi. It was during the busy season at the end of the year. Oshina's mother was very fond of her daughter and did not think her new son-in-law a bad choice at all. In fact she was delighted with him, especially that January when his wages for the following year of work at East Neighbor's arrived at their house. Uhei, however, did not like Kanji at all. While he himself was massively built and went lumbering about his work, Kanji seemed to dart here and there on his slender legs. It annoyed Uhei, too, that Kanji did only as he was told and appeared to lack initiative. But Uhei was himself an adopted son-in-law and taciturn to boot. At the conference of parents before the wedding all he had said was, 'It's none of my affair. You settle it however you want.'

The following May, the busiest time of all for farmers, Kanji fell sick. He had been out in the paddy fields every day, driving a horse through the mud to break up the soil for planting. Suddenly a southeast wind had come up, and the weather turned bitterly cold for that time of year. When Kanji went back to East Neighbor's house that night he complained of feeling weak and collapsed onto his bedding. He swallowed a few Akatama pellets, a medicine they had on hand for the horses, and huddled beneath his quilt. Under no circumstances did he want Uhei to see him sick like this. Nor did he want to lose any pay. If he could just forget how badly he felt and get back to work the next morning he would get credit for a day's service no matter how poorly he performed. But if he stayed in bed until he was well he would get docked for all the time he missed. Despite the horse medicine he had taken his condition showed no improvement. Early next morning he had someone help him home so that Oshina could care for him. Uhei greeted him sullenly. Oshina laid out the bedding, and Kanji lay down on his stomach, his face buried in his hands. Then everyone, including Oshina, set off for the fields. Their work did not allow them time to care for an invalid. Oshina's mother said only, 'There's food here if you get hungry,' as she covered the bowl and left the house. Later on Kanji slipped out of bed to take a look. It was a crumbly mass of barley, all they had left to live on at that time of year. Used to being a household servant where one never had to eat such humble food, Kanji could not bring himself to try it. At noon the family returned from the fields and ate some of the barley themselves. Even when Oshina's mother offered him a little, Kanji refused, remaining face down on his bedding.

'What a time of year to have that fellow on our hands!' Uhei observed with unusual vehemence. 'Look at him there, pretending to be so sick.' Kanji wept after they had left the house again. He stayed in bed for another few days, eating the rice crackers Oshina slipped to him when no one else was looking. Since there were hardly any sweet shops in the area at that time this was the best she could do to show her concern. Kanji found Uhei so unpleasant, indeed so frightening, that as soon as he felt a little stronger he stole away while the family was at work and hid himself in the attic of a relative's storehouse in the village. That night, having somehow figured out where he was, Oshina came to him, with Otsugi tied on her back and a chicken in her arms.

'Don't think bad of us, Kanji-san,' she pleaded, 'I don't mean for it to be that way. It just can't be helped.' Every night she came, bolted the door behind her, and stayed with him until dawn. Still, the very thought of being near Uhei was so distressing to Kanji that he would not go back. For a time he stayed in a nearby village, but wherever he was at work Oshina tracked him down and started pleading with him again. Finally he fled the area altogether. Then, after a short time, he found himself missing Oshina so much that he decided to come back after all. People made fun of him for that.

When Kanji's term of service to East Neighbor was over it was agreed that he and Uhei would divide the hearth at home instead of living together as one family. As their share of the available stores Kanji, Oshina, and the baby received less than a bushel of buckwheat and half a bushel of barley — nothing more. They were unable to make wheat noodles for New Year's, although Oshina's mother did manage to sneak them a little wheat flour from time to time. Despite the hardship Kanji felt happier than he would have been if he had to live with Uhei. Then, after Oshina's mother died, the two men were forced back together, this time with Kanji as head of the household. They did not even own their house and farmyard anymore, having long since sold both to East Neighbor at a cut rate to settle some debts. They were completely destitute. To Kanji Uhei was no longer such a frightening figure. Instead he seemed merely a disagreeable old man. The two men rarely exchanged a word, much to Oshina's distress.

Uhei did not hesitate when South Neighbor came to sound him out. 'The little ones need looking after,' he said, clicking his tongue as was his habit, 'so I guess I'll just have to do it.' Kanji, who had been waiting impatiently at South Neighbor's house for word, was greatly relieved.

'Well, Father,' he said to Uhei as he left for the construction site, 'Goodbye for now.' On that one occasion they spoke amicably to one another.

After Kanji had gone Uhei relaxed, a smile replacing his frown. Sometimes he held his grandson in his arms while the little boy wept. Yokichi often woke up crying in the night, too. Whenever that happened Uhei would roll over onto his side and light the lantern.

'You missing your mama?' he would intone in his deep voice. 'There now, it's light. See, that's your sister holding you. There's nothing to be afraid of.' Yokichi would cling tightly to Otsugi, crying frantically and staring blankly at the wall. She would hold him on her lap with both arms around him until finally he calmed down. Since this happened almost every night she kept a little packet of sugar for him under Oshina's old bedding where both of them now slept together. Sometimes he would cry so violently that he would spit the sugar out, and then he would cry even harder. Impatiently Otsugi would shake him by the shoulders. Finally Yokichi would stop crying, and with his mouth full of sugar again, he would go peacefully back to sleep. Uhei would watch all this intently, by the faint light of the lantern, from where he lay nearby.

Whenever Otsugi held Yokichi in her arms he would fumble at her breasts. Irritated, she would scold him sharply, but he would just smile up at her in his babyish way. Yet once when he was crying and she tried to get him to suckle, opening the front of her kimono just as she had seen her mother do, he would have none of it. Even when she smeared sugar on the nipple he could not be tempted. When Yokichi was hungry Otsugi would feed him a little softened rice mixed with sugar. He would smack his lips after each mouthful and smile up at her, revealing a few tiny white teeth. Then he would lean back until he was almost lying down in her arms and gurgle contentedly. Whenever he wanted more he would reach out his tiny hand toward the soot-covered cupboard. That was where the sugar he liked so much was kept.

Following Kanji's instructions Otsugi cooked herself and Uhei some of the mixture of rice and barley he had put by for them. Other than making a little potato and radish broth she had nothing else to do around the house. Often she strapped Yokichi on her back and went off to the forest to collect firewood, knocking dead branches down from the trees with a bamboo pole. She also made Yokichi a little straw basket shaped like a snail.

Uhei usually wandered off somewhere during the day, and when he came home he always brought a few pieces of cheap candy with him. He would hold them out towards Yokichi and then pull his hand back through the sleeve of his kimono to his chest. Slowly Yokichi would waddle towards him and peer into the sleeve. Uhei would then stick out his other hand. As Yokichi moved unsteadily towards it Uhei would drop the candies onto Yokichi's head, from where they tumbled down onto the ground. Laughing happily Yokichi would reach down to pick them up one by one. They were the hard, black candies called 'bullets'. As Uhei watched the candies scatter and saw Yokichi careening after them, he, too, would break into laughter. Even though Yokichi might stumble and fall he never cried at all. He would put the candies into his straw basket. Then he would hold the basket very carefully, peering into it every now and then. While all this was going on Osugi would be at work preparing supper.

6

Spring stirs first in the air and then in the soil. The strong winds that have come dust-laden out of the west all winter suddenly cease, and soft white clouds hang motionless in the sky, basking in the sun. The moist soil near the irrigation ditches drinks in the warm sunlight and transmits its renewed energy to the roots of the alder trees at the edge of the paddy fields. In almost no time their buds are open and fluttering on their branches. Then an occasional frog, still in its winter hiding place, starts croaking once again. The sunlight grows steadily warmer, and hungrily the soil absorbs the heat. Soon reeds, wild grains, and grasses rise up along the ditches to face the sun. As if intoxicated by the softness of the air the blossoms on the alder trees begin to dance, spewing forth fine sprays of pollen. And the frogs, who are out of hibernation at last, cling to the soft grass and gaze upward in amazement. Suddenly they open their throats and proclaim to the sky their return to life, their boisterous cries echoing far and wide.

The frogs next turn their attention to the world around them, croaking on and on until all the vegetation responds to their message that spring has come. The alder trees, having already shed their blossoms, now display tiny leaves that sparkle in the morning sunlight as they gaze across the paddy fields to the still dormant forest beyond. Hastily all the white, red, and yellow tones of winter change to green as the forest too becomes aware of spring. The barley sprouts upward in the plots of cleared land scattered here and there within the forest, and clusters of black-eyed blossoms peek out timidly from beneath the leaves of the broad bean plants. In amongst the trees the sturdy shoots of pampas grass thrust themselves towards the sun. Every now and then the skylarks who make their home in the shelter of the barley and the grass soar into the sky, singing out that spring is in full sway. This annoys the frogs, who think their voices alone should dominate the air. They hop about, croaking angrily, until the outnumbered birds are once more cowering in their nests. Only in the heat of the day when the frogs are always silent can the skylarks sing in peace. Then, after sunset, the frogs reappear. They croak insistently, ever more loudly, until even the tall evergreen oaks in the forest have shed their old leaves.

By now all the trees and even the weeds that have lain limply on the ground throughout the winter are up on tiptoe, straining towards the sunlight. Since the soil refuses to set them free they remain at right angles to the ground. People, too, who also like to rest in winter, are once more standing upright on the soil like needles in the grip of a powerful magnet. With farm tools in their hands and with their blue trouser legs tied up with straw they begin to prepare the paddy fields for planting. 'We could use some water,' they think, and just then the frogs set up a mighty chorus of croaking, the pouches on their throats so swollen one wonders if they'll burst. Rain falls in silken strands, filling the paddy fields bit by bit. The frogs, born only to croak when it is time for croaking, sustain their chorus as they hop about the farmers' feet, urging them on in their toil. In the afternoon when the frogs retreat from the heat of the sun the farmers too lie down wearily on the grass to rest. Later, in the still of the night, the frogs once more send their voices echoing through the air. The sound reaches faintly through the closed doors of the farmers' houses and lulls them into the deep sleep their aching bodies need. When they leap up at dawn and step outside the farmers hear the frogs once again croaking lustily by their wells and welcoming them to another day. During the night all the vegetation has grown in response to the frogs' serenade. The trees in the forest will keep on growing, no matter what insects attack them, for as long as the frogs continue to croak. As if the gentle rain had brought color from the sky, the leaves deepen in tone, providing cool, refreshing shade on the ground below.

In this way, spring came to the land on the west bank of the Kinu River. Everyone, whether careworn or carefree, was back at work. Kanji was among them.

During the spring he observed the forty-ninth day of mourning for Oshina. Unable to spare a single *sen* he had only bowed humbly before her mortuary tablet in honor of the occasion. When he had gone back to the construction project on the Tone River the gloomy sky had shown every sign of winter. Sleet, snow and rain had sometimes made work impossible, forcing the men to huddle all day inside their chilly bunkhouse. No matter how frugally they tried to live they found it impossible to put anything aside from their wages. That was because of the exorbitant prices they were charged for food and firewood even when they could not work. Then, too, Kanji had incurred what for him were enormous expenses from the time of Oshina's illness until her funeral. He had managed to pay for the funeral itself with the condolence money he had received from everyone in the village and with the savings Oshina had tucked away beneath her bedding. But the doctor's fees and all the rest had taken a severe toll on his purse. In addition he had taken 50 *sen* of the money he had got for selling some of his rice to cover his family's expenses while he was away. Rather than giving the money directly to Uhei, he had left it with South Neighbor to deliver.

Uhei had not been pleased when South Neighbor handed it to him. 'Can't trust me with it without a witness, huh?' he grumbled. 'Well, if that's how he feels, I won't take it.'

'It's not that way at all,' South Neighbor replied. 'Kanji didn't mean any harm.' But Uhei remained unpersuaded.

Wanting to return home quickly, Kanji worked as hard as he could on the project, but all that he earned he had to spend just to keep himself alive. Some of the other men from the area gave up and ran away. Even though Kanji stuck it out a little longer he still ended up with no more money than he had had with him in the first place.

It was night when he finally arrived home, so exhausted that his legs felt numb. 'Thanks for looking after things, Father,' he said to Uhei in an apologetic tone of voice. The children were both delighted to see him. Yokichi clung to his hand, expecting that Kanji, like Uhei, had brought him some candy. But Kanji had felt too poor to buy any presents at all. Now, though, he was sorry he did not have at least a few sweets for the little boy who looked up at him so eagerly, saying 'Eat? Eat?'

'Here, let's have some of Grampa's sugar,' Otsugi said, as she picked Yokichi up and reached for the packet in the cupboard. Uhei had just given Kanji a quick look when he had entered the house. He had not said a word of greeting. It seemed to him that Kanji was just feigning weariness. With a displeased look on his face he clamped his pipe into his mouth. Then, noticing that it had gone out, he rapped the bowl sharply against the hibachi to loosen the ashes. The gesture struck Kanji as a disguised rebuke.

Then Uhei spoke. 'Otsugi! Give the little one all the sugar he wants. You have some too. Your father's gone off and earned lots of money, so you'll have it easy from now on.'

It unnerved Kanji to be treated this way, in his own house and at the very moment of his return. Unable to stand it he withdrew hastily, saying he had to pay his respects to the neighbors.

'Won't tomorrow do?' Uhei muttered after him. It was his habit always to say what he thought, not mincing any words, but never before had he spoken with such contempt.

Feeling sorry for the children Uhei had been willing to stay on and look after them while Kanji was away. It pleased him that his little bags of candy meant so much to Yokichi and made him so important to the little boy. He had been content. But now Kanji was back, and right away the children warmed to him. He felt Kanji had robbed him of all the affection he had won from them. And then there was Kanji himself, whom he had never liked at all. The man could not even talk about calling on the neighbors without cringing and almost whimpering when he spoke.

The manner that Uhei found so unpleasant had stemmed from Kanji's acute distress at having come home with so little money. Feeling that he had failed them all he had only mentioned seeing the neighbors as an excuse to leave the house. Instead he went off and bought a bag of candies. Yokichi was already fast asleep, however, when he returned. Uhei stared at him coolly, wondering at his strange behavior. Then he recalled the matter of the 50 *sen* and became annoyed.

'Got lots of money, huh?' he asked abruptly.

'Oh no, hardly any,' Kanji replied. 'I practically ran away, and I never want to go back. What an awful place. I hated every minute of it.' He spoke nervously, upset that people might think he was well off.

'That so?' Uhei muttered with indifference. 'Well, I know I'm not needed around here. Might as well leave. I don't care how much money you got.'

Kanji turned pale. Uhei thought he did have money after all and was keeping it for himself. The old man abruptly returned to Noda the next day.

Uhei worked as a night watchman in Noda, patrolling a large storehouse compound and striking his wooden clappers to show that all was well. It was not a particularly difficult job, even for an old man like himself. He had the daytime off, and by cutting down on his sleep he was able to earn a little extra money at odd jobs. He never had to go without the tobacco or the occasional glass of sake he liked so much. He even had a nice *yukata* to wear in hot weather. It was not a hard life, except on freezing nights in winter-time when his lumbago would suddenly act up again, causing him such intense pain he could hardly walk. Then and only then he would wish he could be home again with Oshina. With no children of his own he had only had her to look after him in his old age. Now that she was dead he was all alone. There was Kanji, of course, but Uhei could not stand him. He could still manage all right on his own in Noda, and so he had announced he was going back. He had let his pride get the better of him, for despite his contempt for Kanji and despite all his grumbling the old man was desperately unhappy about leaving.

Kanji was despondent. It distressed him whenever Yokichi cried, and every day he thought about Oshina. Sometimes he would think he saw her, carrying her buckets on a pole, out in the yard, or by the well, or even in the house. He would feel her presence so intensely at times that involuntarily he would turn around to look. Holding Yokichi in his arms he would say over and over, 'Your mama's not here anymore. No use your wanting her.' He was also trying to persuade himself that she was gone.

When Oshina had set off to peddle bean curd she had often put an empty bottle in one of the buckets. Some of the sake Kanji liked so much would be gurgling merrily in the bottle when she came home. She had delivered some bean curd to the sake merchant and received a cheap brand of wine in exchange. That way she could please Kanji without having to spend any money. She had only been doing this during the year before she died. Just that summer she had finally become good at peddling. At first she had felt awkward and could hardly bring herself to approach a stranger's door. Her face would turn bright red and she could never think of anything polite to say. But later, as she had often told Kanji, she had reached a point where she could speak easily and even make some appropriate comment about the weather. Unable to bear these memories, Kanji stood at Oshina's grave and wept. He gazed ruefully at the white paper lantern left there after the funeral that was now reduced to a soggy mass by the rain.

Pulling himself together at last Kanji hired himself out as a day laborer so that the three of them would at least have food to eat. He worked often for the master next door, polishing his rice so skillfully that its volume was hardly reduced at all. Occasionally when the master was not paying any heed he would sneak a little rice from the storehouse, hide it somewhere on the premises and take it home with him at night. It did not amount to much, perhaps five or six quarts in all. That was hardly enough for the master to miss, but it made a great difference to Kanji and the children. One day he took some rice and hid it in a woodpile. Another employee discovered the sack and reported it to the master's wife. She told him to leave the sack there for whomever had hidden it, but as a joke the employee emptied out the rice and filled the sack with dirt instead. When Kanji retrieved the sack that night he was certain the game was up. Frightened and ashamed he did not report to work the next morning. For the next few days he tried to remain as inconspicuous as possible, avoiding East Neighbor's house at all costs. Eventually the mistress found out about the employee's joke.

Taking pity on Kanji she summoned him back to work. In addition to a sack of rice mixed with cracked barley, she also gave him some dry millet. 'Our other employees won't touch this sort of thing,' she said, 'so you may as well have it. You can give us back some sticky millet in the fall.' Kanji had always thought he could count on East Neighbor. He worked as hard as he could, which did not please the other employees at all. They could not slack off with him setting such an example of diligence.

Meanwhile spring arrived, and the rains poured down on the fields. Kanji went out to the paddy behind his house and started to turn over the stubble. Otsugi followed him, carrying her own hoe. Now that Oshina was gone Kanji had to rely on his daughter if he was going to keep on working this plot of land. Since it was so convenient to his house he wanted to hang on to it at all costs. If he gave up cultivating rights for a time it would be no easy matter to secure them from the landlord again. He had no choice but to see if Otsugi could handle grown-up work. Kanji drove his hoe deep into the ground and turned up big chunks of earth. Otsugi turned up small chunks only. Kanji moved steadily ahead, his arms in continuous motion. Otsugi lagged farther and farther behind, her efforts with her hoe making only a slight impression on the soil.

'Don't be so bashful about it!' Kanji said impatiently. 'Do it like this.' He took her hoe and struck it forcefully into the ground.

'But Papa! I can't do it that way.'

'It's no good thinking like that. Give it a real try now.'

Otsugi started working as hard as she could.

Yokichi was sitting on a mat laid out near the irrigation ditch. Otsugi called out to him often as she paused to wipe the sweat from her face. 'You just stay right there. Don't you move, or you'll go plop into the ditch . . . Hear that? A frog just jumped into the water . . . Stay right there now! You can play with your stick . . . Don't cry, Yoki. Sister's here in the paddy. You cry and Papa will get mad.' Yokichi poked at the soil on the bank of the ditch with his short, muddy stick. Now and then he would look back to make sure Otsugi was still in the field behind him. Then he would poke with his stick again, laughing merrily whenever the tip struck the surface of the water. Eventually he grew tired of this game and turned to locate Otsugi. Seeing that she was all the way over at the other side of the field he called out to her. She did not answer, so he called again. Then he burst into tears. Otsugi started to go to him.

'Just leave him be!' Kanji yelled at her. 'You can see what he wants when you get back over there again.' Otsugi ignored Yokichi's crying and kept on working.

Kanji moved along steadily until he was at the edge of the ditch.

'Don't cry now. Sister's coming right along,' he said, giving Yokichi a quick glance as he passed by, his arms never breaking rhythm. As Otsugi finally drew closer Yokichi began to cry again.

'What's wrong, Yoki?' Otsugi climbed up the bank, her legs covered with mud, and knelt down on the grass. Smiling through his tears Yokichi held out his arms to show he wanted to be picked up.

'Sister's all muddy,' Otsugi said as she lifted him onto her lap. 'Doesn't Yoki mind getting dirty?' She held him close and went on talking. 'Can't you find any frogs? You know, if you hit 'em with your stick, you'll hurt 'em and they'll start to cry. Crying's for frogs, but Yoki mustn't cry.' Then she looked over towards Kanji. 'Uh-oh, Papa's all the way over there. I better go, or he'll get mad. You stay quiet, okay?' Otsugi set him down on the mat again.

'Stop wasting time over there!' Kanji yelled back at her. 'No more nonsense!'

'See? He's mad, all right. Here now, you can play with these.' Otsugi plucked a few cottonwood flowers and laid them on the mat. Then she made her way awkwardly down into the paddy again. Yokichi poked at the flowers with his finger.

The irrigation ditch was filled to the brim with water from the rains. The heavy branch of a nearby willow tree hung with its tip in the water, moving lightly with the current and creating slight ripples downstream. Thin, scraggly shoots of *toda* grass stood underwater along the banks, swaying helplessly from side to side. A tadpole took shelter from the rush of water among some submerged silvery weeds. Then, like all young creatures unable to remain still for long, it swam out from the bank again, its little tail fluttering desperately as it tried unsuccessfully to maintain its course. Yokichi threw a flower into the water. It spun round and round as it was carried off downstream. Suddenly a frog sprang out from the grass and caught the flower. Paddling mightily with its hind legs it headed for the opposite bank where it turned and stared back across the ditch. After throwing all his flowers into the water Yokichi called out again to Otsugi.

'Ooi!' Her reassuring voice came back to him across the field. Hearing it Yokichi started calling out to her over and over again. Each time she answered him, while continuing busily at work.

Shortly before noon Otsugi returned home to brew some tea to have along with their lunch. Yokichi clung happily to her back. Kanji stayed behind alone and worked. Not until blue smoke had risen above the oak trees and Otsugi had called out 'Water's boiling!' did he put down his hoe.

After lunch Otsugi secured a needle to a length of thread and tied the thread to a pole. This she gave to Yokichi, who played contentedly with his new toy while she and Kanji went back to work. Just as all children will do he flung the needle up into the air and then cast it down into the water. After a while he called out to his sister again. When she had worked her way over to the ditch she saw that both the needle and the thread were gone.

'What happened, Yoki?' she asked as she climbed up the bank. Then she saw that the needle was caught in the willow branch on the other side of the ditch, with the end of thread dangling in the water. Otsugi walked upstream, crossed over the wooden bridge, and bent back the willow branches to retrieve the needle. When she got back she reattached the thread to Yokichi's pole. 'Don't you do that again, now! I don't have time to go hunting for it,' she said in a lightly scolding tone as she returned to the field. Kanji was annoyed. 'But Yoki's thread broke,' she mumbled abashedly. Then she went back to work. Every once in a while Yokichi called out to her plaintively, but she made no reply. If she was far away across the field he would bend over almost double and yell 'Sister! Sister!' at the top of his lungs.

That night they all went to a neighbor's house for a bath. Otsugi showed her hands to the other women who had gathered there. 'Just look at these blisters!' she complained.

'Oh my, yes. Those must really hurt,' one of the women replied sympathetically. 'But with your mother gone, you've got to start working.'

'I hate it, not having a mother!' Otsugi blurted out. Then seeing Kanji nearby she hung her head. Kanji just stood there silently.

'Now, now, Otsū,' the woman said, 'It can't be all that bad. You're just complaining because you don't have anyone to make clothes for you anymore.' Kanji thought that was an awful thing to say, but he just looked on grimly, making no comment.

'Do you think they'll get worse?' Otsugi asked anxiously, looking down at the palms of her hands.

'Course not!' Kanji exploded, no longer able to restrain himself.

When they got back home Kanji picked out a few grains of cooked rice from the bottom of the bowl and kneaded them together with some tobacco ashes. Then he punctured the blisters on Otsugi's hands, let them drain a bit, and applied the paste he had made.

'That stings!' Otsugi whimpered.

'That's because they've just been drained. But putting something on 'em right away makes 'em heal faster.' Kanji stared at Otsugi silently for a moment and then looked over at Yokichi, who was already fast asleep.

'You come to me next time you got blisters or anything. Don't go showing 'em around to other people. You just don't know a thing, do you? Everybody, even me, gets blisters at the start of the season. Here, take a look!' He held out his hands towards her. 'You've just got to forget they hurt and keep on going. They dry up soon enough.'

After another pause he added, 'You're not the only one who's upset your mother died. Look, we're in a bad way, so you'll just have to keep working. There's girls worse off than yourself, you know. Like the ones sent away to Bushū.'

Otsugi was intrigued. 'Where's Bushū?' she asked.

Kanji nodded toward the doors, indicating southwest. 'Off that way, but farther than you could walk in a day.'

'That far! What do the girls who get sent there do?'

'Well, some do weaving, others farm work.'

'That'd be nice, wouldn't it? Learning to weave.'

'Nice! You think so, huh? Well, you go there, they don't let you come home hardly ever. Work you from morning to night, too. You get sick, you have to be dying before they'll let your family know.'

'But if it's so bad, can't they run away?'

'Not many try, because they get caught right away.'

'The police catch 'em?'

'What? No, they've got guards of their own. Don't need the police.'

'But whatever do they do if they can't stand it there?'

'Too bad for them. They've got to stay on no matter what, because of the advance they get.'

'What's that — the advance?'

'Well, if you want to quit before your time is up, you've got to pay back all the wages they give you when you first get there. You can't do that, so you've just got to stay, no matter how you hate it.'

'I sure don't want to go to a place like that!' Otsugi said with feeling.

'Don't you worry, I'm not going to send you. If I put you in service somewhere, though, I could pay all my debts with the money. Then sell Yoki off to the acrobats and I'd be set. But no, it's bad enough already with just your mother gone. I'd miss both of you as soon as you left, so I'll just have to make the best of things the way they are now.'

'Papa, did you say you'd get rid of all your debts if I went into service?'

'That's what your mother and me planned to do, you know. That way we'd get hold of some money. But now, well, I need you here instead. We'll just have to put it off. I'm sorry it's rough for you now, I really am sorry.'

Kanji knew he had Otsugi doing work she was still too young to handle. The next morning he got up first and lit the stove while the exhausted girl still lay fast asleep. Only after the fire was blazing and steam escaping from under the lid of the cooking pot did she get up. Still fully dressed from the night before she stumbled out to the well, rubbing her eyes sleepily. After combing her long, loosely hanging hair and plunging her hands into the cold water she felt wide awake at last. Even so, her eyes were bloodshot and her walk unsteady.

'There, food's ready,' Kanji announced as he transferred the mass of rice and barley to some bowls. Later he fetched the tools himself and they set off for the fields.

The rice sprouts now stuck up above the water level in the seed-beds, their deep green leaves drooping in the heat. There was a light breeze blowing, and pollen from the pine trees covered the ground like a layer of dust. Tiny blossoms clustered on the heads of barley. It was that busy time of year when every farmer feels he has more to do than he can possibly manage. Kanji was seriously worried about falling behind. Tired though he was he worked on and on every day from morning until night. Otsugi dragged along wearily behind him. Only in the late afternoon when she returned home ahead of her father to prepare supper did she have a chance to rest.

Kanji was sowing soy beans in his plot of dry land. Working rapidly he dug a shallow trench between the already established rows of barley. Then Otsugi came along and dropped in the seeds. She was still so small that only her shoulders and the scarf she had tied about her hair were visible above the white-topped barley stalks. Yokichi sat quietly on the ivy near the side of the path. Whenever his sister disappeared from view he called out to her. She responded 'Ooi!' Hearing her voice he would remain still for a time. After digging all the trenches Kanji himself began sowing seeds. He noticed how slowly Otsugi was progressing and cast a glance at the row she was working on. The seeds were unevenly spaced, and in some places she had dropped in four or five at a time.

'What do you think you're doing!' he shouted. 'That'll ruin us!' Angrily he hit her, causing her to fall down among the barley stalks. She lay there crying.

'Can't you do anything right?' Kanji yelled down at her. 'Putting those seeds in like that! I can't believe it!'

A farmer came running from the adjacent field. 'What in the world's going on here, Kanji-san? How can you be so mean?' he shouted. Then he spoke soothingly to Otsugi. 'There, there, don't cry, Otsugi. You get up and get back to work. I'll make it up with your father. Look now, Yokichi's crying. You better go to him, huh?' Yokichi had called out to his sister when she disappeared into the barley. Getting no reply he had burst into tears. Otsugi ran over to him, still crying herself, and gathered him into her arms.

'Her without a mother and all,' the farmer continued, 'Let's have no more of this. What do you expect anyhow? She's just a child, she can't do things the way you want. Why, her mother's spirit must be all upset, the way you're behaving!' Kanji just stood there, saying nothing. Yokichi had stopped crying now that Otsugi was holding him.

That evening while Otsugi was preparing supper Kanji left the field and returned to the house. He crept stealthily into the main room and got his purse. Then he left again. When he next appeared he was carrying a package. The house was dark when he entered, and for a moment he could not see a thing.

That night the three of them made their way through the mulberry field to South Neighbor's for a bath. As usual a number of women from the neighborhood had gathered there for the same purpose.

'It's a good thing, now isn't it,' one woman observed. 'See how Otsū takes care of Yoki? That's what's so nice about girls. They make themselves useful right away.'

'What's the matter, Otsugi?' another woman asked. 'You look kind of gloomy tonight.'

Kanji forced a smile and said, 'It's probably because I took a swing at her a while back.'

'You did what! What an awful thing. You just take better care of her, you hear? Why think of what things'd be like without her. You'd be in some fix if you had to care for the little one yourself!'

'That's right,' another woman chimed in. 'Why, without Otsū Yoki'd have nobody to look after him. That'd be awful, wouldn't it, Otsū?'

'He needs a lot of looking after,' Otsugi replied. 'He never leaves me alone.' Yokichi was getting too big for her to carry so she sat and held him on her lap.

'She's just like a mother, isn't she!' the woman exclaimed, smiling down at the two of them. Kanji stood off to the side, wiping the tears from his eyes.

As soon as they got home he said 'Bring the lantern over here, Otsū. I got something to show you.'

Still looking dispirited Otsugi lit the tin lantern and moved toward him. Meanwhile Kanji unwrapped the package he had brought home earlier. Inside was a neatly folded blue checkered kimono.

'This is for you,' Kanji told her. 'Your mother wove it herself. You know, no one does that sort of thing anymore, but she worked on it real hard, just about every night. See how blue it is? It's dyed real good — to last. Your mother hardly wore it at all, so it's still like new. Bring that light closer and take a good look.'

He unfolded the kimono a bit and sniffed at the odor it gave off. 'Looks like a little mildew,' he said apologetically. 'You just hang it out for a day, though, and it'll be fine.'

Otsugi held the lantern aloft in one hand and stroked the fabric with the other. Her face, still glistening from her bath, was smiling. Kanji had been watching her intently. When he saw that she was happy he went on.

'You like it, huh? You know, all your mother's things are yours. No matter how bad things get I'm not going to pawn them, because they're yours.'

Otsugi set the lantern down beside her and sniffed at the odor as Kanji had done. Then she slipped her left arm into the sleeve. 'Still a bit big for me, isn't it?' she said, waving her arm from side to side. 'I'll put it away to wear later, after I've grown some.'

'It's yours, so you do whatever you want,' Kanji said, still watching her closely. As she fondled the kimono a little lampblack fell onto the ends of her hair.

'Look out there!' Kanji cried as another drop was about to fall. 'You'll catch fire.' Alarmed, he reached out and brushed her hair aside.

7

Kanji's fields yielded a pitifully small harvest that fall. It was not that the weather had been bad or that the soil itself was poor. He had got his crops in late and had not applied much fertilizer. No matter how much energy he expended the results were bound to be disappointing. It was the same for all poor farmers. They spent long hours in their fields doing all they could to raise enough food. Then after the harvest they had to part with most of what they had produced. Their crops were theirs only for as long as they stood rooted in the soil. Once the farmers had paid the rents they owed they were lucky to have enough left over to sustain them through the winter. During the growing season itself they had to abandon their own fields to do day labor for others to earn money for that day's food. They had not forgotten that their own fields needed tending — in a village where everyone worked at farming it was impossible to forget what needed to be done at any given time. They simply had to deal with the immediate necessity of getting something to eat. Even when their own crops most needed attention they might not be able to provide it for days at a time. Nor could they do much about fertilizer. It was no longer possible to obtain free compost from the forests as they had always done in the past. Now the forests were privately owned, and one had to pay to collect leaves or cut green grass. Where people had been at work with their rakes every winter the grass had become stunted, and where the grass itself had been cut the soil gradually deteriorated. Without money one could not obtain good, soft grass at all anymore, unless of course one stole it. Only after others had been through the forests with their rakes and sickles could poor farmers enter to scavenge for leaves and grass. Then they scratched away at the already impoverished soil, leaving it even more exposed and infertile than before.

As the forests became depleted, all sorts of artificial fertilizers appeared in the countryside. But once again only those with money could make use of them. Poor farmers were caught up in a vicious circle. Lacking fertilizer they were unable to grow much more than they owed their landlords in rents. So they had to find other work in order to obtain the food they needed. But when they found such work they fell behind in weeding and cultivating their own fields. If they missed even a few days during the hot, wet summer the weeds would shoot up and stifle the growth of their crops. That alone was sufficient to reduce yields. It was just as if they had uprooted the crops before they had matured and eaten them.

At the end of the harvest season poor farmers withered up like the vegetation around them. There was little for them to do during the fifty or sixty days until the next growing season began but hoe the furrows in their barley fields and hunt for fallen leaves and firewood in the forests. Virtually no paying work was to be had at this time of year. While the frogs and insects hibernated peacefully, farmers had to consume their meager stores of grain just to keep themselves alive from day to day. Inevitably a time would come when they had nothing left to eat.

They had no home industries to sustain them during the slack season. True, they wove mats and sandals for their own use, but since the straw they used was old and brittle, the items they produced had little value. And besides, they were too concerned about the lack of compost to use up all the bits of straw they had scattered about their yards. Even if someone had encouraged them to produce handicrafts for sale, they would have resisted. To poor farmers the winter had always been and would always be a time of suffering. They knew nothing else.

Like other poor farmers Kanji eked out a bare hand-to-mouth existence. He had nothing at all to fall back on in an emergency. Like them he began the winter by collecting firewood and stacking it up against the wall of his house. But then, unlike the rest of them, he had a paying job to perform. For some time now East Neighbor had been interested in clearing land within his forest, and Kanji had been employed to transform one small parcel into an arable field. Despite his slight build he made steady progress, digging the heavy iron blade of his mattock deep into the ground and thrusting the loosened soil behind him. This was work he not only did skillfully but enjoyed as well. When he grasped his mattock he seemed to become one with it. If the blade cut into the root of a tree Kanji's body shuddered too, as if he had actually done the cutting. He had always been good at digging. Indeed, that was why he had gone off to work on the Tone River project. He relied on his strong arms and shoulders for his survival.

He had done land reclaiming in the past, too. One of his first jobs had been clearing a bamboo grove, and he had managed to get the tangled roots dug out in massive clumps of soil, so energetically had he worked. But he had to pay to have the blade of his mattock sharpened before he began, and after he had deducted that expense and the cost of all the food he had consumed to keep his strength up he had found that hardly anything was left of the wages he had received. From then on he let his wages determine how rapidly he worked and how deeply he dug.

He was delighted now that the work he was doing for the master would last all spring, since he was to receive payment in rice and barley as well as a little cash. Not wanting to leave Otsugi alone at home, he had her come along, with Yokichi in tow, to the clearing. While he worked, she collected fallen twigs nearby. Owners of forests did not mind if people picked up little things like that without paying for them.

Kanji worked every day, except when it rained. One day he got the blade of his mattock stuck solidly in a tree stump. When he tried to wrench it free he suddenly found the handle swinging loosely in his hands. There was a large crack in the metal ring that secured the handle to the blade.

'Dammit,' he grumbled, 'there's a day's money gone to the blacksmith.'

He set off the next morning at dawn.

'I've got to go away today,' he said to South Neighbor's wife when he brought her Otsugi and Yokichi. 'Please look after these two till I get back.' Then he turned to Otsugi. 'Don't you go off anywhere now, hear? And keep Yoki from crying.' Otsugi no longer could bear being talked to like that in front of others. She felt humiliated.

Kanji crossed the Kinu River and walked along the embankment on the other side, the blade in one hand. The smith was busy when he arrived, but he finished up quickly. No one in his profession would make a man wait to have such a vital tool repaired.

'Looks like you've really been rough with it. I haven't seen one messed up like this for ages.' The smith pounded the red hot metal with his mallet and thrust it into a bucket of muddy water. Then he pounded it some more with a small hammer.

'Well now, that ought to do it. How'd you get that crack anyhow?' Sweat dripping from his face, the smith looked over towards Kanji. 'Usually the handle breaks before the joint.' Then grinning, he added, 'You sure don't look strong enough to have done it.'

Kanji picked up the blade, which still gave off a metallic smell, and retraced his steps along the river bank.

The west wind was blowing that day from the forests and barley fields on the other side of the river, creating whitecaps on the surface of the water that looked from a distance like little ears of millet. As the wind swept down onto the river it shook the bamboo bushes growing on the west bank. Then when it rose up the embankment on the other side it bent the blades of short, dry grass growing there to the ground. Here and there amid the grass one could see the yellow heads of dandelions. Deceived by spells of warm, windless weather they had started growing again, but now, in the sudden chill, they seemed to be cringing against the soil.

With his mattock blade repaired Kanji could get right back to work. Yet for some reason or other he did not feel particularly pressed.

Downstream a ways a large sandbar stretched out from the east bank of the river, creating a narrow channel for the water to a point below the bamboo bushes on the other side. The wind blew across it as if sweeping up stray particles of sand. From a distance the surface looked completely smooth. Then Kanji detected a number of tiny human shapes, looking for all the world as if they had sprung up from the sand itself. They moved slightly every so often. Intrigued, Kanji climbed down from the embankment to take a closer look. The people were digging into the sand with hoes, leaving the smooth surface rippled in their wake. Here and there little pieces of wood lay on the sand. Most were no more than 6 or 7 inches in length, though once in a while a slightly longer piece turned up. All had the smooth contours of driftwood. The people kept on with their digging, pausing only to blow warm breath on their icy fingers.

Kanji approached one of them. 'What goes on here?' he asked.

It was an old woman who turned to face him. She planted her feet firmly in the sand to brace herself against the wind. 'We're going to dry these and then burn 'em,' she replied, squinting as her dirty gray hair and scarf blew about her face.

'But you won't get much of a fire with this stuff, will you?' Kanji asked.

'Well, no,' she answered. 'They burn pretty quick. Not much heat either. Still, it's a whole lot better than buying firewood. A person can pick up maybe thirty-five bundles here in a day, and for nothing. Why, even an old bag like me can carry off ten bundles at a time, they're so small. It's a big problem these days getting stuff to burn, so we've got no choice.'

'Thirty-five bundles, huh?' Kanji said, his head to one side. 'That wouldn't cost much. Course, what you get from the peddlers is pretty small, too.'

'Not much you say? Where are you from anyhow?' the old woman asked, leaning on her hoe.

'Across the river.'

'Well then, you've got plenty of trees over there, haven't you?' The old woman looked down at Kanji's mattock blade. 'That's quite a thing you got there. Cost a lot, I bet.'

'Yeah, one like this costs maybe three times more than most blades.'

'Must weigh a lot, too.'

'Not more than about eight pounds.' Kanji spoke proudly as he handed the blade to the old woman.

'My, my! Too heavy for me. You can use this yourself? What ever do you do with it?'

'I've been digging up tree stumps. Just had to get it fixed, because I put a crack in it.'

'Tree stumps, you say? Well then, you've got no trouble getting stuff to burn, have you?' the old woman said enviously as she went back to work.

To the west, just across the river, were forests upon forests. They surrounded every village and every bit of farmland, too. Here on the eastern side, however, there were low-lying fields with villages scattered here and there among them. The only trees on this side of the river were planted around people's houses. Kanji had always known that the farmers on this side had hardly any firewood and had to save every scrap of straw and beanstalk for fuel. But this was the first time he had ever seen people hunting for driftwood in the sand. Only rarely did he set foot on this side of the river.

Kanji had lots of firewood stacked up at home, and the more land reclamation work he did the more he acquired. The tool that made that work possible was now in perfect repair. He felt superior to these people who had to grub away for little bits of wood. He did not pause to think about all the troubles he himself faced, nor did he feel any pity towards the people at work before him. He just felt happy. Once more he looked back at the sandbar. All the people wielding hoes were women, with perhaps a dozen children in tow. He gazed down at the traces their digging left behind. The undulating lines of moist sand reminded him of the pattern earthworms made when they turned up the soil in his fields.

As soon as he got home, Kanji reattached the handle to his mattock blade, pounding the metal ring onto it with the blunt edge of his hatchet. Then he grasped the handle and tested it out to make sure it was securely fixed in place. The next morning he was back at work in the forest.

The grain he received from the master kept the three of them going that winter. Kanji felt more at ease than he had in some time. But this very modest improvement in his circumstances aroused envy in others. There are always some farmers who find themselves struggling to survive from day to day. If one among them manages to acquire even a few extra *sen* the rest find out about it right away, for in addition to keeping an eye out for themselves they keep close track of what happens to their neighbors. They derive a measure of security from their belief that everyone is suffering at least as much as they are. But let someone appear to be getting even slightly ahead and they feel desperately threatened. That feeling, in turn, gives rise to envy. For the same reason, too, they take secret pleasure in the misfortunes that befall others.

A mountain of firewood was piled against the wall of Kanji's house. That attracted the attention of some of the other poor farmers in the village, who wasted no time in informing the master. It was even reported that Kanji had brought home the ashes from the trees he had burned up at the clearing. Since he was getting paid pretty well for the work he was doing, Kanji was not supposed to take even a single oak stump away with him. The others knew that, too. Every afternoon, or whenever he felt cold, Kanji burned a pile of wood on the clearing. The blue smoke would rise up slowly from the smouldering tree stumps. As it died away he would hack at the embers with his mattock. Each day he made the fire at a different spot, and he did indeed rake up the ashes and carry them away. He carted off some illicit oak stumps as well, though most of the wood stacked up against his wall he had permission to bring home. But that did not stop people from complaining. In fact, even earlier a rumor had been circulating that Kanji had stolen some newly harvested rice, news that had attracted the attention of the village policeman. Because of all the gossip that reached his ears the master thought he had better deliver some sort of warning. Secretly he arranged for someone to ask Kanji if he had taken any oak stumps or not. If Kanji would just apologize that would be the end of the matter. Unfortunately, Kanji did not realize that this was all the master had in mind.

'You'd better look for 'em somewhere else,' he said angrily to the go-between. 'I'd never do such a thing.'

The master then had a private talk with the village policeman, who one day appeared unexpectedly at Kanji's house. It was raining, so Kanji had not gone off to work. He was sitting by the hibachi, feeding pieces of tree stump to the fire.

'Too bad it's raining, isn't it?' the policeman observed from the doorway, his hand resting on the hilt of his sword. 'You're quite a one for work, I hear.'

'Uh . . . yeah,' Kanji stuttered, getting to his feet quickly. The man's sudden appearance and the way his face was hidden by the hood of his raincloak frightened Kanji. Then, too, there had been a harsh tone in the man's greeting. Casually the policeman walked around to the other side of the house and stood gazing at the woodpile. Kanji hurried after him.

'Quite a lot here, I'd say,' the policeman observed. 'Don't move a stick of it until I come back.'

Kanji blanched. 'But the owner told me I could dig these up,' he said nervously. 'I know where I got every one of 'em.'

'Now isn't that nice?' the policeman observed, fingering his mustache. 'But when I say you can't move 'em, then you better not move 'em!' He turned to go away. 'Sure looks like a lot of oak stumps mixed in with the rest,' he said over his shoulder.

Kanji stood dumbly in the yard, getting drenched by the rain. Otsugi emerged from behind the door where she had been hiding.

'Papa?' she called out softly. 'Papa, I told you not to bring those back here. What's going to happen, Papa?'

After a long pause Kanji replied, 'The Master's turned against me. Nothing can save us now.'

'But how about if you apologized to him, Papa?'

'Yeah, but do you know if he'll accept?'

'Well, maybe South Neighbor could find out for you. Why not ask him?'

'Because it'd be harder than you think, that's why. You're not the one that has to do the asking.'

'Well then, at least shouldn't we get rid of those stumps, Papa?'

'That'd do no good. The police fellow's seen 'em already.'

Then, since he could see no other way out of the trouble he was in, Kanji threw on a battered raincloak and headed through the mulberry field to ask South Neighbor to intercede on his behalf. South Neighbor agreed and reported back that the master would give his reply the next day. Feeling miserable Kanji returned home and huddled in his bedding. Otsugi had gone with Kanji every day to the clearing, so she had known all about the oak stumps he had carried off. Stealthily she removed them from the woodpile. Then at dusk she loaded them into a big basket, lugged them over to the bamboo thicket near the house, and tossed them one by one down the old well. By the time she had finished she was soaking wet from the cold rain. Strands of wet, frizzy hair stuck to her cheeks, and her feet were covered with rotting bamboo leaves.

Returning to the house Otsugi roused Kanji with an excited 'Papa!' Then she whispered, 'I got rid of those stumps.' Kanji stared at her in surprise. Later that night they lit the lantern. Their eyes sparkled in its light.

The next day the policeman returned with one of the master's employees in tow to make a thorough investigation of the wood-pile. There seemed to be far fewer oak stumps than he recalled. Only those that Otsugi had missed in her haste remained behind.

'Weren't there more of these yesterday?' the policeman asked in a menacing tone. 'What've you been up to, Kanji?' He hunted all over the premises but found nothing. The fact of the matter was that he could not tell a piece of oak from any other kind of wood.

'All right now, Kanji,' he said at last. 'Gather these up and follow me!' Kanji shuddered.

'Use a basket or whatever. Load 'em up and follow me!'

Still Kanji hesitated. 'Yes, sir,' he said. 'But where are we going?'

The policeman slapped Kanji angrily across the face. 'That's none of your business!' he yelled. 'Now get moving!'

Kanji strapped the basket of oak stumps to his back and followed the policeman to the backyard of the master's house. He remained standing, the basket still on his back and his eyes on the ground, while the policeman sat down on the veranda. The master himself wanted no part of the charade that was to follow. It was his wife who appeared instead. Kanji felt increasingly miserable.

'Why don't you put down that basket and have a seat, Kanji?' she inquired. Kanji did not move.

She turned to the policeman. 'Are those all the stumps he had?'

'Looks like it,' the policeman muttered, flipping through the pages of his notebook. 'Much fewer than I'd thought there were.'

'Is that so?' the mistress replied politely. Then she turned back to Kanji. 'Well, it can't be very pleasant for you, being brought here like this, now can it?' Tears streamed down Kanji's cheeks and fell onto his feet.

'With all the talk going around about you, something had to be done,' she continued, casting a glance at the policeman. 'It was really very embarrassing for us.' Then she looked at Kanji. 'But as long as you never do this sort of thing again perhaps we can just call the matter settled. What do you say? Shall I tell him there's no need to take you off to the station?'

'Oh yes, Okamisan, please!' Kanji cried out. 'I'll never do it again. Please!' His back already bent under the weight of the basket, he bowed down humbly over and over again. Tears ran off the hem of his kimono onto the ground.

'Will that be all right, then?' the mistress asked the policeman. She was smiling.

'Well now, let's see,' he replied, cocking his head to one side and bringing his sword up onto his lap. 'Think you can behave yourself from now on, Kanji? Because if you take even as much as a dead branch now, there'll be real trouble. Okay, I guess that's it for today. You can hand over that basket and go home now.'

Kanji untied the basket and set it down on the ground.

'Not here in the yard!' the policeman bellowed. 'You ought to know where to put it. Kind of dumb, aren't you? Now look sharp and watch where you're going.'

Kanji edged his way out of the yard, treading as softly as he could.

Outside the gate Otsugi and Yokichi were waiting for him. Otsugi was in tears. Since his sister was crying so was Yokichi. Otsugi held her sleeve over his face to muffle the sound.

Kanji took Yokichi's hand. 'No need to cry, Yoki. Let's go home.' The three of them walked in silence, with several of the master's employees smiling contemptuously after them.

As soon as they reached home Otsugi asked, 'Papa, what happened?'

Wearily Kanji replied, 'Well, everything turned out okay. Your getting rid of those stumps, that's what saved us.'

'They sure were heavy, all those stumps,' Otsugi replied with a smile. 'My shoulders ache all over today.'

After a while Kanji spoke again, his voice choked with tears. 'You'd really be in a fix, wouldn't you, if I wasn't around?'

Soon he could be seen in the forest again, back at work with his mattock.

Five or six days later Kanji went out and bought a sewing box and pin-cushion for Otsugi.

'You can go learn sewing now,' he said to her. 'Take these along with you. You're always saying you'd be ashamed to be seen with your mother's old stuff, so I bought you some new ones. They cost me a lot, too. Nobody will have any nicer.'

Then he picked up Yokichi and told him. 'You'll stay here with me, Yoki. Okay? Because Sister's going off to learn to make clothes for us. You'd better behave while she's away!'

From that time on Otsugi went off into the village with the other girls living nearby. One day she brought home a little kimono she had made for Yokichi, smiling cheerfully as she walked along. Somehow as soon as she had taken up sewing she seemed a lot more sure of herself. She was now 16. She had had to shoulder a lot of grown-up responsibilities in the course of the past year when they had had such a hard time getting by. That fall people had started talking about how smart and capable she was becoming, just like her mother had been. And though he never mentioned it, Kanji thought she was even getting to look more like Oshina every day.

Otsugi was old enough now to be eager for some fun, but Kanji never let her go off anywhere by herself. If there was a village festival, she went in the company of some of the wives living nearby, and she always had Yokichi with her. Then, too, she had to return home earlier than anyone else to make lunch or supper.

'It'd be better if there were no holidays!' she would complain. 'That way I wouldn't have to feel I'm always missing out on things.'

'Well, I've got work to do, so I need you here,' Kanji would reply. It made him unhappy to hear her complaining, but he could never find words for anything but a curt response.

Yokichi was 4 years old now and able to go off on his own to play. That in itself saved Otsugi a lot of bother. Even with the extra time, though, she was unable to keep up with all the clothes he needed and always had to ask a neighbor's wife for help to get them finished. Had Oshina been alive Otsugi would not have been faced with such a task at 16. Nor was that her only problem. Much to her dismay her own clothes were getting too small for her, and some had rips in them as well.

'It's hopeless, not being good with a needle,' she would say with a sigh.

'You'll be able to sew and do all sorts of things when it's time for you to do 'em,' Kanji told her. 'Same thing with going into service. But you've got to be patient. You're only 16, you know. No wonder you're not much at sewing yet! You just stop all that complaining and be patient.'

'But Papa, if I went into service they'd teach me how to make clothes, wouldn't they?'

'Now, look here! It's not time for that yet, and that's that!'

It was perfectly normal, of course, that a girl of 16 was still clumsy with a needle. In Otsugi's case, though, with all that needed doing it was certainly inconvenient. Kanji was well aware of that, but there was nothing he could do about it. That was why he always snapped at her whenever she brought the subject up.

That winter Otsugi went around grumbling that in no time at all she was going to be 17. 'Well,' Kanji had said to her on one occasion, 'maybe I can send you out, come spring.' She had practically abandoned hope by that time and was thrilled by what he said.

One evening, as if suddenly remembering, Otsugi asked, 'How about putting a ladder down the old well and getting all those stumps?'

Kanji was taken aback. 'What ever made you say that?'

'But it's a pity, isn't it? They're just going to waste down there.'

'Are you going to go down for 'em all by yourself?'

'Well . . . no. I'd be scared to.'

'Then why even bring it up? What if we got caught with 'em, then what? Are you willing to go off to jail in my place?' Kanji asked, forcing a smile.

They said nothing more to one another that night.

8

It was Yokichi's fifth spring. He had grown so much in the past few months that Otsugi could hardly lift him any more. Just as the sheath of a bamboo shoot separates from its stalk while continuing to coil around it, so too he gradually struck out on his own while remaining as fond of Otsugi as ever.

He went off often with the other children to the paddy fields. If the day was warm, he slipped on a lightweight kimono and then pranced around impatiently while Otsugi tied up the sleeves and adjusted the length.

'Don't go near the ditches!' she would warn him. 'If you get yourself all muddy, you'll be sorry.' He hardly heard her as he grabbed his little basket and rushed off. The alders had shed their blossoms by now, but leaves had not yet appeared on their limbs. It was still early in the season and the paddies had not yet been ploughed. The soil was slightly moist, feeling warm to the feet. If one looked down closely at the ground between the dry, white rice stubble, every now and then one could spot a tiny hole. That was what the children were hunting for. Finding one a child would thrust both hands down into the sticky soil and overturn a clump. There wriggling confusedly would be a tiny mudfish. While everyone else laughed and shouted the child would try to catch the slippery fish with his muddy hands. After losing hold of it several times he would finally drop it into his basket. The mudfish, uncomfortable in its new surroundings, would struggle for a while before finally settling down. When another fish joined it both would wriggle about together and then be still.

The children wandered from paddy field to paddy field, hunting for these little holes. This was known in the area as *mebori*. No matter how hard he tried and how muddy he became, Yokichi could not catch a single mudfish by himself. The older children would each put one or two of the fish they caught into his basket, however, which is why he always tagged along behind them.

58

The Soil

The irrigation ditch was virtually empty. Here and there standing pools of water reflected the sky, but elsewhere the muddy bottom lay exposed, its surface streaked with tiny grains of sand that glistened in the spring sunlight. The children climbed down through the tangle of dried reeds into the ditch to continue the hunt. The older children got down easily, but sometimes a younger child would lose control of his basket as he descended. His precious mudfish would scatter onto the ground about his feet. 'Found one!' an older child would cry out, scooping up the fish and putting it into his own basket. All the other children followed suit, claiming the spilled fish as their own. At that the little child burst into tears. Then he got his fish back from the others. Peering into his little basket happily, he stopped wailing as suddenly as he had begun. Sometimes, too, a younger child would get his feet stuck in the thick mud of the ditch. The others would dash up out of the ditch. Yelling and gesturing boisterously they would make fun of their stranded playmate below. Clutching his little basket desperately the child would once more burst into tears. Yokichi was often made to cry in these ways. Even among the children family status played an important role, and Yokichi's family offered him no protection at all from teasing. His family was looked down upon by the villagers, and so he was treated with contempt by all the other children. Even so he was happy as long as he had a few fish in his basket when he returned home. Miserable though he was when reduced to tears he was soon cheerful again. Proudly carrying his basket back to Otsugi he was as sweet and lovable as ever. His kimono would be filthy no matter how high it had been hiked up beforehand, for he was always plopping himself down in the mud. He was not at all frightened, though, when Otsugi got angry and spanked his mud-caked bottom. Paying no heed at all to her scolding he would dance around trying to break free of her grasp. 'Look, Sister, look!' he would say, holding up his basket. He was determined to win her praise.

Once he got so excited that he accidentally dropped a fish onto the ground. Covered with dry dirt, the fish began to wriggle uncomfortably. Then just as Yokichi was about to pick it up one of the chickens grabbed it in its beak and carried it off. Yokichi burst into tears.

'You just weren't quick enough,' Otsugi said, laughing, as she held him close. Then she dropped the remaining fish into a tub of water. Yokichi stuck his hand into the water, shouting with delight as the fish darted out of the way. Finally Otsugi put the tub off to the side and washed Yokichi's muddy hands and feet.

Yokichi came home with mudfish every so often. Even though

Otsugi scolded him about getting his clothes so dirty she was happy to let him go off to the rice paddies. 'Take Yoki along!' she would call out to the other children as they passed by. 'Don't make him cry, okay?' Later she would add his mudfish to their soup, and after removing the bones she would give the flesh to Yokichi to eat. She would take the bones and heads for herself, sucking on them for a while before throwing them away.

By now all the paddy fields had been dug up for planting. The children stumbled over the lumps of loosened soil collecting the roots of tiny arrowhead plants. These grew profusely in the area, their white flowers blooming in the shade of the rice stalks in the fall. In contrast to mudfish hunting, Yokichi had no trouble gathering roots. Every day he brought some home. Otsugi roasted a few on the fire whenever she boiled water for tea. Yokichi stood impatiently off to the side, for he was strictly forbidden to touch the stove. Almost as soon as the roots had been laid on he would start begging to have one.

'They're hardly done at all!' Otsugi told him. 'But I don't care. Here!' She took one out and gave it to him. Yokichi stuffed the root eagerly into his mouth. Then finding it still hard and bitter, he spat it out.

'That's what you get for being in such a hurry,' Otsugi scolded him. 'Shame on you, you're supposed to be a big boy now.'

Undeterred, Yokichi started badgering her for another piece. 'Now, Sister? Can't I have one now?' By this time the roots were done, their skins wrinkled and crisp. Otsugi gave him another piece.

'Watch out, it's hot,' she warned as she dropped it onto his out-stretched hand. Yokichi pulled back his hand and let the piece fall to the floor. Then when Otsugi picked it up and gave it to him again he blew on it heavily as he had seen her do. He kept after her for more pieces until finally Kanji got angry and made him stop.

One day Otsugi picked up Yokichi's little basket and found that it was full of roots. 'How about if I boil these for Yoki?' she muttered half aloud. 'They'd be real good with a little sugar mixed in.'

Yokichi overheard her. 'Boil 'em for me!' he implored, rushing over to where she sat and tugging at the scarf she wore.

'Ouch! That hurts!' Otsugi cried, her face contorted. He had yanked a few strands of her hair when he had grabbed her scarf.

'Boil 'em with salt!' Kanji yelled sharply. 'Sugar of all things! If you'd have kept quiet, he'd have never known the difference. You keep that sugar for when he's upset. If you go on using sugar and soy sauce all the time, we'll be in real trouble. We just can't afford

60

it. Even salt costs money, you know. We've got to be careful about everything.' Yokichi hid behind his sister while Kanji upbraided her.

'I don't see why you have to yell at me like that,' Otsugi muttered.

'It's because we just can't afford it,' Kanji said again, dropping his voice. Then he was silent.

For Otsugi this was the second spring since her mother's death. In the intervening months she had learned to cope with all sorts of hardship. She had had no carefree springtime like other girls her age. She had been a mere child when Oshina died, so clumsy that whenever she stirred up the fire she always set the stick aflame. Now she was not only skilled at her chores but physically transformed as well. She had grown both taller and broader, her complexion glowed, and her hair hung far down her back. Whenever her hair got greasy Otsugi would plaster her head with some of the yellow clay from the deposit behind their house. Then, bare to the waist, she would give herself a shampoo at the well. Afterwards her hair would fall soft and full from her face, and she would apply a little sesame oil to make it glisten. Since taking up sewing she had made herself a thin red sash for tying up her sleeves. Somehow she had managed to alter her kimono to fit, and she had washed and starched her cotton jacket. All of a sudden she looked very grown up. Following Kanji off to the fields she would wear her stiff, unwrinkled jacket and drape her red sash over her shoulders. Before starting to work she would hang the jacket carefully from a tree limb. Her appearance did not go unnoticed.

Yellow rape blossoms blanket the fields in springtime. As the gentle rains fall, the frostbritten rape leaves turn green once more, and little protuberances appear at the center of the plants. These are the buds. Taking in the warm sunlight, the buds sent out runners, and soon gaudy blossoms are everywhere, dominating the fields. Otsugi, too, was ready to bloom, but unlike the rape buds she was held back by her parent. Kanji was loath to let her out of his sight. She had no contact with the young men of the village, all of whom were bent, at that time of year, on winning someone's heart. They had been unaware that Otsugi was actually 17. After all, her house was at the very western edge of the village, isolated from most of the other dwellings. Then, too, her family's poverty had kept her somewhat hidden from public view. It was as if they lived in shadow, visited only by the dust-laden winter wind which always announced its arrival first of all to them. Kanji's close supervision restrained Otsugi the way cold weather restrains a flower bud, and it served as a powerful obstacle to anyone who aimed at getting to know her. Still, just as the plants start growing in the spring no matter how much frost they suffer, so too Otsugi's heart could not be stifled totally by her father.

As she trudged along behind Kanji on the way to the fields she could not help noticing the young men clad in blue work clothes who crossed their path. Resting her cheek on the handle of the hoe she carried across her shoulder, she observed them as they passed by. Kanji, walking ahead, knew nothing of this. No greetings were exchanged at all. Otsugi watched the young men without even being aware of what she was doing, but it seemed to them that her eyes were full of feeling. Their only contact with her was during these fleeting moments, always in broad daylight, and always with Kanji present. Like other girls her age, Otsugi was concerned about her appearance, but unlike them, she had no opportunity to overcome her fear of men.

It was early summer now, and the farmers were very busy. Otsugi went off to the fields in the blue checkered kimono her mother had woven, which she had altered the past winter. It had been a difficult task — she had made many mistakes and had started over several times — but finally it fitted her perfectly. The fabric was indeed in excellent condition, for Oshina had never had a chance to wear such a colorful garment during the hard times after her marriage. And the dye had proved as good as Kanji had said it was. The indigo had been prepared the old way — boiled for a week before it was used. It was not like ordinary blue fabric today that would fade in sunlight and run when washed. Once she had thrown away her old, faded winter clothes and started wearing the blue kimono, Otsugi attracted even more attention than before. She tied up the sleeves with her thin red sash, its ends crossed behind her back and tied securely in front. On her forearms she wore blue cotton sleeve-lets, and a newly woven white straw hat protected her face from the sun. She and Kanji were digging up the soil between the furrows in the barley field. They were late in getting to this task, the barley already having come into ears. From time to time Otsugi stood up to scrape the soil off her hoe with her foot. Then she was visible above the gently waving, white-topped barley plants. Her straw hat whirled as she took a quick look around. The hats she and all the other women wore were not only functional but attractive as well. They rested on thick cushions on top of the white scarves that covered their hair and were tied far forward against the sun. During rest periods the women removed their hats to wipe the sweat from their faces, laying them upside down on the ground. The colorful cushions in the center of the white straw and the black cloth ties on either side formed a pretty sight. The cushion in Otsugi's hat was made of strips of red, yellow and green fabric that she had pieced together herself. Only her obi was out of fashion. All the other girls had bright red obis, into which they tucked the bottom edges of their kimonos to free their legs for work. People were bound to notice them out in the fields as their red obis and white hats glistened in the sunlight among the deep green plants. Then, if one drew closer, one could detect a few strands of black hair that had strayed beneath their white scarves. That, too, was a charming sight.

Dressed so colorfully, the young women were like giant flowers adorning the fields. All except for Otsugi, who lacked one vital piece of clothing.

Under Kanji's tutelage Otsugi had become very skilled at farming. The village women often commented on her as she passed by on her way to the fields.

'Look there now! Isn't she just like her mother? Why, even the way she walks is just the same.'

'Got the same freckles on her face, too, doesn't she?'

Sometimes one of them would address Kanji. 'Nothing to raising a daughter, is there?' she would say in a half bantering tone. 'Why, it hasn't been any time at all since her mother's funeral, and here she is all grown up and ready to be a bride herself. Oshina was just about her age when she married you, now wasn't she?' Whenever this happened Otsugi would blush and turn away. Kanji would be uncomfortable, too. Just hearing Oshina's name, or looking closely at Otsugi and seeing how much she resembled her mother, brought on painful memories. At the same time it made him realize how much he wanted to have a wife again. That was one reason he tolerated the women's teasing, despite the grief it caused him. He kept hoping someone would offer to find a woman for him.

The subject had come up shortly after Oshina's death. 'How about it, Kanji-san?' several of his neighbors had asked. 'I have a good prospect for you if you're interested.' But he had been too grief-stricken then even to consider the idea. Only later, as he became aware of how awkward it was trying to manage on his own, did he start thinking of remarriage. He would have welcomed offers of assistance then, but none were forthcoming. His neighbors had never been serious about serving as go-betweens. After all, a man as poor as Kanji, with two children to support, could not expect to marry again. They had just been talking idly. Then as Otsugi grew older and learned to help her father, they decided he did not really need a wife. Even supposing a woman could be found who was willing to join such a poverty-stricken household, she and Otsugi would never get along. If people hinted at the subject thereafter, it was just because they looked down on Kanji and enjoyed making fun of him.

'I keep on hoping for better times, but life just stays the same . . .' People noticed that Kanji was always singing this refrain to himself as he went about his work.

By now the dark fuzzy balls on the chestnut trees had turned to white, blanketing every village in the area in what looked like rising steam. Heavy clouds hung in the sky, breaking apart every now and then to reveal the harsh yellow glare of the sun. It was oppressively hot and humid. Here and there a brightly painted paper carp hung listlessly from the branch of a tree. Soon it would be the day of the Boys' Festival, a time to dress up in one's best clothes and rest, however briefly, from one's labor. There was an expectant mood in the air as people returned home from a long day in the fields and rushed off to bathe while it was still light. A woman selling sweets passed through the village every day, beating a drum and singing as she walked along. It was her song that Kanji sang as he worked. Every day she sang the same refrain over and over, first in a high register and then in a low. She was in her early forties, and she carried a child on her back. On her head was one of the straw hats all the boatmen on the Kinu River wore. The left side of the skirt of her faded kimono was tucked up under her obi. A box of sweets hung on a strap from her shoulder. The sun beat down through the open weave of her hat, burning lines into her haggard face. The child was usually asleep, as if lulled by its mother's voice and the beating of her drum. Its head hung back limply, exposing its face to the sun.

The farmers paid no attention to this shabby woman as she passed their fields on the way to the next village. Soon she was far away. The women who encountered her on the footpaths noted the flushed, sweaty forehead of her child with disapproval, but the woman herself was merely grateful that it slept and remained unaware of how sunburned it was getting. Her only interest was in the village children who came running up to her, copper coins in hand, to buy her candies. The sound of her drum attracted them from afar. There was no need for her to sing, but sing she did, that same sad refrain, over and over again. The women gossiped on and on about who she might be and why she peddled candy. Then one day the sound of her drum and her song faded away across the fields for the last time. The rainy season had arrived, the cloud-bursts pouring down until the heavy flowers on the chestnut trees lay rotting on the ground. The haggard, unkempt figure of the woman was never seen again.

Kanji alone had been captivated by her song. He sang it softly to himself all the time, glancing up guiltily from his work whenever he thought someone might have overheard him. The village women teased him unmercifully whenever they came upon him suddenly at a turning of the path and found him singing.

'It's a pity, isn't it, Kanji-san,' they would say as he passed by. 'You're really pining after that woman. Just about your age, too, and one child's not so bad. But she's gone for good, it looks like.' They would start singing the song themselves as they walked away. Kanji would remain silent until he got home. But he could not keep from singing for long.

All he could think about was getting himself a wife.

9

Despite all his hard work Kanji remained trapped in poverty. He still had not repaid any of the rent rice he had borrowed after Oshina's death. Nor did he have enough food to last until the harvest. By midsummer, when even the water in the well had retreated from the scorching sun, his meager supply of rice and barley had almost run out. Like other farmers he had planted eggplants, squash, and cucumbers to supplement his family's usual diet of grains. Lacking a plot of appropriate land nearby, he had set a row of cucumbers out along the hedge around his yard, driving in a bamboo stake beside each plant. He had stolen the bamboo from the forest behind his house, as he did whenever he needed some. The squash, too, he had planted next to the privy in the far corner of the yard and at the base of the chestnut tree near his house. Only the eggplants had gone into his patch of dry land on the other side of the village, where he planted them between the rows of barley. Unable to prepare cuttings himself and lacking the money to buy good ones, he had acquired the young plants from a local peddler. They were poor specimens, practically worthless in fact, but Kanji had been delighted at how cheap they were. He had counted out the coins carefully before handing them over.

After the barley had been harvested, five short rows of eggplant remained in Kanji's field, surrounded by newly planted upland rice and soy beans. Their lower leaves were yellow, but having been shaded from the hot sun by the barley, they had taken root and begun to grow. Despite the poor soil, which Kanji could never fertilize, each plant had put forth blossoms. In the mornings when it was still cool and the leaves remained moist Kanji trudged off to the field and scattered ashes from his stove over each plant. That served to keep the melon bugs in check, but it could not prevent the aphids from multiplying. Nor did Kanji have the time or energy to hunt and crush the cutworms that hid in the soil, and ate through the stems, slowly killing off one plant after another. His cucumbers did poorly, too, the vines and leaves drying up in the heat before the fruit matured. Only the squash flourished, the big leaves spreading rapidly until the vines completely covered the low roof of the privy. Vines encircled the chestnut tree, too, and fat, round growths hung down from its branches, their exposed bottoms baking in the sun. The rain doors of Kanji's house remained closed against the heat, and nothing moved on the ground below. The only signs of life in the sweltering daylight were the squash and the cicadas, which hummed mightily from every tree trunk.

Everyone faced a similar problem even though no one else's crops were doing quite as poorly as Kanji's. Until their vegetables were ripe at last the farmers had only their dwindling supplies of dried greens and pickles from the previous year to supplement their meals. Faint with hunger from their labor they ate anything, however unsavory it looked or smelled, just to fill the gaping void they felt inside them. Not even pausing to chew, they washed down great mouthfuls of moldering barley with water, for only by getting as much into their bellies as possible could they get their strength back. Although not even a horse or cow will eat hay when it can graze on green grass, poor farmers had no alternative but to consume old, decaying food.

All poor farmers, their mouths parched from toiling in the heat, longed for the taste of vegetables. Sometimes the longing was so great that they stole produce from another's field. Women were especially likely to do this. If they found themselves on a lonely path at dusk and spied something edible in an adjacent field they could not resist picking it and hurrying off with it tucked beneath their aprons. No farmer could prevent such theft, however angry he might be when he discovered it. It was simply impossible to keep watch over the scattered plots of land he tilled. Even Kanji's miserable patch of eggplants was raided once. Looking down the next morning at the damaged stalks from which the tiny eggplants had been torn in haste he was swept by resentment and despair. He would get even, though. If people were going to steal from him, he would take vegetables from someone else. It was only fair. Besides, as long as one didn't get caught, it was the easiest way to satisfy one's hunger.

Most poor farmers felt the same way, and as a result they usually tasted fresh produce well before their more affluent neighbors did. No matter how many vegetables they had on hand, the affluent farmers would not eat a single one. They took everything they raised to market and sold it for the cash they needed. Not wanting to reduce yields, they let their produce ripen fully in the fields, and only at the end of the season would they eat any of their produce themselves. All the vegetables maturing in their fields provided an irresistible temptation to hungry thieves.

One day Yokichi saw some of his playmates eating tasty-looking vegetables. As soon as he got home he begged Otsugi to give him some, too. The next morning a huge squash lay on the dirt floor by the stove. Yet not a single squash was missing from the vines out in their yard.

'Hey, look!' Yokichi cried out as he picked it up. 'Where'd this come from, Papa?'

'Put that down before you smash it!' Kanji snapped back angrily. He had just added a few young, pink sweet potatoes to the barley in the cooking pot.

'Um, so good!' Otsugi said later, when she took a bite of potato.

'Been fertilized with fish meal, that's why,' Kanji replied.

Otsugi had heard about this unbelievably expensive fertilizer. 'The Master always uses fish meal, doesn't he?' she said.

Kanji, realizing what she had just let slip, turned quickly to Yokichi. 'Don't you tell anybody you ate sweet potatoes, ever!' he warned him.

The master's potato and squash fields were not far from Kanji's soybean patch, so it was natural that he did most of his raiding there. He stole only a small quantity at a time. He would spy a nice ripe squash as he passed by in the daytime and come back for it at night, pulling cautiously on the vines until he located it again. Since it was too nerve-wracking to dig down carefully for sweet potatoes, he would just yank out a plant and hurry off with whatever was attached to it. The next day as he walked by the field he would be ashamed to see the mess he had left behind.

As usual Yokichi went off every day to the village to play. Autumn had arrived, and people everywhere were steaming sweet potatoes. Attracted by the odor Yokichi would draw close and watch, a wistful look on his face. Without fail, he was always given a little piece. On one occasion he looked up shyly at the person who had just handed him a piece and said, 'I'm not supposed to say we eat these at home.'

'Why not?'

'Just because . . .'

'Well, if you're not going to tell me, you can just give that piece of potato right back to me.'

Yokichi was upset. 'But Papa said I wasn't to tell we ate any,' he wimpered.

'Your sweet potatoes taste good?'

'No, it's the Master's that taste good.'

'Who said that? Your papa? Or was it your sister?'

'Not Sister! It was Papa.'

'Your papa said those potatoes of the Master's tasted so good?'

'Uh-huh,' Yokichi replied innocently.

There were other hard-pressed farmers who stole vegetables that year, but thanks to Yokichi's slip, gossip in the village focused on Kanji's misdeeds. ·

10

The morning was chilly. The heavy ears of rice in the paddy fields bent to and fro in the changing wind, setting up a mournful rustle. After a night of steady autumn rain the sky was left completely clear, and even the distant mountains appeared close at hand. As sunlight streamed down from above, gently massaging all that it touched, the day grew steadily warmer.

Misled by the spring-like weather skylarks took to the wing again and flew over the fields of ripening buckwheat and upland rice. But now they kept close to the ground, as if their wings had somehow grown tired, and their voices, so bright and cheerful a few months earlier, sounded weak and hoarse. Water poured off the plateau through the open sluice gates and collected in the paddies, submerging the rice plants up to their ears. The village children picked up their straw baskets and fishing nets and headed for the fields again. Splashing their way through the water they sang out gaily in imitation of the skylarks nearby. Deceived by the weather too, the frogs had reappeared in the paddies. Floating on the water's surface they clung to the prickly rice ears and began to croak again. They kept up their chorus until most of the water had drained away and the autumn sun had begun to set. Then they were silent, and would remain so until their instinct to sing was aroused again.

There was little point in going off to work in the fields right after a heavy rain. Most farmers remained at home until the soil had drained. Toward dusk, however, Kanji set off alone with an empty basket tied to his back. Instead of following his usual route, he headed first across the paddy fields and forest behind his house. Then he circled back through the trees to his destination, the area of upland fields where his own patch was located. Once there he strolled about aimlessly until the last ray of sunlight had faded. Uneasy about what he planned to do he wore a large straw hat to shield his face. As soon as it was dark he set the basket down at the side of the path near some tall shoots of sorghum that a farmer had planted in a single row around his field. The basket brushed against the broad leaves of the plants, making a faint rustling sound and causing the leaves to quiver nervously. The ears of the plants bent forward slightly as if to see what was causing the commotion down below. Kanji took out his knife, bent one of the tall stalks down in front of him, and cut off the ear. Once released the stalk snapped upright again and· stood trembling from side to side. When his basket was full Kanji tied it to his back and hurried straight home through the darkness. The next morning he leaned two bamboo poles against the eaves of his house and tied bundles of sorghum ears up on them to dry. The sun hung low in the sky, shining down on Kanji and observing what he did.

That same morning everyone went back to the fields, which were almost completely dry after a day of sunshine. One man among them who went off to cut some of his sorghum found that his crop had been raided. Alarmed and angry he dropped his equipment and headed straight for the village police station. The policeman hurried into his uniform and accompanied the victim back to his field, where they both counted the number of stalks that had been cut. By this time every other farmer knew what had happened, for the victim had shouted it out for all to hear on his way to summon the police; anyone seen returning from the fields late the night before was sure to be the culprit, he had told them. Kanji had been out tending his own field and had heard what the man had said. Immediately he headed for home, untied the sorghum from the poles, and hid it all under some mats in the forest behind his house.

The farmers at work near the victim's field were in an uproar over what had happened.

'This has gone too far! Whoever did it ought to be locked away for a long time. There's too much of this raiding going on.'

'That's right. They ought to make an object lesson of him. Treat him harsh, that's what I say!'

'Search the village and they'll find it for sure. You can't hide sorghum that easy.'

Hearing all this the victim became more angry and determined than before.

'Well, I know how much was taken,' the policeman said as he left the field. 'Now all I have to do is find it.'

'I'll go with you,' the victim said. 'It's my crop after all, so I can spot it easy.' He cut off a few ears to use for comparison and returned with the policeman to the village. Together they visited several houses, and then they arrived at Kanji's. From the start Kanji had been one of the policeman's prime suspects. Yet they could find no trace of the sorghum inside his house. Kanji had already hidden it elsewhere.

Eventually the policeman noticed the bamboo poles resting against the eaves. 'What are these for, I wonder?' he muttered. Meanwhile the victim was examining the damp soil beneath the eaves.

'Hmm, what have we here?' he said. 'Hey look, it's a grain of sorghum. I figure he had the ears tied up here, but now he's carried 'em off somewhere.'

The policeman nodded gravely.

'This grain here, it's one of mine, I know it!' the victim continued. 'He can't grow anything like this. I use fish meal on mine, that's why. I bet there's not a single ear missing from his own field. Just go and take a look!'

Kanji was standing nervously in the yard. It had alarmed him to find the policeman poking about beneath the eaves.

'Hey Kanji!' the policeman demanded, casting a glance in his direction. 'What's this bamboo doing here?'

'Well, I was just going to cut some of my sorghum, you see, and tie it up there.'

'That so? Then what's this little grain doing down here? It's sorghum, isn't it?'

'Well, uh, yes,' Kanji replied, his face turning pale. 'See, I put a bundle up there already and stripped it, just to try things out. It must've fallen then.'

The policeman had the victim guide him to Kanji's field. Kanji trailed along behind them, his eyes on the ground. As the victim had predicted, the sorghum in Kanji's field looked miserable indeed, with only scraggly ears atop the stalks. Not a single ear had been cut.

'See, it's just like I told you', the victim said with feeling. 'Look at this scrawny stuff! He's the one for sure that took mine. I knew it all the time. He's a rotten one, you know.'

'Well, that settles it,' the policeman replied. 'You can go back to work now. Later on I'll bring the report by. You just put your seal to it, and that'll be that.'

'Not quite,' the victim said. 'I'm going to look for my sorghum. It's got to be hidden somewhere.' With that, he set off down the path.

'They've really got him now!' the other farmers gloated. 'He'll suffer for this!'

'I'm done for this time, Otsū,' Kanji sobbed when he got back home. He was panic stricken. Given his distress at being caught, why then had he dared to steal the sorghum in the first place? It was because he had grown used to stealing. Whenever he needed something he just took it. He was too weak to resist the urge even though he knew it was wrong.

Kanji was incapable of doing any more work that day. After a while he went off to the master's house to plead for help. He felt miserable as he crossed the threshold.

The master was not at home, so he spoke to his wife. 'Okamisan,' he said, hanging his head, 'I've done wrong again. I'm ashamed to have to tell you, Okamisan, but I need your help. If they put me away, my kids'll have no one . . .'

The mistress had already heard about Kanji's latest escapade. At the time she had felt disgusted with him, but now, as he stood humbly before her begging for help, she could not bring herself to rebuke him. Instead she felt sorry for him and promised she would help if she could. Hearing that, Kanji's face brightened. He knew that if the master would take a hand in the matter he would have a chance of getting off. Not wanting to go home he pleaded to be allowed to hide somewhere on the premises. The mistress let him into the storehouse, where he crouched down inside a large, discarded tub.

That afternoon the policeman stopped by Kanji's house to get his seal on the official report of the incident. Otsugi could only tell him she had no idea where her father was. Afterwards she burst into tears.

Meanwhile the victim had found the hidden sorghum and led the policeman to it. The bundled ears lay in a heap on top of a patch of dried grass deep within the forest. Nearby were some withered *ominaeshi* stalks and a stunted chestnut tree with several broken limbs. A few small crickets were chirping. It was indeed a lonely spot. The mats thrown over the sorghum were identified as Kanji's.

The mistress went off as soon as she could to have a talk with the victim's family. They were honest, hardworking people, and she found all of them upset at what had happened. The victim's father, in particular, a man of 70, was incensed.

'I've got no use for a thief like him,' he muttered. 'None at all. Why, I bet he's the one that stole some of our eggplants, and I know he's been taking your sweet potatoes, too. Just ripped 'em out of the ground, he did. Honest, that's the truth. I wouldn't lie to you, Okamisan. And he went last night to cut our sorghum, then hung it up on poles bright and early this morning. We found the place where he hid it later, along with a couple of his mats. There's no doubt about it. We got him cold.'

The mistress had anticipated such an outburst. 'You're right, of course,' she replied. 'We got him out of trouble like this once before, and now he's gone and done it again. It's like a kind of sickness, isn't it? I'm as upset as you are about it all, but just think a bit. If he goes off to jail his children will be left with no one. That'd be a shame, now wouldn't it? We're all of us neighbors, you know, so wouldn't it be better to forgive him? It'd save a lot of trouble for us all, and besides he'd be grateful to you for the rest of his life. But if you get him sent off to jail you'll just be making an enemy. You know what they say: "Better to suffer ill than to do ill". Wouldn't it be best to avoid doing something you'll feel guilty about later?'

The old man was still upset, however. 'And besides, Okamisan,' he retorted. 'I get mad just thinking how he's treated Uhei. Why, Uhei and me, we've known each other since we were boys. Worked together a lot too. He brought up that little Oshina like his very own, you know. And then to be pushed aside like that! You know how old he is? If you ask me, Kanji's a swine and ought to be punished!' Angrily he struck his fist against his knee.

'I understand how you feel,' the mistress replied calmly. 'But just remember you may well be sorry later for something you do in anger now. Even little things can start quarrels that last for generations, you know. I can think of plenty of examples.'

Seeing that the old man remained unpersuaded the mistress let the matter drop. After a few moments of silence she turned to his wife and said, 'I hear Orise has presented you with a new grandchild. A boy this time. You must be pleased.' Then she picked up the tea cup that had been placed before her earlier. Seeing that, the victim's wife stepped down into the kitchen to brew her a fresh cup.

'Oh yes, that's so,' the woman replied. 'We appreciate all you did for her, too. And just think, finally a boy on the fourth try! We were a bit uneasy about the match at first, you know, what with him not being very well off and all, but they're getting on just fine. I guess Rise's the best off of all our children. We figured we could count on you to find her a good husband. Look, he sent us this as a present.' Proudly she held up a piece of coarse, handwoven cloth for the mistress to see.

'And have you been to see your grandson?' the mistress asked as she dutifully stroked the fabric.

'Oh yes, Ma'am. I was going to tell you all about it, but then this trouble came up. I just got back last night, you see.'

A hot cup of tea was placed before the mistress at last. Then the victim, who had been conferring quietly with his father in a corner of the room, called out to his mother to join them. 'That's fine with me,' she said after a short time. Finally all three of them returned to where the mistress sat.

'Well, Okamisan,' the victim announced, 'We'd like you to handle the matter however you think best.'

'Please excuse what I said,' his father added, 'I'm pretty hot-headed sometimes.'

'Yes, please,' his mother chimed in.

The mistress stayed on a while longer to chat pleasantly with her hosts, and then she went home. She had known all along that if she just gave them the chance to vent their anger they would soon calm down and agree to do the sensible thing. She was good at settling quarrels.

That night, not wanting to leave them all alone at home, the mistress had Otsugi and Yokichi come to stay with her. Kanji spent the night with the employees, who had been warned not to say a word about his presence to anyone, and then went back into hiding at dawn. The policeman kept watch near Kanji's house all the following day, but he did not press his search as far as East Neighbor's house nearby.

Determined to rescue Kanji if she could, the mistress waited impatiently for her husband's return. Now that she had worked things out with the victim, all that remained was to deal with the police. Only the master could manage that. She waited for him all day, but still he did not come. By evening she could stand it no longer. Summoning Otsugi she lit a lantern and led the way to the top floor of the storehouse.

'Papa?' Otsugi called out softly. There was no answer. Otsugi called again and again, but only after the mistress summoned him did Kanji appear, forlorn and disheveled, from down inside the tub.

'My husband still hasn't returned,' the mistress told him, 'so I'm afraid nothing's been worked out yet with the police. If the police find you in the meantime are you willing to say you didn't steal a thing? That way I think I'll be able to handle everything. How about it?'

'Yes, Ma'am,' Kanji answered meekly, his eyes downcast.

'What's that?' she asked again.

'Yes, but I know I won't be able to stick to that story for long,' he said, trembling.

'Papa!' Otsugi blurted out impatiently. 'How can you say that? Come on now, Papa. Just say you didn't steal 'em.'

'But when they get me in jail they'll make me tell the truth.'

'No such thing!' the mistress said firmly. 'You just keep telling them you cut your own sorghum and everything will work out fine, I promise.'

'If only you'd just do that, Papa,' Otsugi added plaintively.

Both she and the mistress tried repeatedly to reassure him, but to no avail. He stood dejectedly before them, his head hanging.

That night after everyone else had gone to sleep Otsugi and the mistress made their way stealthily through the bamboo thicket behind the house. Every now and then a fallen bamboo stalk cracked beneath their feet. When they finally arrived at the back fence the mistress·grasped the bottom of one of the stakes and tugged at it until it broke. Otsugi did the same thing with another. The stakes were rotten near the ground, and in no time at all they had opened a large hole. Otsugi slipped through it to the other side. All of a sudden there was a violent flapping of wings right above her head. Some pigeons there had taken flight.

'Sure you'll be all right?' the mistress asked from her side of the fence.

'Oh yes, Ma'am,' Otsugi answered from a few yards away. She had already started off.

'Dear me, are you way over there? Just knock when you get back and I'll let you right in,' the mistress said as she turned back to the house.

Within moments Otsugi stood by her own back door. When she stepped inside the house a shiver ran down her spine, even though this was where she had lived all her life. The chickens were up in the roost, clucking peacefully in the darkness. Several mice scurried across the floor, squeaking frantically. Otsugi groped her way to the wall and took down a sickle. When she stepped outside again the hairs on the nape of her neck were all standing up on end. Quickly she took down a carrying basket from its peg on the outside wall and tied it to her back. As she moved away, a bamboo broom that had been propped up nearby fell toward the ground, its handle striking the basket with a thud. Otsugi whirled around in alarm. No moon was shining. The milky way seemed to be drifting just above the treetops that stretched up into the cold night air.

After a short time Otsugi stood beside the sorghum in their own field. The scraggly plants stood limply as if they were asleep. Soon they were rustling noisly as Otsugi slashed off their ears one by one with her sickle. When all of them had been cut she strapped the heavily laden basket to her back again and set off. White buckwheat blossoms were scattered here and there in the fields. It seemed as if the soil were watching her through wide open eyes. Quickly Otsugi made her way along a narrow path lined with sorghum to the low-lying fields and then to the Kinu River. On all fours she made her way through the grass to the top of the embankment, too tense to notice that there was a path just off to one side. The inner slope of the embankment was thickly grown with dwarf bamboo bushes right down to the water's edge. Through the leaves she could catch glimpses of the river, and she could hear the sound of water lapping up against the vegetation. As she started to descend, a clump of soil came loose and tumbled down into the river with a splash. Otsugi moved on to find a safer place, but when she parted the bushes, there right in front of her was the mast of a river boat. People's voices rose up through the darkness. Having anchored their boat at dusk, they had first gone off in search of food. After a late supper they had still not gone to sleep. The voices came from the tiny cabin on the bow where the boatman and his family lived. A baby's cries could be heard as well. Otsugi withdrew once more and ran off down the top of the embankment, stumbling every now and then over the bundles of cut grass someone had left lying along the path.

Gradually the bamboo bushes thinned out, and one could get a clearer view of the river, its water shimmering faintly in the darkness. Crickets were everywhere, their chirping rising and falling in steady waves. At last Otsugi found herself at the ferry landing. Just as she started to descend to the water's edge, however, she once again heard the sound of voices, coming this time from out on the river itself and mingled with the faint sound of splashing. As she stood there puzzled the bow of the ferry boat suddenly emerged from the darkness. Even at this late hour there were people who wanted to cross the river. It was their voices that Otsugi had heard, and the splashing came from the boatman's pole as it struck the water's surface. Otsugi moved back up the embankment and crouched beside a large willow tree. After a few parting words the passengers went ashore and strolled away. A few minutes later Otsugi made her way down to the water's edge, near where the ferry was moored. Suddenly there was a rustling noise beside her, and then the cry of pigs.

'Want to go across?' the boatman yelled, thinking that yet another passenger had arrived. Otsugi dashed away in alarm just as the boatman opened the door of his cabin and stepped outside. He could hear footsteps clearly and searched the darkness for a glimpse of the intruder. Grumbling to himself he went to the pig pen and lit a match. 'Got to be on guard all the time,' he muttered as he returned to his cabin. He raised pigs on the side, and since a litter had just been born he was afraid of thieves.

Exhausted by now Otsugi stopped as soon as she was a short distance from the ferry landing and threw the ears of sorghum one by one down into the river. Then she hurried towards East Neighbor's house, the empty basket on her back.

When she knocked at the door the mistress opened it right away.

'What happened?' the mistress asked. 'You're awfully late.'

'I did just what you told me to, Okamisan.'

'And where did you put the sorghum?'

'I couldn't think of anything else, so I tossed 'em all into the river.'

'Ah, that's very good. Come in, come in!' the mistress said, holding up a lantern. Then she caught sight of Otsugi's clothes. 'Whatever did you do? Just look at your kimono!'

Otsugi looked down and saw that she was covered with mud. 'Oh dear,' she moaned as she tried to brush some of it off. 'It must've been up on the embankment. I tripped over a bad spot once and fell down.'

'I did an awful thing, Okamisan!' she went on in an agitated voice.

'What was that?'

'I lost the sickle! I don't have any idea where I could of left it.'

'The one you used tonight?'

'Uh-huh. I was sure I'd put it back in the basket, but when I'd got rid of all the ears it wasn't there. Papa will be real angry. He gets furious when anything happens to his tools.'

'Well, I don't think you need to worry this time,' the mistress replied with a smile. 'Now, why don't you just go wash up a bit?'

The next day the master arrived home at last. He spoke with the policeman, who told him that since the victim had already signed the report he would have to deal with the chief. Finally it was agreed that if the victim would submit a formal retraction of the charge the matter would be dropped. It was only a petty offense, after all, so the chief was willing to make allowances. The mistress returned to the victim's house with this news, but she did not meet with a very enthusiastic reception.

'What?' the victim moaned. 'Go back to the station house again! Oh no, I'm not going to do that. They'll give me a real tongue-lashing, that's why.'

'But don't you see?' the mistress went on soothingly. 'It's all been arranged. If you just do this one little thing for us, the whole matter will be settled. But if you don't, then everything will fall apart.'

'Not only have I been robbed and lost a lot of time already, but now on top of that I'm supposed to go to the police again and get bawled out! I never heard such a thing!' the victim retorted stubbornly. 'Besides, you say I have to put it all in writing. I don't have the faintest idea what to say.' The truth of the matter was he was terrified of the police and awed by all their complicated procedures.

'Well, you needn't worry about the document,' the mistress said. 'My husband will write that up for you, of course.' She added that she would arrange for one of the neighbors to go along with him for moral support. Finally the victim gave in. Filled with misgivings he set off on his mission. When he returned home, however, he was in good spirits.

'How'd it go?' he was asked.

He recounted his experience with some relish. 'The chief, he's this terrible fellow with a huge mustache. Started off calling me a no-good rascal because I made a lot of trouble for 'em, saying I'd been robbed and all. I was scared to death, but I said to him, "Here, I brought you this statement." He looked at it a bit and then asked me who wrote it. "Why, the Master did," I told him. "Very well then," he said to me. "That'll be all. You can leave now." I heaved a sigh of relief and got right out of there. I hope I never have to set foot in that place again!'

After a pause he turned to the neighbor who had accompanied him and added, "The Master's really something around here, isn't he? All I had to say was he wrote up that piece of paper and that was it.'

Acting on Kanji's behalf, the master paid the victim a small sum of money to cover his loss. In this seemingly bizarre but actually very typical fashion, the matter was finally settled.

'I'll never steal anything again, not anything at all!' Kanji promised with tears in his eyes. He still had not paid back any of his overdue rent rice, nor had he settled any of the debts Uhei had left him with when he took over as head of the household. And now as a result of his latest blunder he had acquired yet another financial obligation to the master. People noted that he was working harder than ever before, taking on any odd job that he could find.

Seizing the first opportunity that arose, the mistress had a chat with Kanji. 'You know,' she began, 'I still find it hard to believe what Otsugi did.'

Kanji looked puzzled. 'She's done something, Okamisan?' he asked nervously, expecting unpleasant news.

'Don't talk like that now! You know about the other night, don't you?'

'The other night?'

'When Otsugi went off and cut your sorghum! I was really concerned about the police, you know. That's why I wanted you to say you hadn't stolen anything if they caught you before my husband came back. Then he could still take care of things. But if you confessed it would have complicated things. After all, there was your own field with all the sorghum still standing. Maybe it really wasn't necessary after all, but I figured the sorghum just had to go. And Otsugi went off and did it without batting an eye. I was really impressed!'

'Yes, Ma'am, she told me the whole story when I asked about a missing sickle. Then we found the sickle later, lying in the grass by the field.'

'Did you now? Otsugi was certainly worried about it. It must have been one of your good ones.'

'No, nothing special. The blade was practically worn out.'

'Well, I hope you didn't get angry with her about it, then. You be good to her, hear?'

'I try, Ma'am, I really do. It's been rough, being alone and all. But my wife begged me to take good care of the kids before she died, and that's what I try to do. Take Otsugi now. She really wanted to, so I sent her off to learn sewing. Then she wanted a new sash, and poor as I am I bought her one. It's because of things like that I haven't paid you people back any of the rent rice I owe. I had to get her mother's kimono out of hock, too, because Otsugi needed one. It's much too good for wearing off to the fields, but it's the only one she's got, so I don't mind. At least she hasn't got it all messed up.'

'Well of course not. She's taking good care of it, and I'm sure she's grateful to you for giving it to her,' the mistress observed. Then she continued, 'Otsugi's become a good worker, too, hasn't she? Especially the other night, it was as if Oshina had somehow come back to life, you know. She was so like her, the way she acted.'

'Uh-huh, I feel the same way sometimes.'

'I hope you don't mind my mentioning it, but as I recall, Oshina was always a great help to you whenever you were in trouble, wasn't she?'

'Yes, Ma'am, she was. I get scared easy, but if there was ever something I couldn't handle, she went off and did it for me.'

'Exactly,' the mistress said, smiling. 'And Otsugi's like her mother in that way too. It's funny, isn't it, how a child takes after one parent or another. And even children in the same family can be so different. Take you and your older sister, for example. The way Otsuta acts you'd never know she and you had the same mother, would you?'

'I've got nothing good to say about her,' Kanji replied bitterly.

'Where's Otsuta now?'

'Living down river somewhere, I think. I don't go see her. She may be my sister, but I've got no use for her. You know, she didn't even come to my wife's funeral. Can you believe that?'

'She didn't? My, my.'

'And that's not all. She swindled me out of a bale of rice once, that I needed for my rent. Said she'd pay me back soon as she got her own crop in, but she never did. My wife was still alive then, and she went off to deal with her. But it was no use. They just had a big fight, with her saying she didn't have it and couldn't pay it back. My wife was real mad, I can tell you. After that we wanted to have nothing to do with her. You know, she even stole money from that son of hers that lost his eyesight.'

'Lost his eyesight? How did that happen?'

'Well, he went off to work in some soy sauce factory in Noda. Then he got sick, because he ate too much, and it affected his eyes. At least that's what I heard. He was about 20 when it happened, and that mother of his wouldn't even let him come home when he had to quit his job.'

'What a terrible thing!' the mistress exclaimed. 'I guess some parents do things like that to their children, but still it's hard to believe. Now that I think of it, though, I've heard somewhere how mean Otsuta was.'

'But that's not all, Ma'am. You see, the boy could still see just enough to do farm work, like threshing or hoeing, and since he was a real steady worker lots of people hired him and took him in. Then after a while he had a bit of money. When his mother heard about that she invited the boy home again. That's what that sister of mine had the nerve to do!' Kanji exclaimed.

'Well,' he continued, 'the boy agreed. After all, being blind he figured he'd be better off back home with his mother than with strangers. But then she spent all the money he brought with him and threw him out of the house again. It's hard to believe, but that's really what happened. I know because the poor fellow came crying to me and told me the whole story. I thought to myself a fellow his age ought to have known better than to let himself get swindled like that. But my wife had just died and I didn't feel like being cruel. So I put him up for the night. Even gave him a bit of grain, hard up as I was. I tell you, Ma'am,' he added, 'since my wife died I've always tried to do good to others.'

'That's very proper,' the mistress replied. Then she asked, 'What ever happened to that poor blind boy?'

'Oh, he's living here in the village. Couldn't find a place anywhere else, but he's doing pretty well, I hear.'

'I'm glad to hear that. And what about the rest of the family? I haven't heard anything about them in a long time. How's Otsuta's husband?'

'Him? Hikoji's as bad as her! Did you know he sold his own

81

daughter to a brothel? Got 150 yen for her, but then he lost half of it at a cock fight on his way home. Can you imagine that? I can't stand the sight of him neither.'

'But that's unbelievable!'

'It's true, though, Okamisan. I wouldn't lie to you.'

'Then he really did that to his daughter?'

'Uh-huh, and then the girl ran off and came back home.'

'Hmm, you know, I think I remember reading about all that in the newspaper,' the mistress said, and then added, 'It's funny about Otsuta. She looks so nice.'

'Yeah, she's a smooth one, that's for sure,' Kanji answered with a shrug. 'That's why she was able to cheat me out of that bale of rice.'

'Yes, it does seem there's nothing good to say about her. Say, didn't her father-in-law fall into the river and drown a while back? It seems I remember hearing about that.'

'Uh-huh. He went off to the river to get rid of his fleas and ended up dead.'

'He wasn't living with his son anymore?'

'No, he'd been living by himself for a time. Seems his house was full of fleas, so he took the floor mats outside to clean 'em off. People didn't like that at all, right there by the fields they were working in. So he went off to the river. He was pretty old, you know, and his eyesight was no good. Guess he wore himself out just getting there and somehow fell into the water. And that's not all, Ma'am. When Otsuta found out he was dead she went off and collected everything the man owned.'

'And kept it all?'

'Well, she certainly didn't divide the things up among the relatives.'

'The poor old man, dying like that. What ever made him think of going to the river with his mats? Why, all the fleas must have been long gone by the time he got there.'

'Too old to think straight anymore, I guess. Old people like that are disgusting, aren't they?'

'What a thing to say!' the mistress said reprovingly. 'Why, fathers-in-law deserve to be looked after by the next generation for as long as they live.'

'Uh, yes, Ma'am. That's so, isn't it,' Kanji replied uncomfortably. He didn't like the drift of the conversation.

'But Otsuta seems to have mistreated her father-in-law all the time,' the mistress continued. 'Why, I remember hearing they used to put sugar on their own bean jam and not give him any for his.'

'Is that so?' Kanji responded cautiously, wishing she would change the subject.

'Treating a poor old man that way!' she said with emphasis. Kanji hung his head.

'Yes, Kanji,' she went on gently. 'Always remember that we have to rely on our children. You'll be a burden to yours one day, so it's up to you to look after them now. You should be glad that despite all your troubles you're still able to earn money and take good care of them.'

They were both silent for a time, and then Kanji asked, 'I know it's a funny question, Okamisan, but how much cloth do you need for an obi?'

'An obi for Otsugi, you mean?'

'Uh-huh. She's been after me for a new one. Says she can't stand the one she has anymore. I tell her we can't afford things like that, not when we owe you people so much and all, but she won't listen. Says everyone has a red one and she's got to have one, too.'

'Ah yes, I see. Well, usually they take about three yards, but it all depends on how they're going to be tied. Now let me think. What are the girls doing with them these days?'

'Otsū says a bit over a yard would do it, but I figured I better check with you just the same.'

The mistress looked down at her own obi. 'Oh, I see. She just wants red fabric for the bow, not the whole thing. Is that it?'

'Yes, Ma'am, she says she can use any old material for the middle part because it won't show.'

'Isn't that clever! The girls certainly are being practical, aren't they? Well, let's say a yard and a half then. That should do it up fine.'

'And about how much would that cost, Ma'am? I can't afford much, you know.'

'Oh not much at all, not for so little.'

'But about how much?' Kanji repeated.

'Well, the price of muslin has gone down a bit recently. It's about 42 or 43 *sen* a yard now, I think. No more than 50 *sen* for first-rate material.'

'That so? I thought it'd cost me a lot more.'

'And that's for fabric cut from the bolt. It can be still cheaper, I think. Not here in the village, though,' the mistress laughed. 'The prices here are ridiculous, and the cloth they sell is awful. I can pick you up a remnant the next time I make a shopping trip. That won't cost much at all.'

'Could you? That would be wonderful!' Kanji said gratefully. 'If you picked it out then I'd know it was okay. As long as it's red it'll be fine.'

'Well then, that's settled. If she really wants it then it's best to give it to her, isn't it? And you can pay for it with just a day's work at our place.' Then the mistress added warmly, 'I can see why she wants it, too. She'll be 18 soon, won't she?'

'It'll be a relief to be done with all her sulking around about not having one,' Kanji said. 'I'm sure grateful to you. I don't know a thing about stuff like this.'

'Well, girls think they're important, you know. They want to dress up a bit so people will notice them,' the mistress observed.

'That's so, isn't it? I don't care at all about what rags I wear, but it's different for a girl. You know, I've really been wondering about what to do, but I knew I could count on you to tell me the right thing.' Kanji thanked the mistress profusely, as if the trifling matter of an obi were some weighty affair.

11

Kanji had almost no friends in the village. It was not that he had picked quarrels with his neighbors. On the contrary, he went out of his way to avoid arguments. Poverty itself was to blame, for it led inevitably to envy and resentment among all those who were struggling to survive. Then, too, even simple gestures of friendship cost money. Kanji and those like him who would not spend a single *sen* unnecessarily were looked down upon by the others and treated coolly. This did not bother Kanji in the slightest. He concentrated all his energies on getting by from day to day. He was satisfied with very little and sought nothing more.

As far as his relations with other people were concerned Kanji was like a drop of oil in water. If the water stirred the oil stirred, too. But if the water remained still the oil congealed into a separate mass. Whether it was the water that kept aloof from the oil or the oil that shunned the water was impossible to tell. They simply did not mix, although they coexisted peacefully. Unless some external force was applied to bring them together they remained apart. As long as nothing disturbed the village he and his two children lived by themselves, next to the oak forest on the western edge of the community.

Although his theft of the sorghum had set tongues wagging, most people soon forgot the incident and paid no more attention to Kanji than they had before. They had too much work to do, and besides, there was always other, fresher gossip to attract them. Only some of the young men of the village remained inordinately interested in the goings-on at Kanji's house. That was because of Otsugi. Having once seen an attractive girl they simply could not forget about her. Still constrained by shyness, though, they could not be open about their feelings. Only at night, under cover of darkness, did their eyes reflect their youthful passions.

At night they came into their own.

A fisherman drops a red clay pot from his boat, which sinks

down to the ocean floor. When the pot is hauled up on board again an octopus may be inside, its tentacles braced against the inner surface of the container. In this way the fisherman can secure his catch even though he is unable to see beneath the waves. For young men of the village, however, the hunt is nowhere near as random. Every day they see the young girls they covet ripening before their very eyes. At night they go off in search of them, their faces covered so no one will recognize them. Not until very late do they return home again to rest briefly before the start of yet another day. Locating the girls is no problem for them, but unlike the fisherman whose clay pot sinks unimpeded to the seabed, the young men have to contend with parents who seek to keep them from their daughters. It is no easy matter to avoid discovery.

If the octopus holds tight to the inside of the pot the fisherman cannot possibly get it loose. Nor will he succeed if he tries to cut it loose with his knife. That is why there is always a little hole in the base of the pot. Just blowing through it onto the octopus's bottom will usually cause it to flee the pot of its own accord. Or if that fails a few drops of boiling water through the hole will always do the trick. The octopus will rush out of the pot in alarm and land at the fisherman's feet. Similarly, even if the young man manages to approach the girl he fancies without detection, he may find her unwilling at first. Then he must resort to all sorts of devices, risking discovery by her parents all the while, until she, like the octopus, can be captured. Once that has been achieved, and the two are deeply drawn to one another, both will work together to overcome all obstacles to their continued meetings.

Just after sunset, when a faint light still lingers in the sky, a girl sits by the well, singing happily as she washes rice for supper. Now and then she pauses for a second, listening for a faint signal from the young man she is awaiting. Or on a cool summer evening she returns to the well after supper and rinses out the scarf she wears every day in the fields until finally he arrives. Then the two of them disappear into the shadows cast by the trees at the edge of her yard. The thick foliage is their only ally, protecting them even on a moonlit night. The bright moon itself looks down at the abandoned wash-basin and seems to smile. If they remain too long in the shadows, the moonlight will finally reach them through the leaves. Should they be too preoccupied to notice, and if it is a persimmon tree under which they have taken shelter, the tree may fling a piece of its still unripened fruit to the ground to warn them. Easily alarmed at such times, they will look around nervously, suspecting that some of the other youths are spying on them. Meanwhile the leaves of the tree will rustle in the breeze, laughing. Until someone calls to the girl angrily from inside her house they will remain together, reveling in each other's company.

Even during the busy season they meet every night without a thought about how tired they will be when they go back to work the next morning. Just being together for a few hours, whispering in the darkness, makes them content. Sometimes their parents will send them off to the forest to work. Then they can savor being together all day as they wander about in search of leaves or grass. Except in winter when the bitter cold restrains their hearts, the forest is their paradise.

In early autumn, when the corn stands ripe in the fields, the young people have the forests to themselves. Only after all the crops are harvested do the older villagers arrive in search of fuel and fodder. Then the young people head off by themselves down narrow pathways through the trees until they are far from everyone else. Deep within their paradise they spread their wings. Only the sound of their singing voices reveals their presence amid the dark green foliage. They may work hard for several hours in the morning and deliver a basketful of grass to their homes at noon, but the afternoon they spend as they choose. If a boy and girl chance to meet they will drop everything and head off together among the trees, away from any footpath. No one passing by would know they were there. Sitting on the cold ground they chat together aimlessly. Or they just enjoy each other's company in silence, listening to the steady chirrup of the cicadas nearby. Mosquitoes swarm about their naked feet, attacking the sunburned flesh at will. They remain together, occasionally stretching out a leg that has gone numb, until the sunlight slanting down through the branches of the trees warns them of how late it is. As pale, gauze-like shadows stretch over their surroundings they stand up hurriedly and head for home, their empty baskets on their backs. They pick up as many fallen twigs and branches as they can as they rush along the paths, hoping to avoid a scolding. Then at dusk they enter their yards and set their baskets down by the grass they collected earlier. No one notices how little the baskets contain, for it is a busy time of day. Fathers are feeding the livestock, mothers getting the fire ready to cook supper.

With a guilty conscience the girl picks up an empty bucket and heads directly for the well to draw water for their soup. Then she sets to work chopping vegetables. Evening primroses open one by one on the fence nearby, fluttering in the breeze like so many yellow butterflies and scenting the twilight air. They gaze fondly at the girl as she hurries about her chores. They, too, know that a young man will arrive later that night and stand outside the door, his face wrapped in mosquito netting, waiting to be let inside. A mat hung over the entry will block the moonlight, and some grass-hoppers set free at just that moment will set up a noisy chirping that masks the creaking of the door as it slides along its tracks. Then the girl will lead her lover through the house, so tiny that it has no sliding doors to set off one space from another. There is no way to avoid the spot where her parents lie sleeping. Afraid that two sets of footsteps on the creaking floorboards might waken them, the girl will carry the young man past their pillows on her back. Exhausted from their long day's work her father and mother will not notice that their daughter's step is heavier than usual.

So it was for almost all the young people in the village. On rare occasions they might be found out and scolded by their parents. But by the next day they had recovered and went on as before with no regrets. Otsugi, however, never experienced such things.

Although Kanji was able to keep a tight rein on his daughter he could not prevent the young men of the village from thinking about her. Once attracted to a girl they pursued her tenaciously, just as chickens will try again and again to reach through a narrow crack in the storehouse door to eat the feed they see within. How intensely any young man thought of Otsugi was completely his own affair. But if he tried to lay his hands on her Kanji could and did intervene to stop him. That made Kanji a villain to all concerned, who complained about his meddling whenever they met together. Each one bragged to the others, too, that only he among them all would succeed in winning Otsugi's heart. Yet no one did succeed, for thanks to Kanji's vigilance, there were no opportunities to approach her.

Finally one young man did find a way to strike up an acquaint-ance. Strict though Kanji was, he could not prevent Otsugi from going off alone to their privy at night. A certain fellow discovered this by chance and saw his opportunity. He reached out and grabbed her as she approached through the darkness, then whis-pered to her softly as he caressed her arm. Otsugi was terrified the first time this happened and trembled with shame until he released her. The young man returned night after night, however, until gradually she grew used to his advances. If Kanji called out to her from the house she always answered him right away. At first he suspected nothing, but after several evenings he was certain some-thing was going on.

One night the door of the house opened with a sudden clatter and Kanji stepped outside. He had been in such a hurry that he had forced the door part way out of its tracks. Angrily he knocked it back into place and set out for the privy. Almost immediately he saw Otsugi walking towards him. At the same time he detected the sound of retreating footsteps. Instantly he grabbed a tree stump from the pile against the wall and flung it into the darkness with all his might. It landed with a thud on the other side of the yard and went tumbling end over end across the dirt. Several more stumps followed in its wake. The young man had already made his escape, but alarmed by Kanji's sudden attack he had stumbled over the gnarled roots of a tree and fallen to the ground. The next day he limped along with a painfully swollen ankle.

Kanji pushed Otsugi into the house and latched the door behind him. Only a few evenings before they had celebrated *Setsubun*, the eve of spring, and eaten parched beans to drive away the evil spirits. A bunch of fresh holly leaves and a dried sardine head still hung in the entry. It was the custom to consume as many beans as one had years of life. Otsugi had eaten eighteen. Despite her age, however, she was still too inexperienced and innocent to defend herself at a time like this. She stood limply in front of Kanji, her eyes downcast. His eyes were gleaming in the faint lamplight.

'Otsū!' he yelled at the top of his voice, so enraged that he was then left speechless for a moment. 'What went on out there?' he finally asked, looking at her sharply. Otsugi hung her head and said nothing.

'Tell me!' he demanded. 'And you'd better make it the truth.' Then as if he were in great pain, he rasped, 'Tell me you'll never give me trouble like that again. Can you promise me that? Can you?' He was silent for a moment and then began pleading with her again, his voice trembling and his manner agitated as if he were torn between anger and despair. Otsugi's muffled crying seeped out through the cracks in the door into the night.

Even though she had gradually come to look forward to those nightime encounters by the privy, she had always felt guilty and ashamed of herself afterwards. Now in deference to her father she vowed never to let it happen again. After only a brief taste of the sweet pleasures that were possible she gave them up and rejected all further advances. That was the end of the budding relationship, innocent and harmless though it had been. Otsugi bowed to her father's will, for to her he was her sole protector. As for Kanji himself whatever satisfaction he gained from his victory was more than outweighed by the painful memories of Oshina which the incident had brought him. He could not bear the thought of yet another loss. Only if all three of them remained together, however isolated their existence within the community, could he feel secure. It had alarmed and grieved him to discover that Otsugi, too, might leave him behind. He regarded the young men of the village as his bitter enemies. They, meanwhile, thought of him as a poisonous snake for what he had done, and all of them joined together to get such revenge as they could. Just as they would not dare approach a snake directly but would torment it by throwing rocks or poking at it with the end of a stick until it bared its fangs, they sought to tease him from afar. At night they would stand by the hedge and whistle at him noisily or sneak up and leave footprints by his door. Later, when they thought he was falling off to sleep, they would call out to Otsugi in high-pitched wails. All this exasperated Kanji, but since he had no way of identifying the culprits he was powerless to do a thing. Getting no response to their teasing, the young men eventually left him alone.

12

Winter stole over the land. With the lunar New Year approaching
and no work to be done in the fields it was the season for
marriages. An array of chests and wardrobes stood outside the
cabinet-maker's shop in town, their simple metal fittings catching
the sunlight.

A bride was coming to the house where Otsugi took her sewing
lessons. On the appointed day all the students dressed in their best
jackets and went off to help. From morning on there was a great
bustle of activity as they did the cleaning and washed the vegetables, laughing as they worked. Otsugi, too, was present, wearing
a red jacket and a light green sash to tie up her sleeves. Every year
when the weather turned warm and farming began again, the
sewing students would abandon their lessons, not resuming them
until the following winter. On a particular day at the start of the
growing season they would all go off to help cultivate their
teacher's upland field. With so many at work at once on such a tiny
plot of land, however, they would only get in each other's way.
Usually about half of them would end up standing to the side,
leaning on their hoes and chatting gaily as they looked around.
Enjoying the attention they attracted and not being needed for anything, they would have a pleasant time. It was the same on the day
of the wedding. Since there were far too many people for the
amount of work to be done they had ample opportunity to relax
and talk.

'I wonder what the bride is like?'

'Must be real nice, coming to this house and all.'

'I wish she'd hurry up! I can't wait to see her.'

At one point the youngest student asked, 'She'll be all powdered
white, won't she?'

'What a silly question!' one of the older girls replied, laughing.

'She might use liquid make-up.'

'I hear there's one as thin as water now.'

91

Then one of them said, 'I may have to help with the serving, but I sure don't want to. I'll feel real stupid out there in front of all those strangers.'

'Just remember the bride will be a lot more embarrassed than you!'

'Oh, I hope I get a chance to see how she's dressed,' another chimed in anxiously.

That evening, just after the sewing students had drifted off towards the parlor, five or six young men appeared at the back door. They had come for the wheat noodles they always received when a wedding took place. A few minutes later they set off again with a large basket of long, thin noodles, a small keg of sake and a bottle of soy sauce. As they passed through the gate they suddenly turned to jear and hoot back at the wedding party at the top of their lungs. Then they made their way noisily to the village prayer hall where the other young men sat waiting for them, throwing faggots onto the fire to warm themselves. The prayer society's cooking pans, teapots, and bowls were strewn across the floor, and a large lantern borrowed from some neighbor sat on its stand nearby. Thanks to the fire and the lantern the room was fairly well lit.

Wheat noodles were provided at every wedding in the village, not only because they were easy to serve but also because their length symbolized a long married life. Buckwheat noodles were avoided because they broke up into small pieces. Always the young men came to claim their share. If the family concerned was poor, the young men never complained about how little they received. But if a family they considered affluent failed to provide them with a generous amount, their resentment knew no bounds. In the past they had gone so far as to threaten to overturn the bride's carriage as it neared the groom's house unless they were given more to eat, but this kind of intimidating behavior was now rare. Almost everyone was willing to set ample noodles aside for them.

Their custom of demanding food at the back door of someone's house served no useful purpose as far as the wedding itself was concerned, but it did provide the young men with an excuse to set aside their rope-making or other night work and meet together for an evening. That alone gave them pleasure. Then, too, a wedding always excited them. Eager to become intimate with women themselves, they resented all the obstacles they faced in doing so, even though those same obstacles served to increase their desire. They could not help feeling slightly jealous that one of their number had succeeded and was now exchanging cupfuls of sake with his bride. Being together on that occasion, eating, drinking, and making merry helped them forget their own disappointment. There were

never enough noodles to satisfy their hunger, but that did not
bother them.

They heated the sake in the soot-covered teapot and poured it
into their bowls. Then they gulped it down, not even pausing to let
it cool a little. It was not that they were particularly thirsty. It was
simply their custom to drink this way. Even if their throats were
burning they had to keep it up. Not worrying about how much they
spilled in their haste, they drank all they had been given. Next they
attacked their noodles, dipping them first in a mixture of soy sauce
and water and then slurping them up.

Aroused by all the alcohol they had consumed they became
increasingly foul-mouthed. Whenever one of them burst out with
some obscene phrase another responded right away with something even worse, as if they were competing to see who was the
crudest of them all. Although they sometimes cowered meekly in
the presence of other people, no such constraints were upon them
now. They were off by themselves and free to behave however they
pleased. Paying no heed to how late it was, they kept on talking
after they had finished eating and had tossed their plates carelessly
to the side. At one point they decided to count up how many
unmarried couples were living together in the village. With gusto
they began rattling off names, hooting and jeering noisily at the
discomfort of anyone among them whose parents' names were
mentioned.

After they had listed all the likely possibilities and their interest
in the game began to flag, one of them shouted, 'Hey, what about
Kanji? Shouldn't we include him and his daughter?'

This sudden inspiration was greeted with applause and cheering.

'Let's ask Kanji about it!' a voice cried out from the corner.

'You try a stupid thing like that,' another voice replied, 'and
you'll end up black and blue all over.'

'Well, how about asking Otsū instead?'

'Then you'd just end up with a broken leg.'

'Yeah, get yourself hit by a ton of firewood!'

Everyone burst into laughter.

'Hey listen!' one of them said, 'I saw Kanji down at the shop on
the corner today. All fired up he was, and downing sake like crazy.'

'How come?' the others asked, pricking up their ears.

'Well,' he continued, pleased to be the center of attention, 'do
you know he let Otsugi go off with the others to help at the
wedding?' Everyone nodded. 'Well, toward sundown he couldn't
stand it any more without her, so there he was in the shop,
grumbling on and on. I just happened in there to buy some sandals
and heard everything he said.'

'I hear he's been there drinking almost every night,' someone piped up.

'That's right,' the young man went on. 'He's getting some money now for clearing land, so he buys himself a bit of sake after finishing up for the day. I asked the shopkeeper all about it. But today he was in there earlier than usual, and I heard some real juicy things.'

'Tell us what!' the others shouted.

'Well, he was grumbling on about how awful Otsū was, staying away and not doing a thing about fixing him his supper. Then he sent Yokichi off to fetch her. But instead of bringing her he just comes back and says she'll be along as soon as she's had some noodles. Well, Kanji explodes and tells Yokichi to go straight back and tell her to come right away. It was really something, seeing him like that, I'll tell you.'

'And did she come?' someone asked.

'Uh-huh. Seems she had left already and met Yokichi on the way.'

'She came into the shop?' two fellows asked at once.

'Nope, she walked right on by. Kanji called out to her, but she just kept going. So then he yelled to her something fierce and started to dash after her. But he was so wrought up he dropped his money all over the floor when he tried to pay his bill. He must've drunk almost a quart. And what a mean look he had! But Otsū wouldn't have a thing to do with him. She didn't even look back.'

'He was scared to leave her at the wedding until dark, 'cause he knew some of us would be dropping by.'

'That's it for sure.'

'The old fool,' an angry voice called out. 'We didn't make any trouble.'

'You know,' the first fellow suddenly observed, 'Otsugi sure looks good with her hair all done up.'

'That's what makes her father lose control of himself!' someone remarked. In the fluttering light of the lantern all the young men shouted boisterously and beat their chopsticks noisily against their bowls.

Kanji expected to earn 30 or 40 yen that winter by clearing land for the master again. Even though he would have to use most of the money to pay off his debts, he had no complaints. Just being able to keep a yen's worth of coins in his purse at all times freed him from worry. While other people gossiped maliciously behind his back, he himself felt that all was well. After years of struggle life seemed easier at last.

13

The loose ends of mosquito nets fluttered in the early autumn breeze. The corn crop had been harvested and the ears roasted crisp over flaming straw. Discarded husks lay everywhere. For the time being there was no more work to be done in the fields. Everyone made ready to celebrate *Bon*, the festival of the dead.

On the first day of the festival Kanji had been busy with chores until early afternoon. Then he hurriedly swept up the yard and cut down some of the largest weeds with his sickle. Meanwhile Otsugi prepared their simple, smoke-blackened household altar. She cleaned the fittings as best she could and set a cup of water, a leaf spread with small cubes of eggplant and a little bouquet of purple loosestrife flowers on the shelf. Towards dusk they closed the rain doors of the house and set off for the graveyard, carrying an unlit paper lantern with them. After burning incense before Oshina's wooden grave tablet and the other nearby gravestones, they lit their lantern and returned home. Oshina's spirit, which had returned from the nether world on this day, would dwell in the flame of the lantern and accompany them. That is why the lantern was lit at the graveyard itself.

For the occasion Otsugi wore a new *yukata* that Kanji had bought for her now that he had a little extra money. Around her waist was a red obi. Earlier that day she and some of her friends had stripped down to their underwear and done up each other's hair. Otsugi was now in her nineteenth autumn. A few white ears of rice scattered here and there in the lush green paddies peeped out at her enviously as she passed by. But there was no one else to notice her. Only after the three of them had arrived home did the other villagers pour out of their houses and head for the graveyard with lanterns in hand.

Kanji transferred the flame from the lantern to the dish of rapeseed oil on their household altar. The light glowed faintly as if it came from far away. The fumes of burning incense flowed over

95

Oshina's white mortuary tablet. In turn Kanji and Otsugi dipped the ends of the little bouquet of flowers into the cup of water and sprinkled the water that adhered to them over the cubes of eggplant. Then Kanji opened all the rain doors while Otsugi stripped down to her underwear and put the glutinous rice she had set aside earlier on the stove to steam. Kanji stripped too and washed the mortar and pestle at the well. It was because they still had to make rice cakes for the holiday that they had hurried off to the graveyard before everyone else.

By the time the rice was cooked it was almost dark inside the house. The moon, which had appeared white in the sky before sunset, was now tinged with yellow, its light casting shadows from the persimmon and chestnut trees in the yard. Standing outside under the eaves of the house Otsugi ladled sticky spoonfuls of rice from the straining basket into the mortar. Every now and then she gave a little bit to Yokichi who was standing eagerly beside her. After licking off whatever had stuck to her finger she went on ladling. Then with steam rising up around him Kanji started to work with the pestle, pounding away at the hot, sticky mass as hard as he could. Whenever the end of the pestle got covered with rice Otsugi would scrape it clean with a wet spoon and push the rice in the mortar back down into a ball. Kanji would then begin pounding again. On and on they worked, the metal mortar gleaming in the moonlight, as the shadows around them deepened. Finally Otsugi reached down into the mortar and began twisting off pieces of smooth, translucent rice cake. These she placed on ginger leaves and lined up one by one on the tray beside her.

The moon, in its thirteenth day and almost full, bathed everything in cool, white light. A faint breeze blew, fluttering the dark green leaves of the persimmon tree nearby. From the forest behind the house came the rustling of bamboo leaves.

Sweating profusely Otsugi hurried inside and set one of the rice cakes on the shelf of the altar. Then she put the other cakes and a bowl of soybean flour in the main room by the lantern. Yokichi sat down right away, impatient to begin eating.

As soon as they had finished supper they heard the sound of drums piercing the night air and calling out for dancers. At the same time the mosquitoes that had been swarming beneath the eaves began to penetrate to where they sat indoors. Kanji tossed a handful of straw onto the narrow veranda and laid some freshly cut grass on top. Then he struck a match and carefully ignited the pile. The rising smoke drove the mosquitoes away. When flames began to dart up as the straw caught fire he doused them out with water. His eyes and nose smarting, he stood amid the smoke, stripped down to his loincloth. With a winnowing fan he directed the smoke towards the house.

Having cleaned up the kitchen Otsugi stood by the well wiping the sweat from her body. Each time she dipped her towel into the wash-basin the reflection of the moon disintegrated into fragments before reappearing on the surface of the water once again. The drums from her own village sounded close at hand as if they were just beyond the yard. Those from distant villages seemed to echo from the sky beyond the forest. Otsugi listened entranced. Everyone else her age would be going off to dance, she thought enviously. In the soft moonlight her skin appeared white. Absentmindedly she reached up and adjusted her hair. Then she slipped back into her *yukata*.

'Where are those drums coming from, Papa?' she asked as she began to tie her obi.

'What? Those faint ones? How am I supposed to know?' Kanji answered without interest, his attention riveted on the smoldering embers of his fire.

'They must be from another village, coming towards us.'

'Now, how can you tell that?'

'Because I heard about it today when I was getting my hair fixed. They're going to come and join ours from somewhere else.

'Well, if you say so . . .'

'Maybe I'll go along and see,' Otsugi muttered. 'I could take Yoki with me.'

'Go off by yourself!' Kanji exploded. 'You think I'm going to let you do that?'

'Well, I bet South Neighbor's wife is going. She could take us.'

'Not on your life!' Kanji retorted. 'What's got into you anyhow. There'll be dancing every night now for days, so what's the rush? You just can't wait to show yourself off, can you?'

Otsugi undid her obi and flung it down beside her.

The next evening, as they did each year on the second day of Bon, everyone fixed wheat noodles for supper. First they added a pinch of salt and a little water to some wheat flour. Then they kneaded the mixture up into a ball, wrapped the ball in a mat and stomped on the mat with their feet. When the dough was firm they stretched it out thin, folded it up and sliced it into narrow strips. All the scraps were pinched up into little triangles and placed on the household altar. These were hats for the spirits of the dead to wear when they accompanied the farmers to the fields to inspect the crops.

As soon as it was dark the drums began to beat again, calling out for dancers. Kanji did not bother with a mosquito fire that night.

Instead he put on a blue unlined kimono and began to close up the house. 'Hurry up and get ready, Otsū!' he called out impatiently. 'I'm taking you off to the dancing.' As the three of them left the yard, the moon emerged from a bank of clouds and hung serenely above the treetops.

The dances took place every year in the shade of the tall fir trees near the village shrine. By the time Kanji and his children arrived a large number of people had already gathered. The wild beating of the drums reverberated among the trees. Men and women were dancing in a circle around the drums, pressing in towards the center and then moving outwards again in time to the drumbeats. The women had attached scarves to the sleeves of their garments to make them appear longer, and around their waists they had tied long sashes whose ends dangled down behind their backs. As they moved about, their sleeves and sashes swung from side to side. The men danced recklessly, brushing up against the women whenever they had the chance. Sometimes a woman would protest, but soon she would be back dancing again, being buffeted by the others as she followed the circle around the drummers. As the number of dancers increased, a second circle formed inside the first. Whenever the drumbeats slackened everyone protested. 'If the drums fail, so will the dancing!' they sang out loudly. Then a fresh drummer would take over, and the pace would quicken.

The dancers all wore bamboo hats decorated with the kind of white wood shavings used for wrapping buns. As they danced about in the semi-darkness beneath the trees the shavings fluttered around their heads, adding gaiety to the scene. Later the tattered strips would lie in the dust along the pathways of the village where they had been cast aside by the dancers on their way home.

Onlookers from the village crowded at the fringes of the dancing. Just beyond them one of the village peddlers had spread out a mat laden with cheap candies, pears, and melons. A sooty lamp lit his wares, among which the dark red slices of watermelon were the most in demand. Thirsty dancers consumed them eagerly, not minding that they were sprinkled with the dust their dancing had raised. Shy young girls clustered in small groups just outside the light of the lamp, each one extending a hand to receive a slice. The peddler, standing in the light at the edge of his mat, had to squint to see where they were. Having obtained their slices the girls hurried off into the shadows of the trees, from where their laughing voices could be heard.

Kanji bought Yokichi the slice of watermelon he craved and sat down at the edge of the peddler's mat. Otsugi remained beside him for a while. Then, wanting to get away from the light herself, she went off with Yokichi and stood beneath the trees. Suddenly Kanji noticed her absence and scanned the shadows until he located her again.

'Otsugi-san! How nice you could come,' a girl nearby called out. Taking a break from dancing she was fanning herself with her sleeve. 'My, but it's hot,' she sighed as she dabbed at the perspiration on her throat and chest.

'Aren't you going to dance, Otsugi-san?' another girl asked.

'Don't want to,' Otsugi murmured. 'My father's here watching over me.'

The girl caught sight of Kanji squinting into the darkness, and thinking that he was glaring at her she hastily turned away.

Sitting as he was in the light of the lamp Kanji was visible to everyone standing among the trees. The older women who had come to watch the dancing pointed at him and smiled derisively. Even the lamp seemed to echo their sentiments as it flickered in the night air, the flames like so many wagging tongues.

At one point Otsugi disappeared among a group of bystanders. Kanji jumped to his feet and moved towards the trees. Almost immediately he located her again, for she had only moved a few steps away. Seeing him standing close by, the other girls drew back slightly.

Early in the evening the fir trees had blocked out the moonlight, providing the dancers with the darkness they desired. Now, however, one portion of their circle was illuminated as the sinking moon finally penetrated the dense cover of branches. The decorations on the dancers' hats gleamed in the light. Gradually the dancing became more and more frenzied. It was as if the participants were totally immune to fatigue. Then a few young men broke off from the circle and descended like a tidal wave on a group of young women standing nearby. With much laughter and shouting the women tried to fend them off. Suddenly one of the young men grabbed at Otsugi's hair. As she cried out in surprise he ran off with her comb and disappeared into the crowd.

'Of all the nerve!' Otsugi muttered angrily when she patted her hair back into place and discovered the comb was missing. Without any hesitation she started off in pursuit of the culprit. Before she had gone more than a few steps, however, Kanji had moved up behind her. He grabbed her by the nape of the neck with one hand and slapped her across the ear with the other. As Otsugi turned around in alarm her father's second blow struck her on the nose. She bent over in pain, both hands pressing against her face. None of the other girls moved a step towards her. They knew how Kanji treated his daughter and shrank back terrified.

'All right, you,' Kanji snarled. 'How come someone took your comb? Don't pretend you don't know, you little bitch! Speak up!' He shoved her so hard she almost tumbled over, but she managed to steady herself with her hands.

'Papa! What's got into you?' she cried, her voice trembling.

'Got into me!' Kanji thundered. 'Of all the nerve! Now, you just tell me how come someone took your comb. Come on, tell me!'

'But I don't know,' Otsugi muttered bitterly, her sleeve shielding her face.

'You expect me to believe a perfect stranger swiped it?' Kanji hissed back at her. 'You slut!' he snarled, giving her a kick. Otsugi fell forwards onto the ground, but she did not cry.

'Ouch!' someone called out in falsetto from the crowd. The dancing had stopped some time ago, and people stood in a circle around Kanji and Otsugi. Suddenly aware of the onlookers, Otsugi reached down and covered her exposed knees with the skirt of her *yukata*.

'The fellow that took it's right here,' another voice called out.

'Make him hand it over!' someone shouted.

'Not on your life!' came a high-pitched reply. 'Cause Papa would give me a thrashing. Papa has to promise to forgive me first.' The crowd, which had been watching in stunned silence, began to stir.

'Hey, Papa!' someone yelled from the rear, 'how about lighting a lantern?' Everyone burst into laughter.

Otsugi sprang to her feet and started to run off.

'Where're you going?' Kanji called out. He tried to grab hold of her, but she twisted away and kept going. Tripping over the toe of his sandal in his haste Kanji stumbled after her. 'Otsū!' he called out anxiously. Bewildered by what had happened Yokichi had been crying the whole time.

There was no more dancing in the village that evening. Those who wanted to continue traipsed off down the footpath, following the sound of drums that were still beating elsewhere. A few of them overtook Kanji along the way and jeered at him as they went past. Their teasing infuriated him, but there was nothing he could do about it. He walked along in silence, Otsugi slightly ahead of him and Yokichi trailing behind.

By the time the three of them reached their house at the edge of the village they were alone, for everyone else had turned off onto other paths along the way. The moon shone brightly, and drum-beats echoed from afar. The night now belonged entirely to dancers. Laughing and singing they made their way towards the distant drums, stealing melons from the fields they passed to slake their thirst. Discarded rinds lay in the grass by the side of the paths. Later that night several young men made their way to Kanji's yard, bent on mischief. Finding that all was dark and still, however, they lost interest and dispersed.

The next morning Otsugi went off in search of her comb. All her friends knew who had taken it, of course. 'I hear you ought to go look in your persimmon tree,' one of them told her. Otsugi hurried back home and found the comb right away on one of the lower branches. Two of its teeth were missing. Otsugi stared at the damage for a moment and then thrust the comb into her hair.

With that the incident came to an end. It was a long time, though, before people stopped talking about it. The village women, in particular, went on and on . . .

'Wasn't that terrible, what Kanji-san did?'

'Like a madman he was, wasn't he?'

'The things I hear about him, well, they're hard to believe,' someone sighed. Everyone knew what she was alluding to. 'Awful, really awful,' they replied.

Among the young men of the village, too, the incident was a frequent topic of conversation, fueling their wildest imaginings.

14

It is summer once more. The hot sun goads the farmers into a flurry of activity. First they cut down their winter barley crops and load the sheaves onto carts. In just a few days' time all the upland fields have been harvested. Then the weather changes, and for days on end rain falls steadily until even the aphids infesting the yellowing plum blossoms have been washed away. The newly planted bean and upland rice seedlings in the barley fields thirstily drink in the cool water and gather strength. Within a few days the soil in the fields is carpeted with their green leaves. Even the trampled down soil in the farmers' yards shows renewed signs of life as the rains bring forth tiny yellow blossoms on the nasturtiums and crowfoots, and on the ridgepoles of their houses grass begins to shoot up once more. Nature is intent upon covering every bit of soil with color. The only resistance it meets is in the rice paddies, carefully cleared and cultivated by the farmers. As time passes and still the paddies remain bare, nature grows impatient. Heavy rains fall, filling the shallow fields and submerging the weeds in the nearby ditches. At last it is time to plant. Knowing that even a single additional day of growing time will increase their harvest the following autumn, the farmers must work as quickly as they can. Abandoning all other chores they drive their horses through the flooded paddies until the soil is just the right consistency. Then with straw capes on their backs to keep off the rain they wade carefully across the fields, thrusting seedlings down into the mud. Though soaking wet they sing happily as they work. One by one the paddies turn pale green. By the time all the planting is done the seedlings have deepened in color, as if nature had applied a powerful dye, and grasses have sprouted on the ridges between the fields. Nowhere is the dark soil visible. Satisfied at last, nature clears the sky of clouds and sends bright, warm sunlight down onto the countryside. Day lilies begin to bloom here and there on the ridges, giving color to the fields even on days when young women from the village do not come to weed the paddies. Now is the time for *Sanaburi*, the end-of-planting feasts to celebrate completion of the major task in growing rice and to reward people for the back-breaking labor they have performed.

Kanji and Otsugi helped South Neighbor with his rice planting and took part in his *Sanaburi*. The leaves of the mulberry trees in the field that separated Kanji's house from South Neighbor's had been picked not long before. In between the trees lay well-established potato plants, each one sporting blossoms. South Neighbor raised a few silkworms on the side and harvesting mulberry leaves for them had put him behind in his farming. Only when everyone else was finishing rice planting was he able to begin, hiring a large group of people to help him get the job done quickly. The weather was fine on the day, and everyone worked energetic-ally. The planting was finished long before sunset. Seeing that all was going well, South Neighbor's wife left for home early, taking Otsugi along with her, to prepare the meal for the feast. Busily she cooked the barley and ground it to make spiced flour.

As soon as they had finished planting, the others headed for the nearest irrigation ditch to get the mud off their clothes. Some jumped into the water without removing their blue work trousers and stood rubbing the fabric between their hands until finally it was clean. Others took their trousers off first and splashed them around in the water. Mud flowed downstream like smoke. Then they descended on South Neighbor's house, laughing and talking noisily. In the shade of a persimmon tree by the back door stood the bathtub, a smoldering fire beneath it. One of the women hired to help out that day lifted the cover off the tub and stirred up the water inside. Then she blew on the fire through a bamboo pipe. The red tongues of flame curled up higher and higher.

The next time the cover was removed the surface of the water was covered with scum — the tub had not been cleaned out thoroughly the night before. Not minding that a bit, however, the workers began taking baths in turn. After just a few dabs with the wash-cloth they emerged from the tub. No one even bothered to scrub the mud off his toes.

'Lots of smoke here!' a man who had just finished bathing said. He stood naked with his back to the others as he slipped his wet feet into his clogs. 'You better take that bad piece of wood out of the fire.'

'Won't bother me any,' the next bather replied as he submerged himself and began to wash. 'Hey, it *is* smoky!' he yelled a few moments later. 'Otsugi!' he called, catching sight of her as she passed by. 'Come here a minute, huh?' He worked as a horse trader in the slack season.

'Now really, Kane-san,' Otsugi replied in a lightly scolding tone. 'If it's so smoky why didn't you do something about it before you got in? Or ask one of the others? I'm supposed to be fetching water, not doing favors for you.' She set her two buckets down on the ground and pulled away the smoking piece of wood.

'He wouldn't have been content if anyone but Otsugi did it for him,' one of the others said.

Kane stood up with a splash. 'Now that there's no more smoke, I don't want to be in here any more. Can't stand all this fresh air.'

Otsugi thrust the smoking stick toward him. 'You're awful! Well, if you don't like what I did for you, here's your smoke back.'

Kane cringed, trying to avoid the stick. 'Okay, okay,' he muttered. 'I apologize.'

Otsugi returned to her buckets.

'Hey, wait a minute, Otsugi!' Kane suddenly called out. 'I've got something to show you.'

'Oh no,' she replied. 'I've had enough of your goings on.' She leaned over and grasped a handle in each hand. Just as she lifted the buckets off the ground Kane called out, 'Well here, then,' and threw something in her direction. It was an unripe persimmon that had fallen into the bathtub. It landed with a plop in one of the buckets, splashing water onto Otsugi's feet.

'You're just full of tricks, aren't you,' Otsugi said, turning to face him. She was smiling.

'Well, at least you got her to turn around,' one of the men by the bathtub said.

'Uh-huh,' Kane replied. 'I'm happy now that I got a look at those freckles.'

'Really! You've got no manners at all, have you, Kane-san? Talking about a person like that.' Otsugi retrieved the persimmon from the bucket and threw it at him.

'Looks like she really loves him, huh?' someone said. Otsugi turned crimson and fled in such haste that water lapped over the rims of the buckets she was carrying and splashed onto the ground. All the farmers standing near the bathtub chuckled at her discomfort. At just this moment Kanji appeared at the back gate. He had gone off across the mulberry field to his own house to change clothes. On his way back to South Neighbor's he had gathered from all the noise that something was going on, and then he had seen Otsugi dashing off. With a suspicious frown on his face he stepped into the yard. No one said another word.

The rays of the setting sun filtered through the bamboo thicket onto the moist soil below. Then the light revealed the mass of white gardenias growing in the semi-darkness near the well. A lantern had been lit inside the house, and the men had sat down in a circle on the wooden floor of a room adjacent to the kitchen. A few young women who had been hired to help with the feast stood by the stove. Small bottles of warmed sake had been set before the guests.

'I'm grateful to all of you for your help,' South Neighbor announced formally. 'Please relax and enjoy yourselves.'

'Thank you,' the men replied in unison. Just as they began filling their sake cups, however, South Neighbor's wife suddenly interrupted them. 'Couldn't you wait just a minute?' she asked, still holding the dish towel she had used to take a pot off the fire. 'I think Father has forgotten the god of the hearth.'

'Why so I have!' South Neighbor replied, somewhat flustered. He picked up one of the bottles of sake and stepped down into the kitchen. A bundle of rice seedlings had been laid across the little household altar atop the stove. South Neighbor poured some sake over them.

'Hey!' Kane the horse trader called out in jest. 'Don't use up too much of that stuff over there.'

'Isn't it awful what people will do to get a drink,' Otsugi whispered. Kane overheard her. 'But sake's made for people, not plants,' he replied. 'Just let me have some and I'll prove how much quicker it works on me.'

Now South Neighbor sprinkled some spiced barley flour over the seedlings to represent blossoms. This symbolized the hope that the rice ears would be full and heavy. When Kane saw him do that he too stepped down into the kitchen.

'Someone get me some wheat flour,' he said. 'Just a pinch will do. Come on now. Otsugi, how about it?'

'Why must you always be showing off?' she chided him. Then with permission from South Neighbor's wife she gave him a little flour.

'There we are,' Kane announced as he sprinkled on the flour. 'Now we have late rice blossoms!' The seedlings on the altar were flecked with white.

'You don't see much of that anymore,' one of the women said.

'Well, I still grow it,' Kane replied. 'Some man at the village office says we aren't supposed to, but if I didn't I wouldn't get any harvest at all, not on that land of mine. The soil never dries up proper, and it's cold all the time. Well, I had a talk with one of the officials after some lecture, and he didn't come out and say it was a bad thing to do. The other man's just stupid.'

'No, you're just stubborn,' one of the women interjected. 'Late rice is really dangerous.'

'Me stubborn? I am not!' Kane retorted. Then he changed the subject. 'Look here,' he said, clapping his hands. 'The blossoms have opened up now. Those flowers are called monks' heads.'

'What?' a woman said. 'There's no such thing as monks' heads on rice.'

'Oh yes there is,' Kane replied in a low voice. 'Kanji-san told me so!' The women tried to stifle their laughter with their sleeves. Trying not to laugh himself Kane stepped back into the other room and sat down again.

As a child Kanji had often been reduced to tears by his playmates. Early on the other children had nicknamed him 'Kannabe', which meant sake-warming pan. Kanji had hated that nickname, and even when he was in his forties he would not say the word *nabe*. Everyone in the village knew that. One recent autumn Kane the horse trader had seen Kanji at work harvesting his rice crop and had asked mischievously what the cut-off ears were called. The standard term was *nabe-ware*. 'These are monks' heads,' Kanji had snapped back at him, not wanting to say the word *nabe* if he could help it. Delighted with his triumph Kane had spread the story throughout the village. 'Hey, there's the monks' head couple!' some people had started saying after that whenever they saw Kanji and Otsugi at work in their paddy.

Finally it was time to drink. Sake was poured around, and the men gingerly lifted their cups to their mouths. 'Help yourself to as much of this as you like,' South Neighbor's wife said, putting down two heaping platters of boiled, salted potatoes. 'There's lots more left.' Quickly the men drained their sake cups and began pouring each other refills, taking care not to spill a drop. They were sitting upright in honor of the occasion.

'Help yourselves to sake, too,' South Neighbor said, 'Don't be bashful.'

'Yes, sir!' they replied, grateful for his generosity. Sake had become so expensive lately that they did not expect much of it to be served at such a gathering. South Neighbor, though, had just sold his first crop of cocoons and had received much more than he expected for his leftover mulberry leaves. To celebrate he had indulged in a yen's worth of sake. Since they needed some soy sauce for the feast as well he had gone off during the noon break that day across the Kinu River to make both purchases. By going directly to the sake distributor he had been able to get a better brand at a better price than in the village.

The sake was indeed delicious. Unused to consuming so much alcohol at one time, the men were soon sprawled comfortably on the floor, talking raucously. Kanji, sitting alone, poured himself cup after cup and was drunk well before the others.

'Me, I'm a carpenter without a plane,' he announced, peering towards the kitchen. 'But I've still got my chisel.' Then he burst into uncontrollable laughter and leered at the women again. Near where he sat was a platter of potatoes garnished with burdocks and fried bean curd. Kanji speared a potato with one of his chopsticks and stuffed it into his mouth. Otsugi stood in the shadows watching.

'These potatoes sure are mighty big,' someone said.

'We grow 'em out in the mulberry field,' South Neighbor replied with a touch of pride in his voice.

'How about that! They sure do good out there.'

'It's where I buried a lot of garbage,' South Neighbor went on. 'The potatoes really liked that, but I'm a little worried about how the mulberries are doing.'

'No need to worry. If the potatoes found that garbage, so will the mulberry trees. It's amazing how far their roots can go. They may be blind, but they'll go straight to where there's food.'

'We got about two quarts of potatoes off each plant.'

'Hmm. Not bad, not bad at all,' several of the men observed.

'These burdocks are really nice, too,' another man said as he picked one off the platter. 'How'd you keep 'em so long?'

'No trouble at all,' South Neighbor answered. 'We just bury 'em out in the yard. That way we still have some to eat at planting time.'

'If I tried that at my house, somebody'd come along and steal 'em,' another man complained.

'Me, I always store 'em in my stomach,' Kane said with a smile. 'That way no one can steal 'em from me.'

Kanji spoke up from his side of the room. 'Got to be careful with burdocks. If you string 'em up on rope to dry they go rotten. The rope poisons 'em somehow.'

'What's that?' a dubious voice inquired.

'No "what's that" about it,' Kanji muttered, uncomfortable at being challenged. 'It happened to me once. Isn't that right, Otsū?' He turned towards the kitchen. The women were standing just outside the light of the lantern, watching the festivities in the other room. Someone nudged Otsugi and whispered, 'Go on now. Answer him!' That was followed by giggles. Kanji squinted into the darkness, a suspicious look on his face.

'She's here all right,' one of the women announced. 'Don't get all upset just because you can't see her.' Kanji was sitting at the edge of the room, near the step down into the kitchen. Every now and then he would lean forward, collect the empty sake bottles and pass them to one of the women.

'Hmm, what's this?' Kane muttered. 'I was sure I'd put it in here.' He hunted around inside his kimono and finally withdrew a small package. 'Ah, here we are. Take a look at this, everybody!' He opened the package and out stepped a praying mantis.

'Just look how mad he gets,' Kane said, chuckling as he poked at the mantis with his finger.

'And just look at that grown-up there fooling around like a little boy!' a woman said. Everybody laughed.

Yokichi had been sitting with his sister, but now he approached Kane. 'Hey, I know what it is!' he said. 'It comes from crows' nests.'

'No it doesn't,' Kanji answered mildly. 'You don't know what you're talking about.'

'But I do!' Yokichi protested as he nudged the mantis with his finger. 'I've seen one coming out.'

'It's no good, Kanji-san,' one of the men said with a sigh. 'You send kids to school for even a few months, they never listen to a word you say again.' Kanji broke into a smile.

Drinking steadily the men now began to talk about horses. Someone mentioned that even the wildest horse could be calmed down by forcing it to swallow a little sake. Then it could be handed over to an unsuspecting buyer. That used to happen often, but now people were more careful. Besides, someone else chimed in, hardly anyone could afford to buy a horse these days. They were buying carts instead. And maybe an ox or cow, even though the animals being imported from Korea were pretty scrawny for the price one had to pay.

'Horse traders are a bunch of crooks!' the man sitting next to Kane said in a light-hearted tone. 'Why, even Kane's tried to cheat me.'

'I have not!' Kane retorted. 'I'm no cheat. And if you ask me, a man who won't pay a fair price for what he's getting is even worse than a thief. This fellow here's been stalling me for a long time.'

'Still, you got to admit there aren't any rich horse traders around,' the man went on. 'That's their punishment for cheating people.'

'Yeah? And what about that white horse I showed you a while back?' Kane asked. 'Offer me a better price! You know the army won't requisition a white animal.'

'It's a good horse, all right, but it's not worth as much as you want for it. I'll add a bag of rice to my offer, but that's all.'

'Not enough!' Kane replied. 'Why, that horse has a pedigree and all. I've got his papers. And a nice blanket, too.'

'Papers! Why those papers of yours just say whether the animal's

a mare or a gelding. I asked a fellow over at the market in
Shirakawa, so I know all about them now.'

'Well now,' another man sitting nearby said in an effort to calm
them down. 'It's time for you two to have a drink.' He gave each
man the other's cup and filled both with sake. 'Bottom's up! Let's
see who's the best drinker, at any rate.' With that the argument
came to an end.

'Say, how old is the head of this house anyway?' someone asked
in a loud voice. 'He's getting a bit gray.'

'Hmm,' South Neighbor said, patting his hair. 'Looks like it,
don't it.'

'He may be going gray,' his wife replied with a smile, 'but he's
not all that old!' She was holding their youngest child in her arms.

'Him and me's the same age,' Kanji broke in.

'You sure about that?' someone asked.

'Sure I'm sure!' Kanji hissed back at him.

'Goodness me,' South Neighbor's wife said.

'And just how old are you, Kanji-san?' one of the men asked.

'Well, like I said, same age as South Neighbor.' Kanji was just
repeating something he remembered hearing a long time ago.

'What kind of answer's that?' the man said laughing.

South Neighbor's wife took a close look at her husband's hair
and Kanji's. 'Kanji-san must be younger,' she said. 'His hair's not
at all gray.'

'Yes, Kanji-san's still just 17,' Kane added. At that the women
almost broke up. Kane turned and saw that some of them were
licking spiced flour off their fingers. 'Better not laugh when you're
doing that!' he said. Immediately they all burst into giggles,
spewing the flour all around them. Choking and coughing they ran
off in search of water.

'Oh, what a horrible thing!' one of them was able to say at last.
'I got it up my nose, even. Did it ever burn! You are really a mean
one, Kane-san. If I had a stick I'd give you a thrashing, that's
what.'

'But I warned you not to laugh,' Kane replied mildly. 'You
should've listened to me.' Then amid all the hubbub he shouted, 'I
think I'll tell you a little story about horse trading.' With one gulp
he drained his sake cup and began drumming it and another empty
cup against the wooden floor to imitate hoofbeats. 'All the way
from Miharu to Shirakawa we bring 'em, a whole string at a time,
all tied together, with blankets on their backs. Listen close now.
This is what it's really like.'

Everybody was still.

'Hai ya, giddyap there!' he shouted. 'We go on and on all day, giddyap there, on and on, until we find a nice patch of grass for 'em, real nice grass. Then we stop. All around there's flowers, real nice rape-seed flowers. Hooi, hooi, the horses cry, they're all tired out, all . . . tired . . . out.' By this time Kane's face was red, and beads of sweat shone on his forehead.

'Sure is a boring story,' someone muttered. 'It's hardly late at all, but I'm sleepy already.'

'Enough of that!' Kane bellowed. 'Get the dung out of your ears and listen. Next morning we set out again, giddyap there, giddyap. The mountains are up ahead, all covered with clouds. Clip, clop, clippety clop. We're going up and over, each slope steeper than the last. Hiin, hiin, the horses cry. They're getting restless, but on we go. By nightfall we're just at the seventh hill, with sixteen more hills to go. The men are all tired, and the horses too, because those rocky slopes are hard-going. It's no easy job bringing all those horses over the mountains, trying to keep 'em from breaking away, or biting at each other, or falling down. Why, some of the trails are so steep they get scared even. Then we have to sing to 'em to calm 'em down, and lead 'em along real slow, real slow.' Kane had tossed his kimono aside and was sitting in his loincloth. His sash, fringed with the same red fabric used to make headbands for horses, lay in a heap on the floor beside him. 'Finally we get 'em to the stable and safe inside. They give themselves a big shake all over and start stomping and whinnying like crazy.' He picked up a dirt-stained towel and wiped the sweat off his body. 'Ouch!' he cried out suddenly, slapping at a mosquito.

Throughout Kane's performance Kanji had sat staring into the darkness of the kitchen as if in search of something. 'Otsū,' he now shouted abruptly, a sullen look on his face. 'Bring me some more potatoes!' He thrust his bowl out in front of him.

'What's got into you, Papa?' she answered. 'There's still plenty on that platter right there beside you.' Then she muttered, 'Just because you're drunk you don't have to act so stupid.'

Kanji put his bowl back on his tray and laughed sheepishly. Then he looked over toward a group of women in the corner of the room. 'Come on over here and I'll pour you a cupful,' he shouted.

'Yes, that's a good idea. Go join the party,' South Neighbor's wife added. But the women did not move. They remained in the kitchen, giggling among themselves.

Yokichi was lying on the floor, sobbing fitfully. Otsugi knelt beside him, patting his back. 'There, there,' she murmured amid all the noise of the party. 'You ate some plums today, didn't you? I know because your teacher told me. You've got a little stomach ache now, huh. Well, just be brave, okay? It'll go away in a while.'

South Neighbor's wife looked up from where she was sitting nearby. 'He's got stomach ache, has he?' she asked as she waved the mosquitoes away from the baby on her lap. 'How about giving him some medicine? I've got some around here somewhere for my own kids. No matter what you tell 'em they're always getting into something that's bad for 'em, aren't they?'

'If he does that again,' Kanji mumbled thickly, 'I'll rip his stomach out, that's what. That'll cure him.'

'Now stop that, Papa!' Otsugi said sharply. 'He's already crying, and here you go scaring him even more.' Kanji silently speared potatoes with his chopstick while Yokichi drifted off to sleep.

Suddenly the singing and talking stopped. 'Let's have some rice!' the men cried. The women set about serving the meal.

'Otsugi is all grown up, isn't she?' South Neighbor's wife observed. 'When a girl's 20 she's real useful, isn't she?' Kanji had spilled a few grains of rice onto the floor and was clumsily picking them up with his fingers.

'Try to be more careful, Papa,' Otsugi told him wearily.

'Kanji-san?' South Neighbor's wife now addressed him directly. Kanji squinted in her direction. 'Kanji-san, isn't it about time you married Otsugi off?'

'I'm not doing anything of the kind,' Kanji replied flatly. 'I still need her at home.'

'If you need someone so badly, why not marry her off and get yourself a wife?' Kane asked with his usual boldness.

'I don't have to listen to that!' Kanji retorted. 'If I wanted to marry again I could find a wife easy.'

'But really,' South Neighbor's wife continued. 'If you don't get her settled soon she'll just get older and older, and then it'll be too late. It's never easy to part with 'em. I've gone through it once myself, you know. But you just have to go ahead and do it.'

'Enough of that!' Kanji said sharply. 'I'm not going to keep her single until she's 30. When the time comes I'll adopt a son-in-law for her.' South Neighbor's wife said nothing more. With a strained smile she stared down at her sleeping baby.

As soon as they had had enough to eat the men thanked South Neighbor for his hospitality and began hunting noisily for their clogs. Kanji too had staggered to his feet. 'Wake up Yoki and let's go,' he mumbled to Otsugi.

Yokichi was by now fast asleep. No matter how hard Otsugi shook him she could not get him to keep his eyes open. Awkwardly she tried to slip his sandals onto his feet.

'Otsū!' Kanji shouted from the yard. Then he reappeared at the back door. 'What's keeping you?' he yelled.

'She's still trying to wake Yokichi,' South Neighbor's wife explained.

'Can't she do anything right?' Kanji exploded. 'Never seen anybody so slow.'

'But Papa, can't you wait a bit longer until everything's cleaned up?' Otsugi asked, looking back at the clutter of dishes in the other room.

'That's all right,' South Neighbor's wife said to her. 'You go along home. Your father's too drunk to wait any longer.'

As they began washing dishes the women talked on and on about Kanji.

'I just can't understand that man!'

'He's worse than a jealous husband, isn't he, the way he acts?'

'He should've got married again, if you ask me. He used to talk about it a lot, but not anymore.'

Each hinted at the same thing, but no one dared say it outright.

A few minutes earlier one of the women had suddenly slipped away. When she returned to the house she was told, 'It's not right going off to spy on people, you know.'

'I did no such thing!' she retorted.

'Then what were you up to?'

'Just a quick trip to the privy,' she said and then she could no longer suppress a smile. 'Otsugi sure gets mad at Kanji when he drinks too much!'

Everybody laughed.

It was pitch dark outside. The frogs were croaking lustily.

15

Frost came stealthily and covered the ground. The cold late autumn air had desiccated all it touched. The leaves of the *udo* plants had opened and a flock of little white-eyes feasted on the exposed seeds, their chirping sounding merry and yet frantic at the same time. Everywhere the foliage had stiffened and withered, and soon all had been reduced to rough, rustling disorder. Winter was severe in these parts, but it took hold slowly, with warm days following upon cold. Then came the first frost. Except for the somber evergreens the trees and shrubs reacted instantly, freezing into the contorted shapes they would hold until they were able to prepare for spring. Winter spread another layer of frost. Relentlessly fastidious, it drove the scattered leaves into the ground.

In the fields all labor was complete. The rice had been harvested from the paddies, and in the upland fields the winter wheat and barley showed brushlike tips of green. Now winter tried to drive the farmers indoors. Busily they plaited bales for their rice and piled the filled bales up inside their houses. Here was their recompense for all their toil since the previous spring. The sight of it made them happy.

It was customary at this time of year, before winter truly wailed overhead, for the villages in the area to hold festivals at their community shrines, each one on a different day. Kanji's village, too, had such a festival.

On the appointed day a single Shinto priest in his white official garb made his way from the horse grounds to the shrine, followed in a rather disorderly fashion by four or five representatives of the parish. Though all wore formal dress none had tied his *hakama* securely enough, and the cuffs trailed in the dirt. One of the men carried a winnow. Behind them came two men shouldering a thick pole from which a large barrel of sweet sake was suspended. For several days before the festival the people in charge of providing the sake that year had made the rounds of the village collecting a

113

few measures of white rice from each household. Each night they had brewed sweet sake from what they had collected, after having cooked a goodly portion of it for their own supper. Not having much time or much leaven they had used boiling water in the brewing. That brought out the sweetness right away, but it meant that an acidic tinge developed quickly. The night before the festival they had got together with a few neighbors for a tasting party. To replenish what they had consumed they had added more water to the barrel. The muddy liquid now lapped to and fro against the barrel staves as the procession advanced.

The thick cuffs of the priest's white overskirt were spattered with mud. Arriving at the shrine he sat down on a mat spread out on the dusty wooden planks of the hall of worship and toyed with a *sakaki* branch. While he arranged the offering neatly on the altar the parish representatives strung the winnow up between two fir trees on a length of sacred rope. The shrine was now decorated for the festival.

Gradually the villagers gathered before the shrine, dressed in their best clothes. As usual the young girls, who wore gaily colored sashes and muslin aprons over their homespun cotton kimono, attracted the most attention. On their feet they wore ill-fitting white *tabi* socks, and a few sported cheaply made clogs. They clustered together, holding hands and talking. For them it was only the opportunity to visit with their friends and to observe the behavior of other villagers that gave the festival meaning.

The priest sat before the altar, on which a few mandarin oranges, cheap sweets, and pieces of dried cuttlefish were arrayed as offerings. He unwrapped the scroll on which his congratulatory prayer was written from a worn and dirty paper that looked as if it had seen much use. The prayer was very brief. Although the priest read it very slowly in a high-pitched voice it took no time at all to complete.

He used the same scroll wherever he went, filling in the name of the village and shrine he was at on any particular day when he came to that point in the text. Today he managed the task without a mistake. Then he moved to one side of the hall and summoned the representatives one by one with his wooden mace to offer a sprig of *sakaki* and clap their hands in prayer before the altar. So timidly did they perform their duties that no handclaps could be heard. One man tripped on the cuffs of his loosely tied *hakama* as he stood up and almost toppled over. The assembled villagers pressed forward towards the hall of worship to watch this and the other sights the ceremony provided.

Otsugi was in the crowd, holding Yokichi by the hand. Kanji

114

stood off by himself in the shade of one of the fir trees. Now that the simple ceremony had ended it was time to distribute sweet sake to all who wanted it. The village children clustered eagerly around the barrel, jostling with one another for a turn at the large tea bowl in which the sake was served. To be sure, home-made sweet sake tasted better than the diluted liquid one got at the festival, but it was fun to be part of a large, boisterous group, and each child drank as many cupfuls as he could get. Some beggars who had been loitering beneath the trees pushed forward into the crowd in search of sake, their bowls in their outstretched hands. One of the parish representatives spoke sharply to them to make them wait their turn.

A while later the priest left the shrine compound, and the crowd began slowly to disperse. The cotton banners near the shrine gate rose high in the air and danced noisily in the freshening wind. Soon the sun lay low on the horizon. Storm clouds spread across the eastern sky and hovered above the forest that surrounded the shrine, as if about to press down on the villagers themselves. For a time the slanting rays of the sun transformed their harsh color to the softer tones of velvet and gave a warm red glow to the nearby zelkova trees. Then the white banners began flapping without pause. Leaves flashed through the air. Darkness enveloped the shrine, and the storm broke. By now everyone had fled for cover and not a single gaily dressed figure remained in sight.

The rain did not stop for several hours.

Later that evening the villagers gathered once again near the shop at which a troupe of blind female singers was staying the night. The doors of the shop front were pulled back and the interior sliding panels had been removed. The singers were still away at dinner. They appeared at all the festivals in the district. Once they had arrived at their lodgings in a particular village they made the rounds of the houses, singing to samisen accompaniment. Here and there one of them would receive an invitation to dinner that night. When the time came someone would guide them there and then come calling from them later. Tonight each had finally arrived at her destination. Now she sat alone and sightless on the edge of her host's wooden floor, waiting for a tray of food to be brought to her. For a while she would be looked after. Then, her hunger satisfied, she would once more cling to her bamboo staff.

At the little shop the singers' baggage and their carefully wrapped musical instruments lay in a forlorn pile on the floor of the main room. A solitary spiritualist sat erect and motionless in the center of the room, the mysterious box that symbolized her profession carefully placed before her. Facing her in the dirt-floored entryway of the shop was a milling crowd of villagers. A few people had stepped up into the main room and begun carousing. But because the spiritualist was an old woman they did not tease her the way they always teased the singers.

'How about giving the spiritualist some business?' a voice called out. A ripple of excitement spread through the crowd. Noticing that Otsugi was present a few of the young men began whispering among themselves:

'Why don't we get her spirit read?'

'Hey, good idea!'

From the rear of the crowd came the shout, 'We can't see!'

'Then come on up,' the woman who ran the shop responded. At that the crowd pressed forward, filling the main room. Kanji and Otsugi had barely enough room in which to sit. The shopkeeper placed a bowl of water on a slightly chipped lacquer tray and made her way across the crowded floor. She placed the bowl before the spiritualist and then turned to ask, 'Well, who's coming forward?' There was a momentary silence. The spiritualist sat waiting, her box drawn close to her knees.

'Okay, why not,' one of the young men said as he stood up. 'How much for doing a living spirit?' he asked as he knelt before the old woman.

'Five *sen*,' she replied softly.

'And I just sit here saying nothing?'

'That's right', she answered. 'The person you're thinking about will be revealed to me.'

'Just twist up some paper and stir the water with it,' someone called out.

'Okay,' said the young man. He made a paper twist and thrust its tip into the bowl. After stirring three times he let go.

The spiritualist had been praying quietly, her hands pressed together before her. Now she rested her elbows on her box and began reciting the names of the deities, summoning them to the séance. A hush fell over the crowd.

'Trust in the white paper, trust in the water, trust in the twist of paper . . . ,' the spiritualist said over and over. Because she was missing a few front teeth her phrasing was somewhat blurred. The slip of paper nodded drowsily as it sank into the bowl. 'Though I can never be yours . . . ,' she began.

'There it is!' someone in the crowd whispered. 'The spirit's come!'

'Don't be angry with me,' the old woman intoned. 'When we meet, let us talk kindly to one another . . .'

A voice cried out from the rear, 'But we mustn't make Papa cry!' People began laughing, nudging their neighbors and glancing

116

toward Kanji and Otsugi. But those two sat absolutely still, unaware they were the butt of the joke.

Suddenly there was a wave of commotion from the entrance of the shop. One of the blind singers had just returned from dinner. The young men playfully tried to obstruct her, but finally she made her way to the main room and sat down.

'Hey, that's no way to treat someone who can't see!' an old man who had followed the singer into the room protested, but the young men merely hooted at him in response. There was another commotion outside as more singers arrived, their faces powdered and white scarves tied over their foreheads. Instinctively they clustered together in a corner of the main room.

Now some of the young men started shaking the sweets counter in the front of the store.

'Don't you steal any of those sweets!' the old man cried out angrily. His face was deeply pockmarked. 'And don't fiddle with that sake barrel either.'

'You've got it wrong,' a voice protested. 'The counter's moving all by itself, and it's got me trapped.'

'You break the glass, you'll make the shopkeeper mad,' the old man retorted.

'But come and look! This case is wearing shoes, I tell you. It's got pots on two feet and bowls on the others. And all of 'em can kick!'

'It's been for a walk, that's for sure!' another voice yelled. 'All of its feet are covered with dirt.'

By now everyone was laughing, even though they knew the pots and bowls were there, and filled with water during the hot weather, to protect the sweets from ants.

'Think I'll get a reading, if no one else will,' one of the young men said as he moved toward the main room.

'Bet you can't pay for it, though,' the old man blurted out.

'Well, I guess you're right,' the young man said. 'Hey, why don't you get a dead spirit reading from your old missus?'

'Because I don't want to! It'd be bad luck.' As the old man spoke he scratched his head.

'How come you been scratching so much lately, old man?' the young man asked. 'You miss your old lady so much it's gone to your head?'

The old man's eyes, dulled by mucous, opened wide in surprise.

'And look at all those holes in your face! Looks like you fell into a soybean press.' Everyone started laughing. 'And how come you're wearing that red scarf?'

'I'm not wearing a scarf!'

'But doesn't the smallpox god like red scarves?'

117

'I don't care if he does. I'm not wearing one.' The pockmarked old man looked bewildered. The crowd laughed uproariously. Even the young girls craned their necks to see him, giggling from behind their upheld sleeves. Thoroughly embarrassed, he made his way to the door and left.

Another young man put his hand on the spiritualist's box. 'What's inside here anyway? Is it really a toy priest?'

'There's offerings in there, you idiot,' someone shouted. 'You know, cut paper and things like that.'

'And you can't see inside,' the old woman said as she pushed his hand away. 'If I showed you what's there I'd lose the power to read spirits.'

While all this fuss was going on Kanji had been inching his way forward. Now with a lunge he sat before the spiritualist. 'Please do a reading for me. It's a dead person's spirit.'

'In that case,' the old woman replied, 'You'll need to put a bamboo leaf in the water.'

'Here's one!' a voice called out from the rear, and a small leaf was passed forward. The crowd fell silent. Kanji stirred the water three times with the leaf and then gently let go of it. The portion above water remained green, but the submerged part glistened like mercury. Once again the spiritualist placed her elbows on the box.

'Thank you for summoning me . . . ,' the old woman chanted. Kanji sat mutely before her, his hands on his knees and his eyes lowered. Otsugi too looked meekly downward. Her elaborately twisted and oiled chignon caught the light.

'I see all,' the spiritualist intoned. 'I disguise myself and go everywhere. No one knows I'm there. I am the raincloak on days when no rain falls. I am the bamboo hat . . .' The audience hung on her every word.

'Not just once, but twice, many times I've caused strange things to happen, to alert you . . .' Her voice began to tremble. Kanji and Otsugi sat absolutely still. 'No matter how difficult, no matter how painful, let the budding blossom bloom. Please, for my sake. Do not let her wither on the branch.'

'Not a day passes when I do not think of you, though I am in my grave . . .' When the spiritualist intoned these words Kanji burst into tears. Otsugi too was crying. 'Just for a moment I have come, now I must return. But I will think of you . . .' The spiritualist spoke slowly now, almost in a whisper. Then she was silent.

'I'm sorry! I'm sorry!' Kanji wailed as he brushed his tears aside.

'She came, didn't she?' one of the younger wives murmured. 'Look how upset he is.'

A few other people had their fortunes told or had live spirit readings. Then the singers began unwrapping their instruments. The spiritualist tied her box to her back and left.

At the first sound of samisen plucking the room became lively once again. Even the lamplight seemed brighter. Kanji could not bear it. He took Yokichi by the hand and went off into the darkness. Otsugi followed after him.

The young men watched the three of them leave.

'I'll be damned . . . ,' one of them muttered.

'The way he cried,' whispered one of the wives to her friends. 'I didn't know he missed Oshina that much.'

'And the things people have been saying about him.'

'All that nasty talk! It's a disgrace.'

For a time after that night Kanji changed his ways and let Otsugi go off occasionally on her own. People in the village noticed and wondered how long it would last. As suspicious and gossipy as ever they watched him closely.

16

That people sneered at him did not bother Kanji much. Any discomfort he felt was more than made up for by the money he had finally managed to set aside.

Oshina had once said to East Neighbor's wife, 'You people don't have any worries at all, do you, Okamisan?'

'Whatever do you mean by that?' the mistress had queried.

'Well, you always have plenty of food, that's how I see it.'

The mistress caught her drift and inquired about the problems she and Kanji had making ends meet.

'It's always a struggle,' Oshina had replied matter of factly. 'We work day and night, and still we never have enough to eat. People who don't have that kind of worry, well, they really have no worries at all.'

In the years since her death things had gradually got better. Kanji was earning upwards of 40 yen each winter clearing land. It was an unbelievably large sum for him, and although much of it would go towards paying off his debts, there was still enough to provide the three of them with food until spring. Otsugi was now almost 20. Yokichi was going to school. Kanji gradually came to feel more at ease in the company of other villagers. Only towards East Neighbor's family did the fear and deference he had once shown towards everyone remain in force.

During these years, he and Uhei had met only once, when Uhei had come briefly for the third *Bon* festival since Oshina's death. Uhei was nearing 80, but despite his thinning white hair his body was as massive as ever, and there was still a luster to his skin. Even after nightwatch duty at the soy sauce brewery he would spend most of the day weeding his master's garden or running errands for him. Whenever the hectic pace got to him he would think of the tea cakes and handtowels he received as gratuities and the extra money the master gave him at year's end. With a little prudence he could put something aside, he would remind himself, but as usual he would fritter his cash away on half-pints of sake.

Since Noda was relatively close to his village quite a number of village youths came there to work in its expanding soy sauce industry — so many, in fact, that wages for farm workers were driven upwards. The turnover was rapid, and Uhei was able to keep abreast of local happenings and gossip by talking to each group of newcomers in turn. He was most curious about Otsugi whom he had last seen when she was 17. Her resemblance to Oshina had been striking then, and as he listened to talk about her he would sometimes wish they could meet again. Pride stood in the way, however. Even though he admitted to himself that he had been wrong in returning to Noda so abruptly after Kanji's return from the construction site, he had no intention of ever apologizing to Kanji for it. And so he had put the thought of going home from his mind. The days and months went by, seeming shorter with each passing year. Winter came, its cold as piercing as the steam whistles of the boats on the muddy Edo River. As usual Uhei's back began to ache. He went to see the doctor who cared for the brewery employees, but the doctor could only tell him that it was difficult to treat what was, after all, the result of growing old. Perhaps a larger dose of the medicine he had tried before might help, the doctor added. Since the medicine did not cost him anything Uhei drank a lot of it, but to no effect. Feeling poorly, he took to staying in bed as much as possible during the daytime.

Sometimes he worried about what to do at the end of the year when the time came to renew or cancel employment contracts. He would persuade himself that if he could just hold on until spring all would be well. Peach blossoms would fill the air, barley would cover the soil with green, and even the white sails of the flatboats making their way up the Edo River would look warm. Everyone would take a day off from work to go wandering among the blossoms, and his pain would be forgotten.

A stickler for tidiness, Uhei had never had to be told when the garden needed weeding. He had kept the ground around the employees' barracks neatly swept and watered, too, and he had planted morning glories everywhere he could. It had helped make his life in service a little more pleasant. Still, for the past two or three years he had known it could not last much longer. Most men his age had stopped working. It was just his peculiar circumstances that prevented him from doing so. Still strong in spirit, he could sense his body getting weaker, his stamina disappearing.

This winter he developed new symptoms. It was rheumatism, the doctor had told him, and going out on fire patrol in the cold of night was the worst thing for him. Uhei kept at it, though. When the time came to renew his contract he hesitated but finally decided to stay on. He had heard from one of the new arrivals that Kanji seemed to be doing well. That sorely tempted him, but he was determined not to return empty-handed. He vowed instead to cut back on sake and fill his purse. Though sake had been a source of consolation to him over the years money was more important now. When spring came and he felt better he would go back to the village.

No matter how hard he tried to keep working, however, the people around him could see that he was faltering. One man in particular, the foreman of a nearby brewery who came from a village near Uhei's and had known him a long time, urged him to retire. The man had been back to the countryside recently and heard about Kanji's improved circumstances. Now he proposed to go and consult with him about Uhei. Uhei listened impassively, his deep-set brown eyes squinting but a faint smile on his lips.

Shortly thereafter the foreman went to see Kanji.

'Well,' Kanji had said coolly, 'he's one of the family so I suppose I have to look after him.'

'Things are going well for you, I hear,' the foreman had ventured politely.

'I wouldn't say that,' Kanji had retorted. 'I've got to keep working or we'll starve. People might think I've got lots of money, but I've still got debts to pay. Still got some of Grampa's debts, too. Be a lot better off without 'em, but I've got 'em so I've got to keep working.'

'Well, once they're paid off, then you'll be in fine shape.'

'Sure,' Kanji muttered.

'And you've got a lot of grain stored up, I see.'

'Got to have that much,' Kanji answered bluntly, and then he changed the subject. 'You know, I took sick when I first came to this house, and all they gave me was some lousy barley. I was treated pretty bad, and I'll never forget it.'

The foreman did not tell Uhei what Kanji had said. Instead he pressed upon him that he would have to go back to Kanji's house eventually. Why wait until he was so sick they would need to carry him there on a litter? He ought to quit and go back while his health was still good. Besides, he was sure Uhei and Kanji could get along. Uhei asked a lot of questions, about the house, Otsugi, the neighbors. There was a warm glow in his eyes.

He had put his mind to it and saved quite a bit of money in a short time. Now he made up two bundles of clothing and shipped the one containing things he did not need right away off on a canal boat. He put a pouch of tobacco in his sleeve, donned work pants and straw sandals and tied the other bundle to his back. As gifts he carried two beer bottles filled with soy sauce and a package of rice crackers. The latter was for Yokichi.

He set off at a slow pace, fearing an attack of rheumatism. After crossing the Tone River he entered mile upon mile of bleak forest. Every now and then he would stop to rest by the side of the path and smoke a pipe. Paying no heed to the little green finches that hopped about in the fallen leaves nearby he inhaled deeply. Occasionally he would gasp as if he had swallowed spittle along with the smoke. He looked tired and disheveled. Standing up and stretching to relieve the pain in his back he shouldered his bundle again and set off, not noticing that the matches he had discarded had set fire to the dried grass by the path.

The winter sun did not last the duration of his 25-mile trek from Noda to the village. By the time he reached the house his hands were painfully cold. He called out at the doorway but all was dark and quiet. The door was locked. Muttering to himself he made his way to the back door. That was latched shut from the inside, but the bolt was not drawn. He wedged his pipe into the gap between the door and the frame and pushed the latch up. Stepping inside he lit a match. The lantern was in its usual place by the pillar. He lit it and began adding faggots to the hibachi so that he could warm his hands and feet. Then he put the kettle on its hook above the fire and removed his sandals. The path had been dry so his feet were not at all dirty. Still he rubbed each one a few times before stepping up into the main room.

Kanji had gone off with the children to South Neighbor's for a bath. He was too tired at the end of a day of steady labor to do much night work, and now that his purse was full he did not have to. Except for a few occasions when he had made rope he spent the long evenings bathing. Often they would sit around talking afterwards, sipping tea made from used tea leaves.

On this particular night South Neighbor's wife had given Yokichi two large peppermint candies. He was sucking on one of them as they made their way back across the mulberry field.

'Think I'll have some, too,' Otsugi said, breaking off a little piece from the candy Yokichi held in his other hand and popping it into her mouth.

'You took too much!' he cried out anxiously.

'Oh, peppermint!' Otsugi cooed. 'So smooth and good. Let's give Papa some.'

As she reached to take another piece Kanji stopped her. 'Hey now, you let Yoki have the rest,' he muttered. No one could spy on them now as they returned home in the darkness.

Otsugi stopped abruptly when she saw the light shining from a crack in the door. 'Papa, what's going on?' she whispered.

Kanji froze and did not answer.

Otsugi peered through the crack. 'It looks like Grampa,' she whispered again. Kanji looked, too. Then he unlocked the door and they went in. Not recognizing his grandfather Yokichi hid shyly behind his sister.

'It *is* Grampa!' Otsugi exclaimed as she approached him. 'You've come all that way today?' she asked by way of greeting.

'You're pretty late, aren't you?' Kanji added.

'I didn't get an early enough start, I suppose,' Uhei replied wearily. 'Didn't mean to be so late, but I couldn't go long without a rest. My legs aren't so good anymore.'

'Have you been waiting long?' Otsugi asked as she began to break up more faggots for the fire.

'Just time enough to get the fire going,' he replied, squinting at her. 'You've really grown up, haven't you. Wouldn't have recognized you if we'd passed on the road. But you didn't forget me, did you?'

'I could never forget you, Grampa,' Otsugi murmured as she reached for the kettle. Uhei was touched by her gentle tone. When he had come for the memorial service three years ago he had brought her a floral hairpin, though who knows what had made him think of it. She had never been so happy and would always remember his kindness.

'Won't you have some tea?' she asked as she went to wash the cups. Uhei had been vaguely uneasy about coming home, but Otsugi's treatment made him relax. He looked over at Yokichi, who was standing in the entryway still sucking a peppermint. 'You've forgotten all about me, I bet. I figured you'd have grown up some, but I wouldn't have recognized you either.' Usually taciturn, Uhei felt like talking tonight. 'And here's something for you,' he added as he tossed the package of crackers onto the matting. 'These are the best crackers in all of Noda! Otsū, can you unwrap them?' Before she could respond he had undone the wrapping himself and placed the box in front of Kanji. He took a cracker and held it out towards Yokichi.

'Yoki, that's for you,' Otsugi said as she put the tea cups down in front of Uhei and Kanji. 'Grampa's brought you a present.'

'Come up here and get it,' Kanji ordered. Yokichi slipped off his sandals and stepped up into the main room timidly, reaching out for the cracker. He bit into it right away.

Otsugi took a cracker, too. 'These come from far away, Yoki. Aren't they crisp and good?'

'I don't like it much!' Yokichi muttered from where he sat, half-hidden behind her. With the flavor of peppermint still in his mouth he found the cracker had little taste. That it was a present from Uhei had made no impression on him.

'What a thing to say!' Otsugi whispered angrily. 'You want me to box your ears?'

Uhei drank several cups of tea while the others munched their crackers. He had lost most of his teeth and could only eat soft food. 'I brought these, too,' he said as he handed the bottles of soy sauce to Otsugi. 'Sorry I couldn't bring more, but I had a lot of other things to carry. It's the best they make at the brewery. You've done your cooking tonight, so you can put 'em aside for now.'

'Oh, but there's a lot here,' Otsugi exclaimed as she put the bottles by the pillar. 'And with all your other baggage, too. This will last a long time.'

Uhei chewed on his pipe. 'I didn't have that much luggage. Just can't carry as much as I used to.'

'You want some dinner, Grampa?' Otsugi asked, casting a nervous glance at Kanji.

'Oh, I'm okay,' he replied diffidently.

'Don't be silly. I bet you're starving.' Otsugi took a bowl and a pair of chopsticks from the shelf. 'How about some pickled greens, too?'

'Don't bother. My teeth are no good, so I couldn't chew 'em.'

'Well then, I'll just cut 'em up small,' Otsugi replied and began chopping. She lifted the lid of the pot. 'Nothing left in the soup, though. Yoki, you ate up all the potatoes, didn't you.'

'Don't need any soup, either,' Uhei muttered. 'I'll just have a quick bowl of rice.'

Otsugi put a tray down in front of him. 'Think I'll add a little soy sauce to these greens . . .'

'Hold that bottle at the bottom or it will come spilling out!' Kanji burst in. He had been sitting expressionless all this while, trying to avoid Uhei's gaze. As he spoke soy sauce came pouring down on the greens. 'Now look what you've done!' he grumbled. When Otsugi put the bottle back by the pillar he spoke again. 'That's no place for it! Put it in the cupboard where it won't get knocked over.'

Uhei downed several cups of hot water as he ate. The cold rice he had been served was so heavily mixed with cracked barley that he could not chew it at all. Instead he gulped it down.

Otsugi reached over to take away the tray. 'Save that soy sauce,' Kanji ordered, pointing to the few drops left on the plate.

'You don't have to tell me that,' Otsugi muttered. 'I'm not going to throw it out. She thought it was bad manners for Kanji to talk that way in front of Uhei.

'Can I have another cracker, Sister?' Yokichi asked softly as Otsugi was washing the dishes.

'You just said you didn't like 'em,' Otsugi scolded him, 'and now you say you want more!'

Uhei handed Yokichi a cracker. 'I bought 'em for him, so he can have as many as he wants.' Yokichi still felt awkward in Uhei's presence. His head lowered, he toyed with his lower lip and glanced shyly at the old man.

17

Eager for a word of praise from the teacher, the students in the village school vied with one another in arriving early for class. Yokichi was no exception. The morning after Uhei's arrival he was fidgeting as usual while Otsugi made breakfast, begging her to hurry up. Finally it was time to set off. His school bag on his back Yokichi reached out for his lunch sack. 'Can I have a cracker, too?' he asked.

'Not that again!' Otsugi scolded him. 'No you can't. Grampa wouldn't like it.'

At the time Kanji was outside chopping tree roots for firewood. Uhei, though awake, still lay in his bedding. After long years as a nightwatchman he was not used to rising early, and his journey the previous day had tired him out. Besides, it seemed right to take it easy his first day home. 'Give him a cracker if he wants one,' he muttered. Otsugi dutifully took a cracker from the package and offered it to Yokichi. He snatched it from her hand.

'What a pest you are!' she chided him, tapping him on the shoulder. 'Now off you go!' Yokichi scampered across the frost-covered yard as Uhei gazed fondly after him. Kanji put a basket of firewood in front of the cooking stove and sat down to eat his breakfast.

'Shall I get Grampa?' Otsugi asked. When Kanji did not reply she called out to Uhei, 'Food's ready!'

'You go ahead without me,' he answered. A while later he got up and went out to the well. For the first time in many years he washed his face with cold water. He could not remember ever having got up so early. His toes were painfully cold. Since there was no fire in the hibachi he had to light his pipe with embers from the stove. It was not at all like Noda where a charcoal fire was always burning and boiling water always available. He tried to eat, but the rice, though warm, was not soft like the rice cooked in the big pot at the brewery. The soup tasted terrible. He could tell that soy sauce

127

dregs had been added to the bean paste to increase its bulk.

Kanji picked up his hoe and left the house, taking Otsugi with him. He needed her help today in tending the barley field. Uhei was left all alone. He felt vaguely depressed as he looked about him in the semi-darkness. Soot hung everywhere from the underside of the roof. He thought of the ceilings in the solidly constructed barracks at the brewery. He·thought of the bustle, too, and the lusty singing of the younger workers as they dashed about half-naked carrying buckets of boiling water across the brewery floor. He was tired, to be sure, but still it seemed to him that in one short day he had grown old and weak. Bedding lay strewn about the floor by the wall. The pillows had no paper coverings and the fabric on them was so stained with dirt and grease that its stripes were no longer visible. The chicken coop suspended above the dirt floor of the entry reeked of droppings. He had known this life before. As a poor farmer he had had no choice but to live surrounded by filth. Then he had gone to Noda and lived in clean lodgings. Over the years he had become accustomed to them. On each of his previous visits, for Oshina's funeral and for the memorial service three years later, the house had been thoroughly cleaned for the occasion. Now he felt disoriented, like someone forced out of the bright sunshine into hiding.

For a while he smoked his pipe, but when the sun rose a little higher in the sky he set off to pay his respects to the neighbors and to those few of his old friends who remained alive. When Kanji and Otsugi returned at noon Uhei was gone. He did not return until after dark. Kanji had been on his way out to the yard and had slid open the door to find Uhei standing there about to open it himself. Shuddering as if he had encountered a snake, Kanji darted past into the darkness.

Uhei appeared stern and forbidding with his pipe clenched tightly in his mouth. Though he moved more slowly now he still towered above Kanji. He rambled off somewhere every day for the next week or so, not returning until late in the evening. Kanji went off daily to the forest with his mattock. Otsugi dashed off to the sewing mistress whenever Kanji did not need her help. She had missed so many lessons for one reason or another over the years that she was still far from expert with a needle.

Kanji usually was ready to leave the house just as Uhei began to eat his breakfast. Otsugi often was delayed, having taken time to light a fire in the hibachi and set out dishes for him. Kanji would put his mattock down with a thud and wait impatiently for her, muttering to himself as he paced back and forth across the threshold. Even though they would be heading off in different directions he was reluctant to leave until she did.

'Go on ahead, Papa,' Otsugi would say sometimes. 'I've got to look after Grampa.' Kanji would glare at her, glance angrily at Uhei, and storm off in a huff.

'Don't worry about me,' Uhei would then say. 'I can manage, so you go along.'

Uhei spent most of his first week home visiting with friends. They would talk on and on about old times, and then he would be asked to stay for a simple meal. Soon, however, the novelty wore off and he began spending more time at home sitting silently and smoking. There was only leftover rice and barley to eat at midday. Sometimes he would go off to the village and buy a square of bean curd. He would have it heated up before he ate it. Then he would order a half-pint of sake and sip it slowly, whiling away the time. Bean curd was one of the few foods his toothless gums could manage.

He had saved up quite a bit of money in his last few months at the brewery. Now he was putting it to use bit by bit to buy food. Time seemed to pass slowly. Sometimes he spent the entire day just sitting crosslegged in front of the cold hibachi at home.

Yokichi would be disappointed when he returned from school and found only Uhei in the house. He would toss his school bag into the main room and dart back to the yard.

'Wait a minute, Yoki! I've got something for you.' Uhei would take a small coin from his purse and toss it to the edge of the matting. Yokichi then stood in the shadows of the entryway gazing longingly at the coin but afraid to touch it. Clumsily Uhei would get to his feet, retrieve the coin, and hand it over. Yokichi would dash off to buy a sweet, and Uhei would find himself alone again.

Occasionally Yokichi would pass by and see Uhei sitting at the village shop smoking a pipe. He would stop and watch from a distance. Uhei always bought him a sweet, but Yokichi would go off a ways to eat it.

'He's a lucky one,' the shoplady would say. 'He's always getting sweets.' It made Uhei happy to hear that.

Slowly Yokichi overcame his shyness. He would call out 'Grampa!' when he returned from school and stand boldly in the doorway. 'Don't you have something for me?' he would ask, hoping for a coin. He would never ask for one directly.

'What is it you want?' Uhei would tease him.

'Please, Grampa! I want to buy something!'

Uhei enjoyed their little game and always gave in at the end.

It took only a short time for Yokichi to be won over. With Kanji it was different. Relations between the two men remained cool, but gradually Uhei grew used to being around him and ceased to pay much attention to his moods. Time passed less slowly now. He was feeling settled. His only complaint remained the food, for not once had he been given anything soft to eat. It was a problem that caused strain in most families. The younger generation wanted coarse food to fill their bellies and keep them going all day. The soft food older people craved left them feeling hungry. But Uhei refused to complain and glumly tried to eat what was set before him. Otsugi had eaten coarse food all her life. Since Uhei always seemed to be frowning no matter what he did, she took no special notice of him at meal times and remained unaware of his discomfort. He could not bring himself to blame her. From time to time he would skip meals at home to eat bean curd in the village.

Even so Kanji soon noticed that the grain supply was being consumed more rapidly than in the past. He knew the old man did not eat much, but the very thought that the supply would not last as long as it used to upset him. Once when Uhei was out he was grumbling to himself about it. Yokichi overheard him.

A day or say later, Yokichi and Uhei were talking together as the old man sat by the hibachi. Yokichi was playing with a coin he had just received.

'Grampa, I heard we're using up a lot of rice since you came.'

'That so?' Uhei took his pipe from his mouth. 'Your papa say that?'

'He said it over and over.'

As Uhei put the pipe back in his mouth his hand was trembling slightly. 'How about that,' he muttered, staring at a crack in the wall.

A chicken had made its way from the yard to the doorway and settled on the threshold. Suddenly it darted up into the main room. Uhei threw his pipe at it. The bird fled outside, hitting the slush that covered the yard with such force that it toppled over. After regaining its feet it tottered out of sight, cackling frantically. The matting of the main room was spattered with mud, and feathers were everywhere. Uhei's pipe had careened off the bird and struck the threshold. Now it lay in the yard.

Yokichi peered at Uhei for a moment. 'Do you want me to get your pipe?' he asked timidly.

'Do that,' Uhei grunted.

He thrust the pipe back into his mouth as soon as Yokichi handed it to him. With a grimace he realized that his tongue was covered with mud. He spat it out and wiped his mouth on his sleeve. When he set about relighting the pipe he found there was a crack in its bamboo stem. Taking a wad of paper from his sleeve he moistened it with saliva and wrapped the paper carefully around the crack. Then he got up abruptly and went out, not returning until after dark.

When Kanji saw the feathers he assumed a weasel had attacked one of the chickens. He hunted all over for the missing bird. He was worried because he knew that if a weasel killed a chicken it would come back for more.

'Grampa hit it and made it fly away,' Yokichi piped up.

'What? Why did he do that?'

'It got up into the room, so he threw his pipe at it. I went out and got his pipe for him.'

Kanji scattered some feed on the dirt floor and opened the coop. The birds tumbled out noisily and began scrambling for food. It took a while for Kanji to count them and make sure that one was missing.

Uhei had had some bean curd and sake in the village. When he got home he was not interested in dinner and merely sat crosslegged and silent by the hibachi. Otsugi tried to talk to him but gave up when he remained mute. Kanji sat as far away as possible, a menacing look on his face. Yokichi was already asleep.

The frightened bird emerged from its hiding place the following morning and rejoined the flock. It was limping slightly. Kanji placed it under a basket and kept the basket by the door for several days as if to remind Uhei of what he had done. Uhei sat sullenly, smoking his mended pipe.

When he was by himself Uhei set about cleaning the house. He swept the soot from the eves of the entryway where the stove was located, and he raked the straw by the doorway free of the traces the chickens had left behind them. He also swept out the main room and ordered Otsugi to roll the bedding up neatly every morning. Kanji did not mind that the house was cleaner, but it made him uneasy to have Uhei poking around. He knew the old man spent a lot of time and money at the village shop, and he suspected Uhei was trying to find where he kept his purse.

By now it was almost the end of the year according to the old calendar. Everyone was busy milling buckwheat flour.

Uhei went from time to time to pay his respects at East Neighbor's. The mistress thought he was losing weight and always asked him worriedly how he felt.

'Not so bad,' he would reply non-committally. The truth was he welcomed her concern.

'And Kanji? Is he taking good care of you?', she asked on one occasion.

'Him? Same as always,' Uhei replied gruffly.

'And Otsugi?'

'Her now. She's not like him. After all, I've known her since she was a baby.'

'And how's the milling going? Do you have a lot of flour for New Year's?'

'Guess so. Him and Otsū have been going off to South Neighbor's every day to do the grinding. He keeps the buckets covered up, though, so I don't know how much he's got.'

'Doesn't Kanji see to it you get some of it cooked up soft?'

'No, we eat the same old gritty stuff every day. I wouldn't mind if I still had good teeth.'

'Well then, I'll give you some buckwheat flour myself. You can make a mush with it. Noodles won't be good for you, but mush — that will really warm you up.' The mistress put a few quarts of flour in a cloth sack. 'Things have been hard for Kanji,' she continued, 'but he's doing better now, so he ought to start being nicer to you. You two have never got on well, have you? When you're old like you are you've got no choice but to make the best of it, have you? Anyway, if he's too mean, other people won't have anything to do with him.'

Uhei put his flour sack away carefully. After Kanji went off in the mornings to clear land he would boil some water and make buckwheat mush. By this time the soy sauce he had brought with him from Noda was all gone. He did not mind, but it had occurred to him that more of it had disappeared when he was out than when he was at home. One day he saw that there was a little soy sauce left in another bottle and added it to his mush for flavor. It was cheap stuff, made from the dregs of first class soy sauce. In the old days he might have liked it, but now it tasted very bitter to him. He was happy nevertheless to feel full and warm. Hastily he washed his bowl and chopsticks and thrust them back onto the shelf. Then he went out.

When Kanji returned home that night he noticed that a bowl was out of place. Suspiciously he looked into the flour bucket. He kept poking around until he found Uhei's flour sack.

'Did you give him any flour?' he asked Otsugi.

'Huh?' Otsugi looked puzzled. 'I haven't touched it.'

'Then he's taken some himself and been cooking with it,' Kanji muttered. 'Just helped himself!' He saw the soy sauce bottle. 'And this is empty too.'

'But it was practically empty before,' Otsugi protested.

'Enough of your back talk!' Kanji yelled. He emptied Uhei's sack into the bucket, still grumbling to himself.

Uhei returned home late, when the lamp was burning low. As usual he ignored the food that had been left out for him and sat down by the hibachi. Looking sullen, he thrust his pipe into his mouth. 'How about getting the fire going, Otsū?' he muttered, the pipe stem still wedged between his gums.

Otsugi lit some faggots beneath the kettle. When the water started to boil Uhei rose awkwardly to his feet and went to get his sack.

'What are you doing, Grampa?' Otsugi asked nervously.

'Looking for a sack,' he mumbled.

'This one?' She held it up. 'It had buckwheat flour in it. We didn't know what to make of it, so we put it back in the bucket. Why did you put flour in the sack, Grampa?'

'Okamisan gave that flour to me,' he said as he sat down wearily. 'Said it would be good for me to eat some mush.'

'Oh, Grampa, then we've done a bad thing,' Otsugi exclaimed. 'I'll fill up your sack right away.' She went to the bucket by the wall where Kanji always slept, glancing at him contemptuously on the way, and filled the sack with much more flour than it had contained before. Uhei started to make a mush.

'Let me do it, Grampa!' Yokichi cried as he reached for the kettle. Uhei let him pour the boiling water into the bowl. Then, very slowly, he stirred the mixture with his chopsticks.

'Is it done yet?' Yokichi asked, his hand on Uhei's arm.

'Stop that begging, Yoki,' Otsugi scolded. 'You've already had your dinner.'

'Oh, he can have some, too,' Uhei muttered, putting part of the mush into another bowl. He ate what remained, then filled the bowl with hot water and drank that.

Kanji did not approach the fire, not even briefly to warm his hands. He sat silently in the corner, scowling. The night grew steadily colder.

18

Uhei greeted the new year at home for the first time in a long while. Only a simple spray of pine branches and bamboo adorned the entrance to the farmyard. There were pine branches on the household altar shelf, too, along with a figure of a shrimp that Uhei had made from twisted straw.

For the first three days of the new year Yokichi wore a clean kimono instead of his usual clothes. Otsugi had had her hair done by one of the neighbors. Even when she did the cooking she wore her best jacket, with the sleeves tied up with a sash to free her hands. Kanji could not bring himself to spend the day at home. Instead he went off to work at clearing land. He enjoyed the labor for he knew that every thrust of his mattock was earning him more money.

As was customary they prepared rice cakes and wheat or buckwheat noodles to mark the year's beginning. Uhei looked forward to the rice cakes because they had been made from upland rice flour and were not particularly sticky. If boiled briefly they became very soft. Only once, though, on New Year's Day itself, did he get them cooked that way. Kanji took all the other rice cakes that Otsugi had made as soon as they were cut into squares and put them away in one of the storage buckets he kept by his bedding. Otsugi was told not to touch them. When he found out that she had disobeyed him and roasted a few for Uhei one day when he was out he exploded with anger.

'But Papa,' she had said in an effort to placate him, 'Yokichi said he wanted some. Then he changed his mind after I'd cooked them up. What else could I do?'

As time passed the remaining rice cakes dried out and became rock hard. Even when heated slowly to puff them up again they remained tough on the outside. Uhei found them almost impossible to chew, but to Kanji they were now just right. He had Otsugi serve them all the time until the supply was exhausted and ate them with

134

gusto. Uhei would suck on his intently, until it got cold, and leave what remained on his plate. Yokichi happily munched on the leftovers when he returned from school.

Kanji also made buckwheat noodles, adding hollyhock flour to the dough to increase its bulk. That way he could eat his fill without using up a lot of buckwheat. Otsugi was told to boil the noodles only briefly. Once drained and rinsed with cold water they were as thick as cedar chopsticks, but the hollyhock flour made them so rubbery and slippery they seemed to have a life of their own. Uhei tried to chew them but they slid out from between his gums.

'You seem to be having a hard time with those, Grampa,' Otsugi observed as she herself tried to catch a noodle that was falling from her plate. 'Papa should've made them more carefully.'

'I couldn't get 'em down no matter how they were made,' Uhei grumbled. Kanji said nothing and continued chewing noisily.

By now the vernal equinox had arrived. Weeds had sprung up along the sunny side of the hedge, and shepherd's purses were in flower in the mulberry fields. If one looked closely one could see new growth on the cedars. The early spring air stirred every living thing in the still drab landscape of winter. The sun, though low on the horizon, cast a warm light. In the mornings, when the sky cleared after a night of rain, its rays would shine obliquely on the fields, and steam would rise from the soil, blanketing everything in a low veil of white.

Since returning from Noda Uhei had taken up with the other old people in the village and joined their Buddhist prayer society. Their regular get-togethers at the prayer hall provided a welcome respite from caring for the grandchildren at home and from the isolation they all felt. Everyone relaxed and had a good time talking, joking, and telling bawdy stories. Especially at the equinox the hall was a lively place, for they feasted on the offerings every household had brought in honor of the occasion. For the first time since coming home Uhei felt he had eaten his fill.

As the weather became warmer he was relieved to find his pains lessening. Indeed, he felt much better than he had in a long time. Taking it easy every day instead of working all night long as he had for years had restored his strength. Uhei did not see it that way, however. Aware only of his circumscribed existence at Kanji's house, to which he attributed his former weariness, he wished he had stayed on in Noda for a few years more.

The soil was now soaked with rain. Even when the sun broke through the clouds the air was so cool that the farmers shivered as they went about their work. Then a mistlike rain would start, the droplets adhering to the ears of barley and making them appear even whiter than before. Suddenly the sky would clear again, and the blossoms on the tangled pea vines would begin to revive. Sunlight filtered through the new leaves in the forest to the soft, lush grass below. From the pine trees came the hum of spring cicadas. Not even Uhei would resist their call to activity. It had bothered him to see Kanji fretting over the dwindling grain supply and always dashing off to do some task or other. Now Uhei too went off in search of work.

Though he moved clumsily he was very skillful with his hands. Soon a number of people were employing him to make straw bales. He made them for the barley harvest and then for carrying manure to the fields. He worked slowly but steadily, taking an occasional break to smoke a pipe. Since he got meals as well as wages from his employers he was able to put quite a bit of money aside.

In the summer he easily found work threshing wheat and weeding upland rice fields. Sometimes he would be gone from the village for five or six days at a stretch. He rather liked moving from one place to another. Along the way if he saw a pretty flower he would ask for seeds or root cuttings and plant them by the chestnut tree or the well at home. At work threshing he wore an old kimono that he had patched himself and a towel over his head to ward off the heat. The skill he had developed as a younger man had not deserted him. When he struck a bundle of wheat against the mortar that sat sideways in front of him the grains would come tumbling off. Then he would raise the bundle high and strike it powerfully against the edge so that even more grains broke free.

He worked on through the busy growing season, helping with the rice harvest and then with the threshing and hulling. He wove more bales. Eventually it was late autumn and there was no more work to do. It was then that Uhei decided to move into a little house of his own. With the extra money he had earned he went off in search of enough posts, boards and millet straw for a simple one-room hut. He decided to build it right next to the eastern wall of Kanji's house so he would be protected from the cold north wind. Kanji had no objections to the project since Uhei was bearing all the expense.

The hut was not difficult to build. The carpenter was needed only briefly. Neighbors helped with the rest, and except for the walls the job was completed in a single day. They even made the thatched roof themselves, using the straw Uhei had bought and the rope he had made for the purpose. The walls took a few days more. Uncharacteristically, Kanji proved willing to help out. As soon as the roof was up he borrowed a neighbor's horse and went off to collect dirt from the barley field of a man who wanted to extend his adjacent paddy and was willing to let Kanji have all the dirt he wanted for free. It took two days to collect enough. Each evening when Kanji took the horse back to its owner he carried along a day's supply of feed. When he had enough dirt he shaped it into a mound, poured on water, added some straw and trod on it to make a thick paste. Meanwhile Uhei split some bamboo that he had got from East Neighbor's forest and wove a lattice to put up between the pillars supporting the roof. The next day the mud was ready, and Kanji plastered it to the outside of the lattice. The wet plaster made the inside of the hut damp and dark. Uhei lit a fire on the floor every morning to hasten the drying. Then the inside walls were plastered, making the hut dark again. Uhei moved in anyway. Despite the labor he had provided, Kanji remained as sullen as ever, and Uhei could not wait to get away from him. There was just barely room for a hibachi in the hut. He had rigged up a hook from which he could hang a pot or kettle. With the rice and barley Kanji had allotted him he started cooking for himself. That was a relief, for he was finally able to eat the kind of food he craved.

Even so there were times when the cold got to him. When Kanji was out he would go and sit in front of the big stove in the old house, adding leaves and faggots to the fire and warming himself to his heart's content. Whenever Kanji noticed that the fuel he had brought in was disappearing too quickly, his grumbling would be aimed at Otsugi.

Soon after setting up on his own Uhei realized that he must do something to earn more money. He started making rope and straw sandals. Rather than using Kanji's straw he went out and bought good-quality straw wherever he could find it. A small bundle that cost him one *sen* would make about two and a half short lengths of rope or five pairs of sandals. He could make twenty lengths of rope in a day, or he could make five pairs of sandals. The rope sold for about 7 *rin* a length and the sandals for 1½ *sen* a pair, so if he worked steadily all day he could make enough of either to clear 6 or 7 *sen* profit. Since it only cost him about 2 *sen* a day for the food he had to buy, he would have 4 or 5 *sen* left over. That was when he worked all day, of course. Sometimes he had to go off peddling what he had made. And other days he just felt like taking it easy. Even so he made enough to feel secure.

Kanji continued to ignore Uhei, but Otsugi kept dropping by to call him for meals whether he came to eat them or not. Sometimes, when he was too busy working to cook, or did not feel like it, or was just tired of being alone, he would go, and soon he was eating there often. Just hearing Otsugi's voice or gazing at the freckles on her face made him feel better and quenched the anger towards Kanji that sometimes welled up in him as he worked.

If Kanji was away when the hens laid eggs, Otsugi might bring Uhei one. She did so only occasionally so that Kanji would not notice, and she never brought more than one. Uhei ate the eggs gratefully and was careful to break up the shells and dispose of them where no one would notice. He also looked forward to seeing Yokichi, who came by regularly hoping to get a coin. The doorway was so narrow that even his small body blocked the light, and Uhei could no longer see whatever it was he was working on at the moment. Usually he gave the boy a 5-*rin* piece. Sometimes Yokichi would try to open Uhei's leather purse himself, but the metal catch was too strong for him. Upset, he would fling the purse down and cling to Uhei imploringly. Once or twice he got so wrought up that he knocked Uhei over.

Kanji knew Yokichi got money from his grandfather and never gave him any himself. Uhei was aware of that, but rather than resenting it he was pleased that the boy depended on him. By now, however, all the money he had brought from Noda was gone, and he had nothing but his income from making rope and sandals to support himself. Only by scrimping here and there could he still afford an occasional cup of sake. Drinking it cheered him up and made him wish that he and Kanji got on well enough to have a drink together. For his part, Kanji did all his drinking at the village shop on his way home from a long day's work. He never brought any sake home with him, and he never let Uhei see him when he had sake on his breath.

Whenever the pain in his back became severe or his hands were too stiff to work Uhei would lie down for a while to rest. He had never said anything about his rheumatism, so when Kanji passed by and saw him like that he thought Uhei was just being lazy. Eventually Uhei would get up and go back to work. Despite his infirmities he had not lost his talent for weaving and plaiting straw. He tied the finished articles up in a bundle and went off peddling them on days when the weather was good.

It seemed to Kanji that Uhei did pretty much as he pleased. That he bought a piece of salted salmon occasionally and grilled it on his hibachi was proof that he had no worries. The very smell of the fish cooking over a smoky fire irritated Kanji and made him keenly aware of his dislike for the old man. At the same time Uhei was keenly aware of being lonely. Especially after dark as he lay under his quilt he could hear Kanji and the children talking next door. It had occurred to him before that they always seemed tense when he was with them. When by themselves they talked amiably to one another. No matter how far under the quilt he buried himself he could still hear their voices, Otsugi's slightly coquettish and

Yokichi's childish and unrestrained. He envied their intimacy and at the same time resented it. He would find himself wishing he were living with them again and be overwhelmed with sadness. Now that his rheumatism was acting up again he felt especially sorry for himself. Just hearing Otsugi or Yokichi call out to him and raising his head from the pillow to see that it was morning and he had survived another night would bring tears to his eyes.

Kanji had so many chores for her to do that Otsugi had no free time at all during the daytime. She would come to Uhei's hut in the evenings and massage his back. She came no matter how tired she was. Kanji always noticed when she left the house for any reason and would yell out to her if she did not return promptly. He did so even when he knew she was with Uhei.

'There's no need to yell like that, Papa,' she replied on one occasion. 'I'm right over here. What do you want?' Her gentle rebuke echoed in his ears and reduced him to silence. A while later he slid the door open noisily and went outside. After a few moments he pulled the door to, as if he had gone back inside, but left it open a bit. Then he made his way barefoot towards the hut. There was no lamp lit and all was dark inside. He retraced his steps, slipped back inside the house, and closed the door as quietly as he could. He was scowling, but as soon as Otsugi came in he felt better.

'You shouldn't stay out so late,' he muttered gently.

'Don't worry, Papa,' she replied coolly, 'I'll still be able to work tomorrow.'

It upset Uhei that Otsugi got into trouble on his account. 'You don't have to bother tonight,' he would usually say when she came to give him a massage. But the truth was he looked forward to her visits. It was now his second winter home. From time to time the pain in his back subsided, but it always recurred, slowly sapping his strength.

He was not as happy living in his hut as he had thought he would be.

19

'My but it's hot!' Otsuta exclaimed as she strode into the yard. 'Everything sure looks neat and tidy here,' she continued with studied casualness. 'Not a weed in sight. And that's quite a harvest you've got there. Just look at all those stalks!' She moved towards the chestnut tree in whose shade Kanji and Otsugi sat threshing summer buckwheat.

Two mortars were rolled over sideways in front of them. As they did with wheat, they would strike a stalk against the side of the mortar and the triangular grains would fall to the ground, some bouncing away into the bright sunshine. But unlike wheat the buckwheat stalks were moist and sticky. Just peeling one free from the bundle took effort. The stalks had to be struck again and again before all the ripe grains would fall. Those that were still green would resist to the end. The yard had been swept clean for the occasion. Uhei had already seen to it that no weeds remained unpulled.

Kanji was stripped to the waist. As usual he wore a broad-brimmed hat to ward off the sunlight that penetrated even the lush foliage of the chestnut tree. Its strap of braided flax was tied beneath his chin. Drenched every day by sweat the fibres were stained and had begun to lose their resiliency. Kanji took pride in his strap and would need to get a new one made before the autumn.

When he had seen his elder sister at the gap in the hedge Kanji had frowned and pretended not to notice her. Now Otsuta had made her way across the yard, carefully avoiding stepping on any buckwheat grains, and stood beside him. She wore an old-fashioned tie-dyed cotton kimono with one sleeve unshouldered and dangling at her waist, revealing her undershirt. The lower edges of the kimono were tucked up in her sash. Over her shoulder she carried a faded sateen parasol. Kanji could no longer ignore her presence. He stopped working and looked up, a strained expression on his face. 'What do you want?' he asked. Sweat trickled down his chest, washing away the dusty flecks of buckwheat chaff and leaving streaks of clean flesh in its wake.

'Oh, nothing in particular,' Otsuta answered lightly. 'I was just passing by and thought I'd drop in to see how things were. It's been a while, after all. Is this Otsugi here? She's quite grown up, isn't she. It really is hard keeping track of young folk. You don't see 'em for a bit, you don't recognize 'em anymore. Not like us grown-ups. We always look the same!' She rambled on, as if trying to find a way to start a conversation.

Otsugi bowed slightly, one hand holding the edge of her hat. Despite the heat she had not abandoned modesty. Her kimono was neatly secured, with just a bit of her white undershirt showing at the neck. Her sleeves were tied up with a sash, and her hands were gloved. As she went off to make tea Otsuta strolled to the well and filled a washbasin with water.

'You've got good water,' she said, half to herself. 'Nice and cold. Not like the lukewarm water in my well.'

Kanji paid no attention and started back to work. Otsuta began to wash herself. Soon smoke rose from the eves of the house and drifted off into the sky.

'Tea's made, Papa,' Otsugi announced as she came outside.

'Hmm,' Kanji muttered. 'There's tea if you want some,' he said, still busily at work.

'Won't you have some?' Otsugi chimed in.

Otsuta wrung out her handkerchief and flapped it in the air. The edge struck some wilted touch-me-not flowers that grew by the well and sent them cascading to the ground. Nearby stood some tall sunflowers and a row of phlox.

'Well, well, look what we have here,' Otsuta observed. 'Never plant flowers myself, much as I like 'em. These must look real nice in the cool of the morning.' She closed her parasol and made her way into the house. Kanji followed. Otsugi had wiped the sweat from her face and combed her hair before calling them. 'It's very hot, isn't it,' she said politely as she served the tea.

For a time the three sat in silence. At East Neighbor's a group of men were threshing barley. 'Hooi!' one of them would chant, and the others would chant in reply as they stuck the sheafs with flails. Deep thuds echoed through the forest. As if entranced by the sound the three tea drinkers remained still. Otsuta gazed at the tea leaves in her cup and smiled. Then she looked out at the yard. When he was sure their eyes would not meet Kanji stared at the elder sister he had not seen for so long a time. She must be well over 50. Her small, round face looked younger than her years, despite deep wrinkles. Her hair was very dark and glossy. It was clear she dyed it, for the roots were faintly white. Kanji sipped his tea. Otsugi, too, glanced curiously at her aunt from time to time.

Otsuta looked at the two mortars in the yard, their sides stained green from the soft buckwheat stalks. 'Looks like a good crop,' she said, commenting on the first thing that struck her eye. 'The grains are nice and big.'

'It's been raining like crazy,' Kanji replied coolly. 'The stalks just shot up. Still, it's not a bad crop.'

Otsuta tried a new topic. 'Those flowers are really nice, aren't they.'

'That may be, but they used up more of my night soil than I could spare.'

'You didn't plant them then?'

'Are you joking? Grandfather put 'em in. Last year I had some corn growing there, but it wasn't worth making a fuss about.'

'So he's returned from Noda. I haven't come by for a while and didn't know.'

'He came back about two years ago.'

'How's he doing? He must be pretty old.'

'Oh, he's healthy all right. You'd be surprised how healthy he is. Works only when he wants to and goes off peddling to make a little cash.'

'Still, it must be handy to have him around to help when things get busy.'

'Not at all. He's never been any help. For that matter, I don't ask him for any.'

'Is that so? He was quite a worker in his prime, but you could tell he didn't much like doing it.'

'And what's more, he doesn't like being with me either, so he's set up on his own. Spent a lot of money doing it, and I had to do most of the work. Well, he's the grandfather around here, so I have to do whatever he wants. But I really can't make him out at all.'

'So that little hut out there is his? When I saw it before I thought it was a manure shed. He has been behaving strangely, hasn't he! If only old people would try harder to get along with the younger generation life would be much easier, wouldn't it?'

'I've got one more mouth to feed, too, and that's not easy, believe me. He makes it worse, too, the sour face he puts on when he's eating my food. I can't bear looking at him!'

'My, my, you have got trouble. You think he'd at least try to be polite.' As she spoke Otsuta stared at the bales piled up under the chicken coop. 'You've really been working hard. Just look at all those bales. I'm no flatterer, but it looks to me as if you're doing just fine.'

Kanji finally began to warm to the conversation. Breaking into a smile, he said, 'Things are a little better now, that's for sure. I could say a lot about how bad off I was for a spell, but now we're getting by okay.'

'And Otsugi looks like a good worker, too. I saw her out there threshing buckwheat. She really throws herself into it, doesn't she? And isn't she nicely dressed! That's your training, I expect.' Otsuta looked over at Otsugi. 'She looks just like her mother, doesn't she.'

On hearing that Otsugi grabbed a bucket and hurried out to the yard.

'You know, I was really worried when my wife died,' Kanji muttered softly. 'I didn't think that girl would ever be any use.'

Otsuta smiled wanly at the reference to Oshina. 'I just couldn't come then, you know. I'd gone off a long way away. You probably think bad of me for it.' She let her apology go at that and abruptly changed the subject. 'I noticed before what good care you take of your tools. That sickle has a real nice shine to it. And it looks good and sharp, too. Tools will last forever if you treat 'em right the way you do.'

Otsuta walked over to Kanji's mattock. 'Now this is really a big one! Don't think I could ever use one like this. Just lifting it must be a chore.'

'Take a look at these, Sister,' Kanji said proudly, showing Otsuta the palms of his hands. The skin was thick and calloused. It was clear he could wield the heavy oak handle all day and never get a blister.

'Anybody can buy a big mattock if he's got the money, but you don't get hands like these unless you really use it. Mine got this way after a couple of years. Used to hurt a lot, but now I can clear more than an acre a winter. It's the Master's land, out in the forest. Some places I can put in upland rice. Got about an acre of it growing now, in fact. What with all the rain this year I think it'll do fine. I wasn't able to plant any before.'

Otsuta was impressed. 'Growing that much must be a lot of work.'

'Not really. The soil is fresh cleared, so there aren't any weeds to worry about, and you don't need fertilizer.'

'An acre! You're going to end up with a lot!'

'As long as there's enough rain when the ears are forming, maybe about four bales a quarter acre, I figure.'

'How about that! We can't grow upland rice where I live. Too much flooding.'

'This is a good place, all right. No trouble with floods.' Kanji had relaxed during the conversation. This was his sister after all.

He forgot about the past. 'Get us some of those pickled scallions, Otsū!' he said, feeling expansive. 'We put 'em up before the dog days set in, so they ought to be good.'

Otsugi took some pickles from an old sake cask and placed them in a bowl. Kanji picked one up and munched it noisily.

Otsuta had been smiling throughout the conversation. For a moment she seemed about to say something else, but neither Kanji nor Otsugi noticed. Starting to pour herself some tea she saw that her cup was already full. She drained it with a gulp. 'It sure is nice to hear how good things are going for you. You're my brother, after all, and we ought to care about one another,' she said as she got up to go to the privy.

When she sat down again on the ledge up to the main room she announced as casually as she could, 'Actually I came here to ask you about something.'

Kanji stiffened, and the uneasy expression he usually wore returned to his face. 'What about?'

'No great matter, really. It's that blind boy of mine. I'm seeing about getting him a wife, and I thought . . .'

Kanji interrupted. 'So that's your business, isn't it? If you want a daughter-in-law, it's not for other people to object.'

'Well, that may be, but we ought to talk about it, don't you think? Afterwards it's too late for complaints. So I thought I'd better let you know what's going on.'

'I'm in no position to make complaints,' Kanji replied, relieved that that was all Otsuta seemed worried about.

'Well then, that's just fine. He's 27 now, you know. I've tried to take good care of him, but well, I've had troubles of my own and haven't always been able to do what I'd like for him. It's the same with you, I expect. You have to care what happens to your own kids.'

Kanji said nothing. With his toe he traced a pattern in the dirt floor below the ledge.

'Then he went blind,' Otsuta continued in an earnest tone, seeking to arouse Kanji's sympathy. 'Still, he'd been a good worker before that, and he still is. You know that already. It's a relief to me, believe me, that someone was willing to arrange a marriage for him despite his being blind. What counts in life, after all, is being able to work. Like you. Everyone talks about what a worker you are. And I've seen the girl. She's not much to look at, but looks don't matter when you're blind. It's the feelings that count, and she seems like a kind one.'

'Well, that's good,' Kanji muttered, on his guard again.

'And, you know, since he's got work right here in the village it just doesn't make sense to bring him and his wife back to my place after the wedding. Better for him to be where folks already know him, him being blind and all. I was thinking about renting a house for 'em here. Looked into it a bit, but it turns out I need someone here to stand guaranty for him. Can't do it myself, because I don't live here. So I thought maybe you'd do it.'

'What!' Kanji shouted. 'Oh no, I'm not doing anything like that.'

'But why not?' Otsuta looked downcast. 'There's nothing to worry about. He's steady and reliable, after all. It's just a formality.'

'That's what you say! But what happens if he falls behind in the rent? I have to pay up for him, that's what! That'd ruin me. Oh no, I'm not having anything to do with it.'

'You're getting all wrought up over nothing. He'll have help, after all, so he won't have any trouble paying 30 *sen*, even 50 *sen* rent. Look, how about if you just do it for a month or two? See how it goes. If you don't think he'll make it, you can drop him.'

'Not even that!' Kanji retorted. 'I won't listen to any more of this.' He went out to the yard and started back to work.

'My, aren't we the busy one,' Otsuta called after him.

'You're damn right!' Kanji answered. 'And I still have the paddy to weed. Nothing but rain since the dog days, so I'm behind on that, too. Nobody's got any spare time this time of year. Just listen to all that flailing over at East Neighbor's.'

'Some reception I've got,' Otsuta grumbled. 'I didn't think a brother would act like that.'

'If I did what you want I'd be ruined,' Kanji shouted as he pounded the buckwheat stalks against the mortar. He did not even glance towards Otsuta.

Otsuta had a mean look in her eyes when she stood up. 'Whatever else I am I'm not a thief, Kanji,' she snarled.

Just then Uhei appeared in the doorway. Otsuta's manner changed abruptly. 'Why, it's the father of the house!' she exclaimed. 'Haven't seen you for a long time. I hope all's well with you.'

'Come along with me,' Uhei muttered and led the way to his hut. 'I've been out and just got back. What's going on anyway?' he asked with his usual bluntness.

Otsuta stood in the doorway of the hut and told her story. '. . . and so I asked him to stand guaranty. The rent'd be next to nothing. No bother at all. And for a nephew who's blind! Well, Kanji, he'd have none of it. Said it was too big a risk. That's the response I got! You're an old man, so you know how important it is to have someone kind to rely on. We all depend on the next generation, don't we. And this bride for my boy, she's really kind. I could rely on her, I know I could. It may sound selfish putting it that way, but it's how I feel. I want a nice, sweet daughter-in-law, or I might as well have none at all.' As she spoke she dug little holes in the ground with the tip of her parasol. Every once in a while she cast a glance in Kanji's direction.

'Hmm, you've got a point there,' Uhei muttered, his hand on his pipe.

From where he sat in the yard Kanji was sure that Uhei was giving Otsuta encouragement. He picked up a bundle of buckwheat stalks and tossed it away angrily. With a thud it landed on the touch-me-nots by the well, forcing a branch to the ground. 'That sister of mine knows how to tell a tale,' he grumbled. 'She's probably talking about how well she looked after her own father-in-law . . .' Otsuta overheard and looked sharply at Kanji.

'Be quiet, Papa, please?' Otsugi urged. 'Lunch is ready,' she announced.

'Well, in that case I'll be on my way,' Otsuta said to Uhei and opened her parasol. 'I know when I'm not wanted. You'd better be careful, too. You don't want to become a burden, after all.' Still upset, she could not stop talking. 'You'd think he's got plenty of grain baled up to stand guaranty for a measly 30 *sen* or so. He's got no good reason to refuse.'

'Won't you have some food?' Otsugi asked timidly.

'Don't need any!' Otsuta walked off across the yard, making no attempt this time to avoid trampling on the buckwheat grains. As she neared the gap in the hedge she turned and announced in a voice dripping with sarcasm, 'The way you take care of your family, not to mention the fine reputation you have here in the village, why, it makes me proud to be related to you.' Then she walked away.

The noise rose again from East Neighbor's, as if mocking the now silent yard next door. Kanji concentrated on threshing and said nothing more. Otsugi stood watching from the yard until Otsuta's parasol disappeared from view.

Uhei sat with his pipe clenched in his mouth. After a while he noticed the fallen touch-me-not branch and lumbered over to the well. With a vengeance he kicked the bundle of buckwheat stalks away. Then he thrust a small bamboo stake into the soil and tried to prop the branch up on it. The branch broke from its stem. Angrily Uhei picked it up and threw it away. Nearby stood the sunflowers, their stalks straight despite the heat and their broad flowers gazing down contemptuously into the yard.

20

Autumn again. A hint of withering was visible in the green tree-tops. The sun had grown weary of long days sending forth bright, scorching heat, and both the sky and the land below assumed a muted tone. From time to time clouds rushed in from the south, pouring down rain that transformed the dusty soil of the upland fields to mud and splashed it onto the lower leaves of the crops. Then the foam-flecked water drained away. The sun reappeared, but only long enough to dry the sodden flowers on the bindweed vines that coiled up the trunks of the mulberry trees. Again and again the showers came, harassing the farmers who had been up since dawn hulling barley and now had the grain spread out on mats to dry. Would the showers end that day? If not they knew they would continue for three days or five days or even longer, for at this time of year it always rained for an odd number of days.

Soon after the showers began the melon vines withered and died in the fields. As clouds tumbled this way and that in the sky above, leaves began falling from the trees with a mournful rustle. More clouds raced through the cold night air, devouring the moon and an instant later spewing it out behind them. The autumn wind was blowing. Even the sturdy oaks lost their dignity as they bent with its gusts and revealed their inner leaves and bark. For days the down-pours continued, chilling the air and tormenting the vegetation. Flood waters filled the rivers and lapped savagely against their banks.

Finally the sky cleared. Like someone suddenly aged by an ordeal the trees and bushes were bleached white, their remaining foliage fluttering helplessly in the wind. Though covered with mud the spiderwort entwined in the roots of the bamboo along the Kinu River embankment clung tenaciously to life and put forth tiny flowers. Crickets cringed beneath them, chirping faintly. The gray starlings that had flown far away to escape the deluge now swooped down from the sky in search of branches on which to light. White flowers adorned the poisonous traveler's joy vines that flourished in the thickets and in the bamboo along the embankment. As if convinced only they had been invigorated by the storm they danced proudly in the wind like tiny sails.

Kanji's village stood on a plateau, and thanks to the tangled bamboo roots that shored up the embankment, damage was slight. Still, it took days for the rain-water to drain from the rice paddies and from the more low-lying fields. Kanji worried incessantly about his crops, but in the end he found them relatively unharmed. Hearing about the devastation that had occurred elsewhere in the district he rejoiced in his own good fortune. It was clear and warm the day he harvested his soybeans and carried them back to the yard. The burs on the chestnut tree had begun to open. The ground was bathed in sunlight. Having stood a long time in water the soybean plants were laden with mud.

Kanji and South Neighbor often exchanged labor. In haste to get his beans finished while the weather held he had called upon South Neighbor's wife for help that day. The plants had been arranged in neat rows to dry, and soon the pods had begun to pop open. With Otsugi and South Neighbor's wife standing on one side and Kanji on the other the three flailed in turn at the pods, and the glossy pale green beans came tumbling out. Then it was time for lunch. For a while thereafter they sat talking in the shade of the chestnut tree.

Suddenly Otsuta strolled into the yard. 'Just look at all those soybeans!' she exclaimed. 'I can see you've had no problems here.'

Kanji glanced up for an instant and looked away. Calmly Otsuta went to the door and set down a bundle that had been slung over her shoulder. 'Whew! That was heavy.' Wiping her brow with one hand she set her parasol upside down in the doorway and placed the bundle inside it.

South Neighbor's wife stood up.

'My, my, it's been a long time,' Otsuta addressed her politely.

'I hear you had terrible flooding over your way,' South Neighbor's wife said. 'Is that so?'

'You wouldn't believe how bad it was,' Otsuta replied energetically. 'It's been almost a month since the rains stopped, but we're still in a fix. Nothing but floods all the time where I live. I don't know why we stay on there. You were lucky here, weren't you.'

'It wasn't like that at all,' South Neighbor's wife admonished gently. 'Why, some people here got hit pretty hard.'

'That may be,' Otsuta retorted, 'but there's no sign of it now. Over my way some people lost their houses and had to take shelter on the embankment in little huts they made out of straw mats. They could manage all right as long as the weather held, but when it rained it was awful. And my own house was full of water. We had to put big barrels on the floor and lay planks on 'em to stay above it. Finally found a way to do some cooking, but we were stranded there, cut off from everything. The whole neighborhood was like that. Some people even died. Believe me, I feel lucky to be standing here alive.'

Otsuta was delighted to have an audience and continued to describe her experiences in detail. 'It was next to impossible to lie down and go to sleep with all that water lapping up around our ears. We were scared we'd get swept away and drowned. You could just reach out and touch the water! Finally we tied a little boat up inside the house. Kept it right by our pillows, we did. Really! And we were freezing cold and all crowded together on those planks. You had to watch out or you'd bump your head on the ceiling! But we held on and got through it. We were lucky the house was still standing.

'Nighttime was the worst part. At least during daylight you could see all around you. You could see the frogs that came swimming up. And the snakes! Now, they were really awful. Tried to scare 'em off with a stick, but they'd keep coming back. We kept a little lantern going at night just to be on the safe side, and I guess that attracted 'em. But it was still pretty dark so you couldn't see 'em until they were right up beside you. You'd look over and one of 'em would be right there, its head out of the water, staring back at you. Gave me a real fright, it did.'

Kanji could not help becoming interested in Otsuta's vivid account, and with South Neighbor's wife present it would not do to go on ignoring her. 'You've had a rough time, sounds to me,' he said as he stood up and led the way to the house. All the rain doors had been shut to keep out the dust from the flailing. Even with the main door wide open it was still dark and hot inside. Otsugi lit the fire and began making tea.

On her way to the door Otsuta picked up a handful of beans and inspected them. 'These look really good. No doubt about it, you were lucky here. All my land's down by the river, you know. We had some beans growing around the rice paddy, and afterwards we picked 'em and laid 'em out on the embankment to dry, but it was no use. The pods were all shrivelled up, no bigger than beans themselves.' She reached down to get the bundle she had brought with her and went inside. 'With water all around us we couldn't do any work, so we all rigged up poles and went fishing. Right in my own yard I caught a few carp!' Otsuta said as she sipped her tea. 'Somebody just passing by would have thought we were all a bunch of lazy good-for-nothings.'

Otsugi and South Neighbor's wife listened wide-eyed. Kanji was frowning, but he too listened intently.

'Afterwards it was still pretty awful. Nothing but mud under the floor and everywhere. We finally got it cleared out, but the floor boards are still waterlogged and covered with mildew. We still haven't been able to put any matting back down. And I can't tell you how rotten the fields smelled when the water finally started draining away! I'd just been worried about my crops, but the paulownia and the oak trees in one of my fields took quite a beating, too. Leaves are all gone. I'm not sure they'll recover.' As she spoke Otsuta undid the bundle she had brought with her. Inside were three cans of boiled beef and a few lumps of table salt wrapped in paper.

'Everyone who was flooded out got some of these from the village office. Pretty tasty too. I've been wanting to get over here to see how you folks made out, and I thought I'd bring some along for you.' She folded up the cloth in which the items had been wrapped.

'Well now, isn't this something!' South Neighbor's wife exclaimed as she examined one of the lumps of salt. 'Is it really salt? I've never seen anything like it. What a nice present for you, Kanji-san.' Otsugi too was fascinated by the salt. Kanji scratched off a little piece and popped it into his mouth. 'It's salt all right,' he said with a smile. 'How about putting these things away, Otsū.' Then he turned to Otsuta. 'I take it your crops really suffered.'

'Yes,' Otsuta replied glumly. 'The rice is a total loss. In fact, everything is.'

'Even your vegetables? Must be something growing you can put in soup at least.'

'Are you joking? The only green anywhere is the weeds along the river. We're really in a bad way.'

Kanji was moved. 'I guess I can give you some eggplants and some squash.'

'And I can let you have some onions,' South Neighbor's wife chimed in. She scurried home to collect them.

'How about a little rice, too, Papa,' Otsugi suggested. 'We'll be bringing in the upland rice pretty soon, so we'll still have enough'.

'I suppose you're right,' Kanji muttered. He went over to the half-empty bale and measured out about nine quarts of rice into a China rice sack.

'You could add some barley, maybe,' Otsugi said. Kanji looked over at Otsuta. 'You mind if I put the barley in with the rice?'

'Not at all,' Otsuta answered softly.

Kanji added some barley to the sack. Then he went and got three large squash and set them down on the dirt floor.

'I really appreciate all this,' Otsuta said. 'You know, I think I'll just take the rice today and come back for the squash tomorrow.' She looked at Otsugi. 'Could you loan me a big wrapping cloth? The one I brought with me is too small for all this.'

'Hmm, we don't have one, do we, Papa. But I think Grampa does.' Otsugi hurried off to Uhei's hut. He had just returned from somewhere and was sitting down, smoking a pipe.

'Oh, you're here!' she blurted out. 'I thought you were away and I'd have to take it without asking. A big cloth, I mean. Aunt needs to borrow one to carry the rice we're giving her. Is that okay?'

'Sure,' Uhei muttered and leaned over to get the cloth. Then he followed Otsugi back to the house.

'We've been flooded out, you see,' Otsuta told him as she tied up the rice sack in the cloth, 'and Kanji's come to the rescue. Just look at these huge squash he's giving me, too. I'm coming back for 'em tomorrow.'

Just then South Neighbor's wife returned with a bunch of onions.

'I'm really grateful for all this,' Otsuta said, looking at Kanji. 'And now onions, too! You're all very kind.' She sat down again and sipped her tea. 'Why look, your chestnuts are ripe!' she exclaimed, catching sight of the tree outside.

'The burs just started opening a few days ago,' Otsugi replied cheerfully, taking some chestnuts from a bowl she had nearby. 'You're welcome to some, if you want. And soybeans, too, as soon as we've got 'em shelled.'

'Well, well, I guess I might as well take a few.' Otsuta wrapped the chestnuts up in her handkerchief. 'And I think the father of the house ought to have one of these.' She picked up a can of boiled beef and handed it to Uhei. Not wanting to appear rude, Otsugi had ignored her father's order to put Otsuta's gifts away and had left them arrayed on the matting. Kanji looked on in dismay as Uhei examined the can. He felt as if he had been robbed.

'Well, I'll see you all tomorrow,' Otsuta announced as she tied the heavy bundle to her back and set off. 'This has really been a good trip,' she said to herself but in a voice loud enough to be overheard as she left the yard.

Kanji turned his gaze to Uhei, who stood next to him holding the can of beef. Resentment welled up inside him. 'Don't forget to bring my rice sack back tomorrow!' he yelled out to Otsuta.

That night there was a crisis in Kanji's house. Yokichi stole one of the lumps of salt, thinking it was a new kind of sweet. He broke it in half and gulped a piece down. A moment later he was in agony, his throat burning. Kanji and Otsugi rushed to his side in alarm. When Kanji discovered what the boy had done he exploded. 'Idiot!' he shouted. 'How can anyone be so stupid!'

'Getting angry isn't going to cure him, Papa!' Otsugi shouted in turn. Yokichi was sprawled on the floor, crying furiously and clawing at his chest. Uhei heard the uproar and came over.

'Try giving him water,' he ordered calmly. Otsugi instantly obeyed. Yokichi clung to the ladle she handed him and gulped the liquid down.

'When a chicken's got something stuck in its craw you force water down it quick,' Uhei muttered. 'Works a lot better than screaming and carrying on.' He gave Yokichi more water, and they put him to bed. All night they sat uneasily by his pillow, not getting a wink of sleep themselves. The next morning the boy felt fine again and went dashing off to school.

Later the same day Otsuta returned. Unaware of the trouble the previous night she was in the same good spirits as the day before. Kanji, deprived of sleep, was glummer than usual.

'Are these the same that were out here yesterday?' Otsuta asked uncertainly as she bundled up her squash.

'Guess so,' Kanji muttered. In fact he had substituted three smaller ones.

'Thought there'd be some beans, too,' Otsuta said, but Kanji remained silent. An unhappy expression on her face, Otsuta put the bundles of squash and onions on her back and, after a few words with Uhei, set off for home. Kanji stood staring at his nearly empty rice bale.

For him and for all farmers the weeks before the autumn harvest were a time for worry and sometimes tears. There before them, almost ripened for the taking, was nature's bounty, but how much of it would be theirs, and how much lost to jealous storms and frosts? Just as anyone would fear losing a purse full enough to satisfy all his material needs, so too farmers feared what they might lose of their crops. As it happened, however, there were no more storms that particular year. For days the sky was obscured by low-lying clouds, and a warm, dry wind blew day and night. Even the stiff, razor-sharp leaves of the pampas grass in the forest were caught by the wind, and their soft, pale red tips rippled to and fro. Then the sky became radiantly clear. The upland rice glowed golden brown in the sunlight. Washed by the autumn rain and dried by the autumn wind, the buckwheat had gradually bleached; now it was white enough to illuminate a moonless night. Here gold, there white, the fields undulated across the plateau and sloped down to the river. Around each field, like a thin fence, stood a row or two of full-grown sorghum. From the river one could see their tips rising above the bamboo-covered embankment and waving in the southerly wind. Like beckoning hands they urged the boats upstream. Mountain peaks were visible in the distance.

Unfortunately, Kanji's upland rice grew not in the open, rolling countryside but within the forest on the tiny parcels of land he had cleared. The sparrows preferred the isolation there and attacked his crop in droves. He had strung nets of polished cotton thread over each field and hung bright strips of paper to scare the birds off, but to no avail. They had pecked away happily at the soft, sweet rice inside the partially formed husks. The ground was littered with chaff. Kanji thought the wind had blown it down and remained optimistic as he harvested the crop. As soon as he started threshing, however, he realized with dismay that his yields would be much lower than he had predicted during summer.

How could he have let himself be talked into giving Otsuta that grain! Just thinking about it drove him to rage. He was too fond of Otsugi and Yokichi to take his anger out on them, so he focused on Uhei. His hatred of the old man, festering for months, now knew no bounds.

21

When Kanji came running up to the bank of the Kinu River a thick
fog had descended, shrouding the water just a few yards from
shore. There was no boat. Kanji assumed it was on the opposite
side of the river and shouted impatiently to summon it. The boatman's reply came back loudly from near at hand. Taken by
surprise, Kanji froze and said nothing more. A moment later the
prow of the boat emerged from the fog. Kanji got on board.

To avoid a sandbar that had formed in mid-river after the early
autumn floods the boat set off on a widely curving course. Kanji
was annoyed that the boatman was poling so slowly. 'Maybe I
should just wade across,' he muttered.

'Go ahead, if getting soaked to the skin is what you want,' the
boatman answered curtly and continued poling without haste.
Suddenly the bottom of the boat heaved, and Kanji almost toppled
over. He was sure the boatman had done that on purpose. For the
rest of the trip he crouched nervously and made no sound.

Because of the shoals extending from the sandbar the boat could
not dock at its usual place. Kanji wondered where the boatman
would decide to let him off. Finally the prow hit against the bank
where some scraggly purple willows stood amid a tangle of box-
thorn and smartweed. Despite the clutter it was clear the boat had
docked here on numerous occasions, for a series of indentations
made by the feet of other passengers led upwards. Kanji grasped a
willow branch and stepped out of the boat. Branches and leaves
brushed against the rolled mat he carried on his back, but soon he
was on the bank. Fields lay before him, the mud brought by the
floods now dry and cracked. Cut stalks of sorghum stood forlornly
in the fog. When Kanji looked back the boat had already disappeared.

He followed a trail to the top of the embankment. Suddenly the
fog lifted and Kanji looked around in disbelief at the damage the
floods had caused. Then a few tiny specks caught his eye. They

were little boats that were anchored far upstream. Kanji made out the bamboo poles rising from their decks and knew they were salmon fishing boats. The fishermen were waiting for the dead of night to go after salmon with their nets. They might have no success for nights on end, but they would stay awake, waiting. Even in the dark their keen eyes could detect the salmon making their way through the water·and just as the fish went by they would snare them. At dawn they would wrap each of the silvery fish they had caught in bamboo leaves and take them off to market. If they had caught nothing they would lie down wearily to sleep. Only in daylight when the crafty salmon took refuge in still pools along the river bank could the fishermen afford to rest. At the moment the boats were motionless. Except for the smoke rising from distant villages all was still. Kanji stared at the scene for some time. Then he gathered himself together and set out along the embankment towards the north.

The embankment stretched far into the distance, following the undulating course of the river. Soon it was lined by rice paddies and the path became narrower. That was because the grass on the inner slope of the embankment was piled with damp, newly harvested rice. Only the stalks of the wild rose bushes that grew here and there remained uncovered. The roses had long since fallen, and a bright red berry was visible on the tip of each little branch. Starworts clung tenaciously to the wild rose stalks, their flowers damp in the morning air.

The heavy odor of the rice assaulted Kanji's nostrils. He stripped off a few grains from one of the ears and chewed on them to see what the crop was like. Suddenly annoyed with himself for wasting time he hurried on along the path. He wore leggings and straw sandals. The rustling of the mat on his back urged him onward. Eventually he descended the embankment slope and struck out towards the east.

The path he now took made straight for a forest on a plateau in the distance. Along the way were parcel after parcel of paddy field, interrupted only by the occasional clump of trees that indicated a village. Kanji had travelled this way before, but then the path had wound this way and that. He was amazed at the vast amount of land adjustment that had been carried out in seemingly no time at all. The system of irrigation ditches that he passed was also new and fascinated him.

At long last the sun had risen in the sky and everything was bathed in light. Yet there was not a trace of vivid green in view. The rice in the paddies that had not yet been harvested glowed yellow brown. Only a few small leaves remained in the tops of the mulberry trees in the dry fields that were scattered here and there. The trees clustered around the villages, too, were covered in dark red leaves. The sky alone was intensely bright. Indeed that explained it. The sky had taken all the green from the vegetation below. The following spring it would return it in the form of rain. Then the dampened branches would take on color again. Weeds would sprout up in the fields despite the efforts of farmers to prevent it. The more it rained the lusher the weeds would grow. No doubt about it. It was because the late autumn sky had absorbed all the green that everything on the land was dry and drab.

The bright sun was now directly overhead. Kanji walked with his eyes downcast, holding his bandaged right elbow close to his body and staring at the water in the narrow ditch beside the path. The blue sky and a few white clouds were reflected in the water. As if they had lost their way and anxiously sought a place to rest, the clouds dashed along, keeping pace with Kanji. Staring at them made him dizzy. He had not slept the night before. Only the anger pent up inside him drove him on. He must show his injury to someone. Usually so loath to take time off from work he was too befuddled even to think of the losses he might incur. The sun shone hot on his right cheek but otherwise the day remained cold. Silenced by the chill the frogs that lay submerged in the water of the ditch watched Kanji go past. He was the only person on the path. A few farmers were at work in the fields, but as if hiding from his gaze they were bent over, intent on harvesting their rice. Kanji's lonely trek was like a mere speck of dust to them, unworthy of notice.

At the end of the expanse of paddy Kanji passed through a village where people were laying out the rice crop on their hedges to dry. Everyone paused to take note of his passage. As soon as he became aware that he was being looked at Kanji carefully cradled his injured elbow in his other hand.

Beyond the village he emerged onto the wooded plateau where dry fields had been reclaimed among the trees. Kanji looked closely at the soil and at the crops as he went past. Beyond the next village a broad expanse of dry fields opened up before him. In several fields newly harvested upland rice lay in piles. He trod on some of the stubble to test its quality. Nearby a few farmers were plowing the soil in preparation for planting winter barley. The neatly cultivated black earth, not yet dried out by the sun, was pleasing to the eye.

Kanji remembered that he had not yet finished preparing his own barley fields. He remembered, too, that a sudden cold spell last year had forced him to abandon sowing and that the harvest from the seeds he had planted a mere two days later had been markedly reduced. As a rule he made it a point to plant on the day ordained for planting. Yet here he was wasting a day on account of his injury. That bothered him, but at the same time he felt compelled to have the injury looked at. He longed for a little sympathy.

Some lush radish leaves dotted the black soil of the fields Kanji now passed. They were the only bright green in sight. All the other plants had ceased growing and lay drooping on the ground. The chirping of insects too had subsided into the soil, driven down by the autumn weather. Even the green radish leaves could not resist autumn much longer and soon would be flattened against the soil, never to rise again. The soil itself had nothing left to do but grow cold and freeze.

Kanji finally arrived at the bone doctor's gate. The house, surrounded by a bamboo fence and overarched by a tall woodbine tree, looked dark. A wooden litter lay inside the fence. Kanji shuddered as he realized it had been used to transport someone with severe injuries. Suddenly ashamed of his overly elaborate attire he timidly made his presence known. In the entrance hall sat a number of other patients waiting to see the doctor. One man had his bandaged arm in a sling. Another lay sprawled on the floor, his face pale and drawn. Kanji lurked behind the others, waiting his turn. The medicinal smell that filled the room made him uneasy. When the doctor glanced his way Kanji felt he had been glared at.

The doctor sprinkled a little yellowish brown powdered medicine onto a wooden slab, kneaded some white paste into it, and moistened the mixture with what looked like sake. Then he cut off a strip of white paper, smeared it with the medicine, and pasted the paper to the injured part of the patient he was treating. The others sat silently, watching his skillful hands. Kanji stood on tiptoe behind them so that he too could see what was going on.

Eventually a boy of 12 was carried up to the doctor by a young farmer in work clothes. The boy started sobbing, terrified, as soon as he realized what was happening. Paying no heed to his cries the doctor sat crosslegged on his cushion and calmly examined the boy's left arm. It was broken above the elbow and dangled uselessly. 'You hold him here,' he directed the farmer, pointing to the boy's chin. Hesitantly the farmer moved behind the boy and took hold of his chin.

'Hold on tight,' the doctor ordered. He put his foot against the boy's abdomen, grabbed the broken arm with both hands, and started to pull. They boy burst into tears, screaming in pain. The doctor stopped pulling.

'You must be his brother,' the doctor said to the farmer. 'Might as well let go. This isn't going to work.' Out of sympathy for his sibling the farmer was unable to grasp the shrieking boy tightly, and the more the boy cried the looser his grip became. The doctor decided to send for one of the young men who lived nearby. The farmer sat sheepishly on the floor, his face drained of color.

'He fall out of a tree?' the doctor asked.

'That's right,' the farmer replied. 'I got upset and brought him here right away. I'd been working in the fields and didn't even stop to change my clothes. It was a persimmon tree. I came running when he fell. He was lying there all pale, but I got his color back a little. Then he started crying. I tried to lift him up, but he kept screaming that it hurt. So I pushed up his sleeve and there was his arm just dangling like that. I couldn't believe it.'

'It happens almost every day, doesn't it,' an old woman sitting nearby remarked. 'People fall out of trees and end up here. When children get hurt that's usually the reason. Having a boy is nothing but trouble! Still, anybody can have an accident. One little mistake, and that's it. Me, I fell over putting on my clogs and broke my wrist just like that.'

'But he's good at climbing persimmon trees,' the farmer went on. 'Climbs 'em all the time, except just after the rain. Too slippery then. But it hadn't been raining. I think he saw a snake on the branch he was holding and got scared. There was this funny sound just before he fell, and the next thing I knew he was lying on the ground.'

Kanji was listening intently, alarm in his eyes.

'When snakes climb trees it usually means rain is on the way,' a patient chimed in from across the room. 'Just when us farmers have a lot of work to do! I sure hope this good weather holds for a bit longer.'

At last the young man the doctor had summoned arrived and took hold of the boy's chin. As before the doctor yanked on the broken arm. There was a frightening crack.

'That should do it,' the doctor announced, letting go of the arm. He rubbed the skin for a while with his thick, soft-looking fingers, then stuck on a strip of paper smeared with medicine. With some thin strips of wood as a splint he applied a bandage.

'How long will it take to heal?' the farmer asked anxiously.

'Won't be quick,' was the doctor's curt reply. The farmer, his face still pale, took the boy up on his back and left. After a few more patients, finally it was Kanji's turn.

'You've taken mighty good care of this, haven't you?' the doctor muttered as he removed the towelling Kanji had wrapped around his elbow and examined his wound. The blow from the iron fire tongs had left a welt a few inches long.

'What happened here? You have a fight with your wife?' The doctor had picked up a free and easy manner of talking from the farmers he treated every day, and it was not unusual for jokes to burst forth from his burly frame.

Kanji forced a smile and said, 'It couldn't be that. My wife died on me about seven or eight years ago.'

'Is that so? Well, somebody hit you, that's clear. You're not so old. Maybe you were trying to make it with someone, is that it?' The doctor stroked his mustache as he spoke. That Kanji had put such an elaborate bandage on such a minor wound brought a derisive smile to his lips.

'You're joking, sir. Our Grampa hit me,' Kanji said in a rush, as if revealing a painful secret.

The doctor said nothing more as he applied a little medicine and a simple bandage.

'Do I have to come again?' Kanji asked with a worried look on his face.

'Just put some of this on it, and it will heal up fine,' the doctor replied, handing Kanji a packet of medicine. 'You can manage it by yourself.'

Ever since he had arrived at the doctor's house Kanji had felt uncomfortable. He had never imagined there could be so many injured people in one place. Now as he made his way back from the shade of the woodbine tree to the bamboo fence he was swept by a feeling of release. Recalling the boy with the broken arm, he thought uneasily of Yokichi's interest in the persimmon tree in the yard at home and hurried off as fast as his legs would carry him.

When he passed by the farmers he had seen that morning and saw them still at work the resentment he had forgotten briefly welled up inside him. He had been relieved to hear the doctor say his injury was not serious, but now with each step he became more and more unhappy with that diagnosis. He was going to treat his injury as serious when he got home, and that was that.

The sun was poised to set when he arrived back in the village. Unable to keep quiet any longer about what had happened to him he made straight for South Neighbor's. As soon as he encountered the head of the house he announced in as matter of fact a tone as he could muster, 'Grampa hit me with his fire tongs, and I've just been to see the doctor. With all the work I have to do these days, he couldn't have picked a worse time.'

South Neighbor had thought it strange that Kanji was got up in leggings and sandals. He knew he had to say something in reply to such a direct statement. 'My goodness, Kanji,' he said, trying to sound surprised. 'What made him do that?'

'When I came back from the fields yesterday he was feeding the chickens. I took a look and saw he was giving 'em some of the grain he had put by for food. There was rice mixed in it! I told him he couldn't give 'em that! I've got special feed for the chickens. You give 'em that, I said. Well then, all of a sudden he hauled off and let me have it with his tongs. Said I couldn't stand to have the birds eat anything decent same as I resented him having food. Can you imagine that! He caught me off guard and sent me sprawling. Didn't have a chance to get away, and that's how I got hurt like this. Right when there's all the planting to be done, and who knows how long it'll take to heal up. Well, I had no choice but to go off to the bone doctor's this morning. All that way, and then there were so many other people I had to wait a long time. I meant to make a quick trip, but look how late it is! The days sure have gotten short, haven't they?' At long last Kanji had been able to unburden himself.

'And the wound will heal up okay?' South Neighbor felt obliged to ask.

'Well, I hope so,' Kanji answered hesitantly.

South Neighbor had not been paying close attention and did not catch the uncertainty in Kanji's reply. 'And how's Grandfather?' he asked.

'I left first thing this morning and haven't been back yet, so I wouldn't know,' Kanji replied, his voice gradually growing louder as he spoke. 'But he can't be very pleased with himself, can he? He can't be feeling good after the awful thing he did, wounding me like that!'

'Well, look now, if that's how you feel, I suppose I'd better go and talk to him and see if I can patch things up. You can't really mean what you said, putting all the blame on him. You just don't go around blaming parents, you know. That's really too much.'

A little while later South Neighbor appeared at the door of Uhei's hut. 'I feel a little awkward about this, but Kanji asked me to come,' he began. 'It's about what happened last night. Kanji's willing to let it pass, I think. You two don't need to make it up formally or anything, but well, how about forgetting all about it and trying to get along? After all you're family, and you can't let a little thing like this break things up. Well, how about it?' Trying to be a peacemaker, South Neighbor spoke as gently but as frankly as he could.

Uhei was silent for a moment. Taking his pipe from his mouth and holding it in a hand that trembled slightly he said, 'Not a chance. That swine, he treats me like dirt. He couldn't bear giving me food, so I had to go out and get my own. You know, if he can't

stand me, he's the one should leave. He came to this house after I
did, you know.'

'I can see you're angry,' South Neighbor broke in, 'but like I said
before you're family. Don't just look at the bad side, there's good
things too. Won't you let me fix things up?'

'What good things?' Uhei grumbled. 'I've kept quiet about it, so
no one around here knows, but for a while Kanji hasn't even had
any bean paste on hand, not a bit. We were going to make some the
end of last year, you know, and I bought some salt with the money
I earned. I can't chew anything tough anymore, so without bean
paste I'm in a bad way. Matter of fact, I've always liked it, ever
since I was young. Now I need it to keep up my strength. Not
having any has been rough, I can tell you. But he hasn't made any,
even though he had all the things he needed, just had to mix the
malt with that salt I bought and boil up the beans. Nothing to it.
You know what? He's hoping I'll die. He's just waiting for the day.
And he may not have long to wait.' Uhei paused a moment and
then grumbled, 'I hit him because I've had all I can take from him,
that's why.'

'I see,' South Neighbor said, feeling awkward. 'I certainly didn't
know about your problem. We may be close neighbors, but then we
don't go poking into each other's cooking pots, do we? That wasn't
right, what Kanji did. You're the father of the house, after all. If
you like bean paste he should make some for you. It's simple
enough. Tell you what, I'll see that he does it. Then you'll feel good
again and there'll be no more trouble between you. You know,
when you two don't get on it's the kids who suffer the most. How
about it now? I'd hate to have to bring the Master into this, so let's
settle it ourselves, okay?'

Uhei put his pipe back into his mouth and said nothing. South
Neighbor went and fetched Kanji. Ordinarily Kanji would not have
been interested in a reconciliation, but Uhei's violence had
frightened him.

'Well now, you two need to work this out,' South Neighbor
announced. 'Maybe you were too busy, Kanji, but you've got to
make some bean paste straight away. Then everything will be okay,
and you two will get along fine. No more trouble at all. Isn't that
right, Father?'

Kanji stood dejectedly, his head bowed. Uhei refused to look at
him. Then he stiffened slightly. 'You can go to blazes!' he growled
at Kanji. 'You stingy swine!'

South Neighbor decided it was time for him to leave. He knew
from past experience that if he got too deeply involved in a family
quarrel both parties could end up holding a grudge against him.

'Well, I guess that's that,' he said as he started to return home. 'I'm sorry I couldn't be of help.'

Kanji had looked in vain for a little sympathy from the doctor and from South Neighbor. But the doctor could see how trivial his wound was and had done nothing but tease him. Nor had South Neighbor felt moved to comfort him. Instead he had stepped in to try to resolve his dispute with Uhei. That was not what Kanji had wanted, but it was all he got.

None of the other farmers seemed able to understand what he wanted either. For several days he idled about, his arm elaborately bandaged, but everybody was too busy with planting to stop to talk to him. Indeed they thought he was a fool not to be working at this time of year and made snide comments about him behind his back. Finally Kanji himself realized that he was courting disaster by not getting his crop in and went back to work. He said nothing at all to Uhei, and Uhei, sullen as ever, paid no attention to him. Although their behavior upset Otsugi she knew she could do nothing about it.

Eventually news of Kanji's clash with Uhei spread through the village, but only those who were parents or grandparents took special note of it. Realizing that there was no simple solution to the long-standing conflict between the two men, they were unwilling to intervene. The young men who had been so exercised about the way Kanji treated Otsugi paid no attention to the incident at all.

22

It was a while before dawn and the farmers lay shivering in their bedding, thin quilts pulled up over their chins. The clanging of the bells reverberated through the air, summoning the old people of the village to the prayer hall. They got up quietly so as not to disturb their families, slipped into their padded kimonos, and with a shudder stepped out into the cold. Some picked up a bundle of faggots from the pile outside their door as they made their way clumsily through the semi-darkness. It was time for the *Tennenbutsu*, the chanting ceremony in praise of the sun, that was held each year in mid-February according to the old calendar.

The chanting was supposed to begin the moment the sun rose over the horizon, and two old men from the congregation had been selected to see to it that everyone else assembled in time. They stood at the crossroads striking with all their might the bells they held in their icy hands. The sliding doors of the hall had been removed and a fire lit in the hearth to stave off the biting cold. An iron kettle hung from a pothook over the flames. The old people milled about, clearing their throats. Finally they heard the crowing of the second cock. The time had come. The two men in charge took up their drums by the open doorway. Everyone else sat down behind them and began chanting to the slow rhythm of the drumbeats, their aged voices rising and then sinking as the drummers beat loudly and softly in turn. Again and again the chant was repeated until first the distant trees and then the nearby trees became clearly visible and the eastern sky deepened in color like a ripening tangerine. The chanting voices of the old people grew more distinct as all about them became light. Frost gleamed white on the ground, and the paper covering the sun altar in the prayer hall yard shone red and blue. A stalk of green bamboo rose from the center of the altar, its tip adorned with colored paper streamers. Around the altar stood four or more bamboo stalks which were linked by ropes from which hung colored strips of paper that fluttered in the breeze.

163

In the old days the altar had been made of fine wooden pillars such as those used inside houses, but that had been lost when the hall was destroyed in a violent storm. Many houses in the village had been destroyed as well, and for a time no one gave any thought to rebuilding the virtually useless hall. Some people who were too poor to pay for cutting timber in the forests began taking boards away on the sly. Finally the present hall, a much reduced version of the old one, was reconstructed. At the same time a crude altar was fashioned from sawn boards. Even though the new hall was cramped the old people were happy to have a place of their own again where they could contemplate the boundless pleasure and comfort that awaited them after death.

When the chanting ended the old people gathered around the hearth. Soon they could hear the sliding doors of the nearby farmhouses clattering open and the frantic clucking of chickens. Blue smoke rose from every roof. It was time to return home to eat.

When Uhei reached his yard Kanji and Otsugi had already left to work on the plot of land they were clearing. Uhei stood still, staring at the empty, shuttered house. Decrepit though it was, there always seemed to be a little life to it when voices could be heard within. Now it appeared utterly forlorn. Kanji had got up right after Uhei's departure and lit the fire in the stove. While Otsugi made breakfast he quickly donned his work clothes. It was a long walk to the field he was reclaiming that year, and as the area was greater than the fields he had worked on in past years he knew there was no time to waste. They set off every morning as early as possible, Otsugi with the cuffs of her trousers bound with straw against the cold.

Uhei moved towards the entrance of the house. The latch was down. He did not bother to try it for he knew that Kanji had as always used the key. He moved to the back door and tried the bolt. It would not budge. Clicking his tongue as was his habit, he slowly made his way to the door of the hut. Inside it was dark, and the bedding he had thrust aside earlier was cold. He lit a fire in the hibachi and noticed the box and the pot nearby. Both were cold. Otsugi had left them for him when she had called him to breakfast and got no response.

Despite his padded kimono Uhei had returned home chilled to the bone, hoping to find some warm food on the stove. It had not occurred to him that the doors would be locked. With a sigh he put the pot on the hibachi. As soon as steam began escaping from the lid he ladled some of the soup out and tasted it. It was still cold. He added a few faggots to the fire and scraped the rice into the pot.

Frowning, he held his hands near the flames to warm them while he waited for the pot to boil.

He looked haggard and wizened; he had lost a lot of weight, and his shoulders sagged. His bones ached with rheumatic pain.

A pungent smell aroused him. He stirred the sizzling pot and began to eat, savoring each mouthful he swallowed. At last he began to feel warm again. As he waited for the kettle to boil he laid his tobacco pouch on his knee. It was empty. He had been short of cash ever since his failing health had forced him to stop working and had decided to give up the tobacco he loved so much. He had promised the Buddha he would do it the next day and prayed for recovery from his illness in return. Then he had spent virtually the entire day smoking up the remainder of his tobacco. He had even turned the pouch upside down and tapped out the last few shreds. Thereafter he regretted his decision to stop smoking, and his hand kept reaching for his pipe. At the same time he was reluctant to break his vow so soon. He tried smoking dried mulberry leaves and butterbur leaves, but unlike tobacco both burned up instantly and sent acrid smoke into his mouth. Next he tried the grape leaves someone had recommended, but he did not like them either. In frustration he stamped his pipe to pieces beneath his feet. The pouch, however, he could not bear to part with. He put the few coins he had left inside it and tucked it into his sash. That had been some time ago, but even now he would forget and reach for the useless pouch.

At last the sun shone directly into the yard. Uhei slowly made his way back to the prayer hall following a narrow path that ran east beside the rice paddies. To his right were scattered plots of mulberry trees. The sun had melted the frost on the southern side of the furrows, but all he saw as he walked along was endless white.

That afternoon every household in the village brought an offering of colored rice cakes or other food to the prayer hall, which the old people arranged in front of the shrine. When a veritable mountain of offerings had accumulated the drums sounded again and part of the food was distributed to the children who had gathered in the yard. Then the old people themselves sat down to eat and drink sake, enjoying a rare opportunity to satisfy their hunger. Only Uhei did not drink anything. He left before the others, taking with him the box that had contained his own family's offering. In it had been a little rice mixed with red beans, the only thing Otsugi had had time to prepare.

On this first of two days of revelry Uhei had felt uncomfortable and unhappy. 'I'm sorry about the cold food I left you this morning, Grampa,' Otsugi told him that night. 'I forgot you were going out, but I bet you had lots of fun and lots of good things to eat down at the prayer hall.' Somehow her gentle tone cheered him up.

23

The chanting was repeated at dawn the next day, and more boxes and parcels of food were delivered to the prayer hall. The yard swarmed with children, some with school bags on their backs, others carrying the infant brothers or sisters they were caring for.

'All right now, everybody inside!' an old woman announced, and the children scrambled to find seats in the hall. Several old women were whispering among themselves as they opened the offerings that were piled before the shrine.

'Well, can you imagine! Look, this one is full of sushi!'

'Better put it aside.'

'Let's put this one aside, too.' As they worked they slipped three or four parcels behind the shrine.

Meanwhile another old woman told the children, 'Be quiet now, everyone, or you won't get a thing.'

'Let's not give anything to the ones with runny noses, either,' yet another woman teased. At that all the children sniffled and hastily wiped their noses on the sleeves of their kimono. A sheet of white paper was placed in front of each child, and extra pieces were laid out to be put in the emptied food boxes before they were returned to their donors.

As the women began distributing the food a voice bellowed at them, 'Don't touch that food with those hands you been wiping your own noses with!' It was an old man sitting by the hearth who spoke. He wore a double strand of rosary beads around his neck. Despite his slight build he had a very powerful voice.

'My, my, I suppose we should wash.'

'Well, I don't wipe my nose that way!'

After dipping their hands in water and wiping them on their aprons the women went back to distributing the food. Up and down the room they moved, placing a bit at a time from the boxes they carried on the paper before each child. The rice with red beans had been made from inferior ingredients and tended to crumble when it was served out, but the children were still delighted as the pieces accumulated, each one a slightly different shade of red. If a piece rolled off the paper they hurriedly replaced it. There were cakes, too, but unlike yesterday's these were made of pounded millet, not rice. Seeing them pile up also delighted the children. The women kept bumping into one another as they made their way around the crowded hall. Laughing and chattering among themselves they lost all traces of the self-restraint they displayed in their own homes.

'That's the end!' they announced as they stood up and tapped on the bottom of the empty boxes. The children hastily wrapped up their food and dashed for the doors. There was a great tumult of shouting and wailing as some slipped and dropped their precious parcels. Then all settled down in the yard to eat, pinching up bits of food in their fingers. In no time the ground was littered with discarded paper.

Most of the old people now sat around the hearth, stoking the fire in preparation for heating up some sake. The gallon barrel that someone had donated lay nearby. A woman poured some sake from the barrel into an old earthen teapot and hung it over the fire. It was dark inside the hall now that a few of the sliding doors had been closed to keep out the cold. Several old women were clustered by the Buddhist shrine.

'Stop stealing, you old hags!' the slightly built man with the rosary bellowed. 'You bring those goodies over here!'

'Nonsense! We haven't taken a bit. Just got the wrapping off in fact.' So saying the women brought the box over to the hearth. Arranged inside were pieces of *inarizushi*, each rice-filled bag of fried bean curd tied up with a strip of *kanpyō*. It was clear that a few pieces were missing.

'It's not right to eat sushi alone,' the old man teased.

'We weren't alone. There were at least three of us!' one woman retorted.

'And besides, you'll drink more of that sake than we will,' said another.

'Let's just see how the sake is doing,' the slightly built old man muttered as he held his hand against the teapot. 'Ouch!' he cried out, 'it must be boiling.' As he set the pot down on the *tatami* matting he added, 'Me, I don't want any sushi myself. You fill yourself with that, then the sake tastes bad.'

Everyone sat down in a line. Cups were set before them, as were the sushi and the boxes of boiled potatoes, burdocks, carrots, and other vegetables that had been donated. There were no tables or trays. The slightly built old man poured some sake from the teapot into the little serving bottle and returned the pot to its hook. 'Ugh!' he exclaimed as he raised his cup to his lips. 'This smells burned. Sake's just like tea. It picks up bad smells easily.'

'Well, what did you expect?' someone piped up. 'There was too little in the pot, so it got burned. Put more in next time.'

'I'll pour in a lot this time,' one of the women said, reaching for the teapot. 'I don't do much drinking, so you'll have to excuse my mistake.'

'You'd better rinse out the pot with water in between.'

'Why don't you just warm up the serving bottles in the kettle instead?'

'Such good sake, it's a shame to ruin it.'

Everyone was speaking at once.

'What a lot of bother that would be,' the old woman muttered as she hung the iron kettle back on the fire. 'We could only heat up a tiny bit at a go.'

By the time the barrel was empty everyone who had been drinking was thoroughly intoxicated and talking noisily.

Uhei sat solemnly by the hearth. Missing his pipe, he fidgeted with the faggots and clicked his tongue against his gums. He had drunk nothing but had concentrated on eating his fill of sushi and vegetables. No one paid the slightest attention to him, but he did not mind. On the contrary, he felt better than in a long while now that he had eaten so well.

The revelers began to dance, staggering to and fro to the unsteady beating of the drums. Slowly they made their way out into the yard, tottering this way and that and carousing all the while as if an entire year's worth of pent-up laughter was suddenly being released. Whenever one of them stumbled the others piled up behind, stepping on their neighbor's feet as they tried to press forward. Their cheeks were flushed bright red, making them appear almost young again. This was the one time of year, the time of the sun chanting, when they could let go and forget they were old, neglected, bored. Gone was their usual reserve. Like a breath of spring the sake had woken them from their long winter's sleep and given them renewed life. The paper streamers on the rope around the sun altar fluttered in accompaniment to their merry-making. The sun shone bright and warm. Here and there in the yard stood clusters of children and adults, watching in amusement.

Only Uhei did not join in the festivities. He sat in the now empty hall not noticing that the fire in the hearth had burned to ashes. The raucous voices from the yard seemed far away. Yokichi spotted him from outside where he had been standing watching and approached.

'Don't you have something for me, Grampa?' he said.

Although Uhei heard Yokichi's voice, for a while he did not respond.

A short time previously, just after the vernal equinox, the west wind that usually blew only at dusk had descended on the region with a vengeance, raging for days on end. It was reported that the shallows of the Kinu River had frozen. Uhei had felt chilled to the bone. Suddenly he had noticed that he had lost the use of his fingers. Every muscle in them felt stiff and if he tried to make rope or straw his fingers would throb with pain. Yokichi's visits to his little hut no longer brought him pleasure, although he remained fond of the little boy.

'I'll have something for you tomorrow,' he would reply to the boy's requests, not wanting to refuse him outright. After a time Yokichi became so dejected that Uhei could bear it no longer. He gave him a 1-*sen* coin, twice the amount he usually gave. Yokichi, who had been afraid he might be rebuffed yet again, was absolutely delighted.

Unless one has completely forsaken the world it is painful to realize that one's days are numbered. The old people might find things to laugh and joke about, but not one of them could forget that death approached. Uhei could think of little else.

After his fingers had failed him he had reached for the parcel he had brought with him from Noda and taken out his brightly patterned *yukata*. Pieced together from the towels he had received from time to time from his employer, the garment had once been his pride and joy. Now he pawned it and all his other valuable possessions. Outside the warm sun was melting the ice in the river, but Uhei gained no solace. He had no hope that his frozen fingers too would thaw. He got very little for the contents of his parcel, but it was enough to buy a little of the soft food he craved every now and then. Some of the remainder fell into Yokichi's tiny hands. From time to time Uhei would peer into his tobacco pouch where he kept his money, anxiously looking for the reassuring glint of the few silver coins among the copper. No matter how it pained him, though, there was nothing he could do to prevent the contents of the pouch from dwindling. He sank into a deep depression, and in that same depressed state he now sat by the hearth of the prayer hall.

The others staggered in from the yard, disrupting his solitude. The barrel of sake they had chipped in to buy was opened and the serving bottle put in the kettle to warm. The drinkers sat down nearby. Silently Uhei threw a 5-*rin* coin toward Yokichi, who lingered a few feet away. When one of the old men playfully reached for the coin Yokichi pounced on it and snatched it up.

'Can't I have one more, Grampa?' he begged. Now that he had got used to receiving 1-*sen* coins he felt vaguely dissatisfied with only 5 *rin*.

Uhei said nothing.

'What a thing to ask!' the slightly built old man with the rosary snapped. 'You've already had plenty to eat. You want me to open up your belly and scrape out that rice and red beans so you have room for more? Just look at you! You've done so much eating you've got sores around your mouth.' After a pause he yelled, 'You want money — go get it from your papa!'

'He won't give me any,' Yokichi mumbled.

'Well, that's because he's deaf and doesn't hear you asking. You try yelling at him in a big voice like mine. Then if he doesn't come across, you box his ears.'

'But he'd beat me up if I did that.'

'Useless brat, why don't you go away? We don't need you around here.'

Dejectedly Yokichi retreated. 'Here you go,' Uhei muttered and tossed another 5-*rin* coin after him into the yard.

Meanwhile some of the old women closed a few more of the sliding doors and sat down in the shadows in front of the shrine. Within moments they were joined by some of the younger village wives who had been waiting outside. Now ten in number and sheltered from the prying eyes of passersby they were going to indulge in a few rounds of 'drawing for treasure', their favorite game.

Eight strips of waste fabric lay in the center of the circle they formed. Before each player lay 2 *sen*'s worth of coins. The first dealer gathered up the strips, wound them tightly around her fingers and tossed them onto the *tatami* matting. Everyone else grabbed for the end of a strip and, if successful, began reeling it in. Whoever reeled in the only strip with several tiny 1-*rin* pieces tied to the end was the winner. She collected a coin from each of the others and dealt the next round.

The women played intently, their hands moving swiftly as they bent forward in unison and their faces reflecting their delight or disappointment at each outcome. Had they not been afraid of being discovered at an illegal pastime they would have been yelling and screaming.

There were fewer old people in the hall now that the dancing had ended and those who did not want to gamble or drink had gone home. The women who had joined the men at the hearth for more sake were all thoroughly tipsy.

171

'Hey now, you used to like me when I was young, didn't you?' one of them mused as she leaned on the neighboring man's shoulder.

'Let's have none of that!' the old man with the rosary roared from nearby. 'I was pretty wild in my time, but I didn't chase women!'

'No need to get huffy,' the woman retorted. 'What do you expect at a sake party?' Then she broke into laughter. 'You want some?' she asked, holding out a cup to Uhei. As yet he had had nothing to drink and had remained lost in his own thoughts, oblivious to the noise around him. Attention now focused on him.

'I don't drink anymore,' he muttered.

'Oh come on,' the old man with the rosary urged, holding out a cup. 'Don't just sit there moping. Have a little and cheer up.'

'No, I've quit. Gave up my pipe too because it was bad for me. And I don't have the money for drinking. If I have a little I'll just want more, so the best thing is not to touch it. Sake costs too much these days.' Uhei spoke in a matter-of-fact tone.

The old man emptied his cup in one gulp and yelled, 'Don't talk such boring nonsense!'

'You have some now,' one of the women coaxed. 'It's special sake for the sun chanting, so it'll make you feel good. A little bit will cure you.'

'That's right, you quit all that brooding,' another woman added. 'Brooding isn't going to stop all the trouble you have with Kanji.'

'It's all that brooding that caused his rheumatism, if you ask me.' The old man spoke with such gusto that the rosary around his neck trembled. 'But the cure is easy. Just rub yourself down with a snake. I'll do it for you if you want.'

'I don't like snakes,' Uhei said with a grimace.

'Afraid of snakes! I suppose that proves what they say about you big men. Me, I'm not the least bit afraid of 'em. Look,' he said as he staggered to his feet, 'this is what you do.' He bared his back and with a towel stretched between his hands he started rubbing it.

'I'd been suffering from rheumatism for eight or nine years when I heard about this cure and decided to give it a try. I was going to knock this big snake down from the persimmon tree I saw it dangling from, but the old woman said to leave it alone. So I just sneaked up later and grabbed it when she wasn't around, and then rubbed myself down with it like this. Cured me straight away, it did!'

'Those are big moxa scars you have there,' one of the old women exclaimed, pointing to his back.

'Yup, I burned three hundred sticks there once because I had the

172

runs so bad I couldn't sleep. Even kids know better today, but dysentery was a big problem when I was young. You must remember that big epidemic we had, Uhei. I was going to the privy sixteen times a day I was so sick. The whole village was sick, and some people died of it. I was the only one strong enough to go for the doctor. I finally got better after two weeks, and that's only because I was strong to start with. I drank a whole bottle of sake every day, I did. The doctor said it was bad for me and gave me some sort of herbs instead. I made a tea with 'em and drank five bowls at a time. Had to hold my breath while I did it because it tasted so bad.' The old man wiped the sweat from his face. Although he was past 70 he did not have a single gray hair on his head and his flesh remained lean and taught.

'Once I ate up this big gamecock I'd caught and got an awful fever,' he continued. 'But I was strong and got over it in a couple of weeks. Went right out and hulled about four bushels of barley. I may be small, but I was strong through and through. Uhei, now, he was strong working, but otherwise he was a weakling. When he got dysentery that time he just lay around moaning. Scared to death, he was. I said he was worried his wife was going to get him. Me, I hate worrying, so stop your worrying and have a drink.'

'That's right, we don't want anyone moping around,' an old woman said as she offered Uhei a cup.

Another women offered him a cup as well. 'You'll get drunk right away from sake a woman gives you. Just try this and see.' It was not that they wanted to cheer him up. They were making fun of him for behaving strangely and trying to get him to do what they were doing.

'I can't pay my share,' Uhei mumbled.

'No need to worry about that,' the old woman next to him said.

'We've got money over here if you need it,' called one of the women playing 'drawing for treasure'.

'We don't want any of that money!' the slightly built old man yelled back. 'I hate gambling and everything to do with it.'

'I don't have any money left,' Uhei muttered, as if revealing something he had kept pent up inside of him.

'So what?' the slightly built old man responded. 'Kanji's got a thick purse these days, so if you need any you just tell him to hand it over. Or just take it. That's what I'd do. Letting a son-in-law lord it over you! That's what I mean when I say you're really a weakling.'

'Nobody's lording it over me.' Uhei protested. 'I just want to be on my own.'

'Some son-in-law he is too! Everybody knows he's a thief. Got to keep a sharp lookout all the time, or he'll run off with your crops.'

'That's not why he has money now,' Uhei grumbled.

'Now, don't get upset. I was just remembering the time he cut our sorghum. I was against letting him off that time, but I had to give in because the Mistress was there. If I was you, though, I'd make him toe the line. Be tough with him, like I am with my son. You know, he had the nerve to complain about having to get up at dawn on New Year's and eat roast potatoes by the hearth, but my family's been doing that for as long as I can remember, and as long as I'm around they're going to keep on doing it.'

'Well, you're his father so you can have your own way. It's not like that with me and Kanji,' Uhei muttered.

'And you're a fine one to talk about toeing the line!' one of the old women added. She was better dressed than the others. 'All that trouble you caused when you were young, coming home drunk all the time in the wee hours and practically knocking the doors down. Then having the nerve to yell at your family when the hot water to wash down your horse wasn't ready. Farmers can't live like that, not getting any sleep. You're lucky you produced a good heir.'

'But I made out fine because I was strong. Uhei was no match for me in wrestling, big as he was. And it wasn't just my arms. My teeth were strong, too. I could chew up a peach in one gulp, pit and all. Once I even bit a brass pipe in two. My teeth are still as good as ever. Just look! And what's more, I never lost a fight. I could knock anybody down and then twist his neck like this so he couldn't get up. Anyway, the Master saw to it I didn't have any more trouble with my family. He kind of took me in hand and straightened me out. I owe him a lot, I really do.' The old man was quiet for a moment, his head hanging. Then he raised his cup above his head, drained the sake into his mouth and swallowed it in one gulp.

Just at that moment one of the village wives rushed in from outside. 'The patrolman is coming!' she hissed to the women by the shrine. They froze at her words and then began scooping up all the fabric strips and coins before them.

'Let's just see if we can join this nice, happy group here,' one of them said as she moved to the hearth.

'If we let that bunch in they'll try to get *us* gambling,' the old man with the rosary grumbled.

'Oh, don't you treat us like a nuisance,' one of the women said. 'We may be old, but our families still need us. Why, that daughter-in-law of mine doesn't know how to do anything.' Holding a cup of sake to Uhei she added, 'We're going to pay for more sake out of the kitty so why don't you stop being so glum and have a drink?

Uhei finally yielded and took the cup in his hand.

'That's better!' the old man exclaimed. 'You drink that up so you can deal with Kanji. He's a bad one, that's for sure. Just like an animal.'

'Really now, you've got no proof about all that. It's just talk,' the well-dressed woman reproached him.

'It's a fact, though. I don't tell lies. And that girl is no good neither. You know, I asked her a while back if she ever thought about her mother, and she told me she never did. Can you believe it?'

'Now, that's not fair,' Uhei broke in. 'She's really good to me. She just said that because she's tired of everybody teasing her. There's no crime in that. She's had a rough time, but she still remembers her mama.' Uhei emptied his cup and added sadly, 'It wasn't just her and Kanji who suffered when Shina died. I cried too. I'd raised her since she was 3, you know.'

'Yes, her dying was bad luck for you too, wasn't it,' one of the old women murmured. 'But even so you've managed to live to a ripe old age.'

'Maybe so, but I've got so weak I can't earn any money. Had to pawn the clothes I brought with me from Noda. I bet I don't last until summer, but I don't care. Not at all.' Uhei spoke in a monotone and downed cup after cup of sake.

'It's sad about the girl,' one of the women mused. 'She's all grown up and still no husband.'

'She's not my real grandchild, and I don't know what Kanji's planning for her,' Uhei grumbled.

'Well, someone has to talk to him. If he'd only agree it's time to send her off, there'd be no problem finding her a husband.'

'There's no one can convince him of that!' a woman replied.

'How about the Master?' someone asked. 'I bet he could manage it.'

Uhei's cheeks were finally flushed red. He looked pleased with the suggestion. 'The Master could make her a good match, I'm sure of it. I thought of it myself a while back, but somehow I don't feel right bringing it up.'

'What you really ought to do,' the slightly built old man yelled, 'is bash Kanji one.'

'I did that a couple of months ago,' Uhei replied cheerfully. 'Knocked him down with my fire tongs.'

'That's the way! And if he doesn't give you what you want you just take it.'

'After I knocked him down he went out and bought a barrel of

175

bean paste,' Uhei added proudly. 'It was poor stuff, made with wheat bran, but now I can have soup whenever I want.'

'Him being stingy with food, and you're bragging about that? I'd kill him if I was you, that's what I'd do. It's a crime not to give parents all the food they want, so you'd be in the right.'

'He hasn't said a word to me since then,' Uhei muttered.

'Won't talk, eh? You just grab him like this then. That'll get his mouth working again.' When the slightly built old man pulled his lips wide apart with his fingers everyone burst into laughter. Even Uhei joined in.

There was a slight spring to his step as he made his way home that night and sat down in front of the hibachi. He felt better than he had in a long while.

'Bring me some rice and barley, Otsū!' he yelled all of a sudden. 'And make it quick.'

'What ever's got into you, Grampa?' Otsugi did not take him seriously.

He glowered at her.

'Well, I'll make some tomorrow if you still want it. It's really too late now, isn't it?'

Uhei said nothing more. By the next morning the effects of the sake had worn off and he was himself again.

24

Uhei had never been a troublemaker. Despite his burly frame and stern appearance he had always behaved rather timidly. He had even had a soft spot for women.

One of the things that people remembered about him as a young man was that he seemed too easy-going about work. The other was his fastidiousness. He would always put a fresh towel, kimono and sash in his saddlebag when he went off on horseback to cut grass for someone. He would tie his horse up in the forest, change clothes and go off wandering for a while, but he would always come back in time to do the work expected of him. Nothing else about him stood out in people's memories.

His strength and ability earned him a good income, and since he remained a bachelor until the rather late age of 30 he was able to spend his money on himself.

It was during these years that he contracted syphilis. For a time he was very ill, but the symptoms eventually subsided. Quite naturally he assumed that he was cured and soon he took a wife. She became pregnant right away, but the fetus died and emerged rotten from her womb. It was what everyone in those days called a 'poxed baby'. Two or three more children died in early infancy. That they too were called 'poxed babies' did not mean people understood they had died from the germs still carried by their father, nor that there was anything to fear from future pregnancies.

Oshina's mother was a poverty-stricken widow who barely managed to sustain herself and her toddler of a daughter. Even if she had been more skilled at farming than she was, she would have been hard put to make ends meet on her own. Her plight aroused Uhei's sympathy, and a certain softness in her manner attracted him. Eventually the two grew close.

At the time Uhei's wife was ill with the disease that ultimately would kill her. Toward the end of a pregnancy a few years previously her belly had begun to swell dramatically. After a few days

177

she had found she could no longer bear even to lie on her side and had leaned against the piled up bedding instead, barely breathing. She had been suffering from an excessive build-up of amniotic fluid. At the time not even doctors could do anything about that. Nor had Uhei even considered summoning one. Fortunately the water had broken free of its own accord at last. Several quarts had come gushing out, inundating the matting on which the frightened woman had collapsed. Having lost its haven the fetus had begun coming out too. It was, of course, dead. Only a tiny hand had emerged from the womb.

Uhei's wife had by then been thoroughly exhausted. At her urging Uhei had wrested the fetus from her body. That cruel task had been his to perform because they lacked the money to pay for another person's help.

She had not died right away but had lingered on for about three years, her body racked with pain and fever. Only rarely, when the weather was especially warm, had she left her bedding to hobble outside into the dazzling sunlight.

Eventually the gossip about Uhei's relationship with Oshina's mother reached her ears. It may also have been because of the heat wave that descended about then, but she went into an immediate decline. Uhei was not by her pillow when she died. A few cases of dysentery had broken out in the village a short time before, but even so everyone had gathered for a funeral and without the slightest anxiety had taken a meal together afterwards. As a result the disease spread rapidly. Uhei, who numbered among its victims, had dragged himself to Oshina's house and placed himself in her mother's care. He simply could not bear to go to his dying wife's side, for the thought of seeing the pain and fear in her eyes was too much for him. She died in agony, unaware that he was ill. Uhei cried when he heard the news. Only close relatives and neighbors went to the funeral. Uhei was there too, leaning on a stick.

The epidemic had subsided by the time of the *Bon* festival that autumn, but there were also more departed souls to be greeted. Here and there in the graveyard lay the crudely made platforms on which coffins had been carried. As was the custom then, towards evening on the sixth day of the month people went to cut down weeds around the graves. Like Uhei, most of them had barely recovered from the dysentery that had laid them low.

Uhei held his sickle loosely in his still feeble hand and swept the blade under the platform on his wife's grave. Suddenly he shuddered and pulled his hand away. A snake lay belly up at his feet, its flesh gashed by his sickle. For a moment the snake remained motionless. Then, very slowly, it slithered back under the platform.

Uhei's face was pale in the gathering dusk. He stayed at home for a time after that, trying to get his strength back. Even the slightest exertion exhausted him, and at night he was drenched in sweat.

On the eighth day of the month when the villagers carried paper lanterns to the graveyard to welcome the spirits of the dead, the weeds they had cut just two days earlier had sprouted up again. Out of curiosity they gingerly lifted the platform on the grave of Uhei's wife. The snake was still lying there. After they had gone home the smoke from the incense burners they had lit rose fitfully into the lonely twilight as if writhing in agony from the flames below.

Four days later the villagers met again at twilight in the graveyard to see the spirits off. The snake still had not moved from under the platform. Indeed, being wounded, it could not move freely. The flesh around the gash, bloated like a pair of snarling lips, was blackened and covered with dirt. Whenever it sensed that people were looking the snake became frightened and wriggled a little. It's Uhei's wife come back from the grave, people said.

It did not take long for the news about the snake to reach Oshina's mother. Thereafter she insisted that Uhei spend every night at home with her. Oshina was then 3. She soon grew fond of Uhei and bound him to the house forever.

After a time people forgot about the snake, for nothing happened to keep the story alive. When Oshina's mother died years later, only a handful of people vaguely recalled the incident.

It could be said that Uhei had never done evil intentionally. It is true that when he was young he and the other hired hands used to kill and eat the stray cats that went after the village chickens. But that particular part of his past did not get talked about. He did nothing else that could excite the malice or the envy of others in the village, and so he deprived them of the only grounds they had for thinking ill of him. Living in isolation on the western edge of the community he aroused no interest whatsoever. Indeed, taciturn as he was he had virtually no contact with his neighbors. His presence meant nothing to them.

25

For weeks the west wind that had blown from time to time through
the early autumn treetops had lain asleep beyond the distant snow-
covered mountains. Now it awakened, suddenly realizing that
winter would soon be over and its chance to give vent to its powers
ended. Every day the wind raged across the land, sweeping particles
of soil up into the air.

At dawn on this particular day the sky was clear. Frost lay thick
on the trees and on the ground. As usual Kanji went off with Otsugi
to work on the plot of land they were clearing. Otsugi wore a jacket
loosely over her shoulders. The wisps of hair that peeped from
beneath her white kerchief seemed to shiver as she walked.

For a time the snow on the distant mountains sparkled in the
morning sunlight. Soon, however, the mountains were enveloped in
clouds. Every day the clouds came, rising up from behind the
mountains and filling the sky above. Like giants on a rampage they
would swoop down onto the land below, kicking out with their
massive feet at all they encountered. It was almost time for their
assault, almost time for the treetops to cry out in pain.

Tall ungainly oak trees, planted years ago as a source of firewood and charcoal, bordered the path that Kanji and Otsugi
followed. Every winter now, saws cut into the oak's limbs. As if in
fear of what lay in store for them, they held on to their life-giving
leaves long after all the other deciduous trees had shed theirs. Only
after the wood-cutting season had ended and acorns nestled in
shallow cups on their remaining branches did they give in to the
cold and surrender their desiccated foliage. Their fear had disappeared just as thorns disappear from the trunk and branches of a
grafted pear tree that no longer has any need to concern itself with
progeny or self-protection. Whipped by the late winter wind the
fallen oak leaves scurried for whatever cover they could find.

Kanji and Otsugi made their way across the rice paddies, where
snipes dived down into the stubble in search of food. Through the

trees ahead they could see clouds roiling in the sky above the distant mountains. Within moments a crash resounded in their ears. The giants had arrived, borne by the wind.

The west wind came every morning now, savagely ripping leaves from the evergreen trees and grinding them into the slush. All day long it blew, sucking up every bit of moisture and permitting not a drop of rain to fall. Only at night could the soil fight back and acquire another blanket of frost. That too would be melted by the morning sun, and the wind would sweep down to remove every trace. The more violent the wind the thicker the next morning's frost. The thicker the frost the denser the roiling masses of clouds on the mountain peaks and the swifter the wind. Not until winter gave way to spring would the struggle end.

Today the air was already filled with yellowish brown dust that shrouded the landscape like mist. The trees were bent forward as if trying to escape and find sunlight again. Oblivious to the chaos about him, Kanji saw nothing but the mark left by his mattock as it dug deep into the ground a few feet in front of him. His body dripping with sweat, he thrust forward and pulled back, thrust forward and pulled back, raising clumps of soil. Otsugi pounded at the clumps with the back of her rake, breaking them down and smoothing out the soil. She worked diligently, trying to ignore the dirt that flew into her face and whipped through her hair.

Uhei had been finishing his breakfast when Kanji and Otsugi had hurried off to work. He remained sitting by the hibachi. When the west wind struck, causing the dilapidated house to tremble, the embers of the fire were still warm. Soot cascaded from the roof, and the yard was soon aswirl with dust. To the wind-borne giants the ramshackle houses in the villages scattered throughout the plain were as insignificant as mushrooms peeping up through fallen leaves. All day long they trod on them with their massive feet.

Eventually Uhei went back to his hut. Through the partially opened door he could see the soil in the mulberry field beyond the yard rising up into the air like so many twists of paper and disappearing into the yellowish brown cloud of dust. South Neighbor's house would appear faintly and then be lost again to view. Buffeted by the wind, the well bucket seemed about to fall from its hook on a stake by the chestnut tree. Uhei stared at it absentmindedly for a time and then lumbered outside and made it fast. Returning to his hut he shut the door behind him and lay down under his bedding to rest.

At noon Kanji and Otsugi returned home for a hurried meal. Shortly after they left again Yokichi came clattering back from school on his poorly fitting wooden clogs. He wore no socks, and his feet were cracked like sharkskin. The water in the kettle was still slightly warm. Yokichi scooped some rice out of the pot into a bowl, poured on some water, and began eating hungrily. There were some dried fermented soybeans in a soup bowl nearby. He stuffed some of them into his mouth and helped himself to more rice. He had not bothered to sit down. Rice grains tumbled from his bowl onto his chest and scattered onto the dirt floor where he stood. Full at last, he thrust the bowl back onto the tray where he had found it and banged the lid down on the cooking pot. Just at that moment Uhei came in. Otsugi had called him earlier, but he had not felt like getting up.

'How come you're home so early?' he asked.

'Teacher said we could go, seeing as tomorrow's Sunday,' Yokichi answered, sniffling. Two damp red streaks ran from his nostrils to his upper lip.

'You had something to eat?' Uhei moved towards the stove. 'Just look at the mess you made on my tray,' he muttered. 'Your papa sees that, he'll get angry. He's got a temper, your papa has.' Uhei picked up the spilled grains of rice and fermented soybeans and carefully put them into the soup bowl. Otsugi had set out a tray for him before going back to work and put a bowl of dried fermented soybeans on it just for him. Finding them closest to hand, Yokichi had used Uhei's bowls and eaten his beans without a thought.

Uhei lifted the lid of the cooking pot and found the contents cold. The tea kettle was equally disappointing. He did not feel hungry enough to eat, but he did feel cold and his right shoulder throbbed with pain whenever he moved it. It seemed to him as if all his illness had concentrated in that one spot. It never occurred to him it might only be that he had been sleeping on that shoulder. Indeed such a thought could not occur to him, so fixated was he on his illness as the source of all his problems and so contemptuous was he of his failing body. His hands felt slightly numb. Thinking that a hot drink might thaw him out he squatted down in front of the stove and held his palms over the ashes. They were still faintly warm. He took some leaves from the big basket nearby and thrust them under the tea kettle. Yokichi squatted down beside him and threw leaves onto the ashes too. Ashes and leaves scattered about their feet. With a bamboo stick Uhei stirred the ashes, but the leaves would not ignite. He looked around for some matches but could not find any. When Yokichi refused to go to his hut to get some Uhei had to go himself.

So stiff were his hands that by the time he got a match near the fire it had burned out. He had wasted half a dozen matches when

Yokichi reached out for the box. Uhei let him take it and sat down wearily, a frown on his face. Yokichi could only get smoke from the match he struck. In a fret he threw the box at Uhei's feet. It was nearly empty. Still frowning Uhei tried again, carefully cradling the match between his hands as he bent towards the stove. After two or three attempts he finally got a fire going in the leaves. Clumsily he poked at the leaves with a stick to keep the fire going.

Flames lapped out from the mouth of the stove, warming Uhei's hands. He reached for more leaves from the basket and added them to the fire. Yokichi stood beside him and decided it would be fun to start a fire of his own in the other mouth of the stove.

He and his playmates were always starting fires in the dry grass by the pathways. As the flames spread to the nearby wild rose stalks and took hold of the reeds that flourished there they would yell in delight and terror. Finally fear would overtake them, and they would set about extinguishing the flames by pounding them with sticks, throwing dirt on them, or sometimes even by beating them with their clothing. Now Yokichi grabbed some leaves and thrust them into the opening. Meanwhile Uhei heard the kettle boiling. He rose and reached for the tea cup on the tray, but he did not get a good grip on it and it fell to the ground. Slowly he picked it up, cleaned it off, and ladled in some hot water. As he reached to put the lid back on the kettle he suddenly heard the roar of flames. Yokichi screamed just as he turned around. Somehow the big basket of dried leaves had caught fire. Yokichi had tried to pound the flames out just as he and his friends did out-of-doors, but instead of dying the flames had leapt up and licked his cheeks. That was when he had screamed.

Shocked at what he saw Uhei dropped the tea cup once more. Then he thrust Yokichi aside. Without thinking he picked up the fire tongs and began raking the burning leaves apart. He moved so slowly that this did no good at all. It would have been much better had he simply thrown the whole basket outside where the wind would have sent the burning leaves scattering harmlessly over the ground. Now there was no time for that. The flames leapt up again, singeing his hand and cheek. He could not see. By the time he recovered, the flames had spread to the bundles of straw hanging from the roof beams. Seconds later they were licking at the inside of the roof itself as if trying to escape from the dark interior of the house. The bundles of burning straw fell to the ground, rekindling the fire in the smoldering leaves below. Uhei stood dazed as the burning straw fell about him. By the time he fled outdoors the underside of the roof was red with fire. Smoke poured from the eves as flames shot into the air. The wind raged overhead, more violently than before, as if it were trying to snatch the flames away.

An instant later the entire rim of the roof was ablaze. Seeing that and recognizing the catastrophe that was occurring Uhei collapsed dejectedly to the ground, smoke rising from his tattered kimono where the flames from the falling straw had singed it. He lay motionless, like a clod of dirt, as the dust blew all around him. Nearby Yokichi wailed in pain from his burns.

Trying yet again to remove the flames that were blocking its path the wind swept across the thatched roof with all its remaining might. At that the fire dove under the thatch and grew steadily stronger. The wind now hurled huge sparks to press the flames to the side and keep them from rising straight up into its sky. Most of the sparks were cut off by the swaying trees of East Neighbor's forest, but some found their way down the gap opened up by the surveyors years ago and landed on a corner of East Neighbor's roof.

The sooty bamboo poles under Kanji's roof had exploded from the force of the blaze, resounding like rifle shots. Neighbors heard and came running just as the ridge pole collapsed and flames shot up defiantly into the air. By then East Neighbor's house had caught fire, and everyone rushed to the scene. Large and solidly built, the house was not going to burn down quickly. Aided by daylight the villagers had time to remove most of the furnishings to safety before the blaze took hold and sent them scurrying away.

Growing steadily stronger the flames now towered above the cedars that surrounded East Neighbor's compound. From the tree-tops the wind assaulted them, driving them down and to the side. The flames fought back, roaring louder than the wind, and sank their talons into the branches. As the resinous needles sizzled the bamboo roof poles of the house exploded. So intense was the heat that the crowd of would-be firefighters was driven steadily backward, the thin stream of water from their pump impotent before the blazing inferno. With a crash that resounded across the paddies and through the forests the massive ridge pole crashed to the ground, spewing flames in all directions. Down swept the wind, and the flames retreated. Now and then a single tendril of fire would break free and soar above the treetops, only to be beaten down once more. Smoke filled the air.

The crowd of villagers milled about in near panic. No one even cast a glance in the direction of Kanji's yard.

Meanwhile Kanji wielded his mattock in a far-off clearing, surrounded by yellowish brown mist and totally unaware of the diaster that had struck. Only when he saw a man from his village hastening along a nearby path and asked him what the matter was did he learn about the fire. Hearing that it was at East Neighbor's house he set off immediately, with Otsugi in tow. A moment later something struck his foot. Looking back he saw that his purse had jarred loose and fallen to the ground. Impatiently he undid his sash and retied it with the purse safely inside the knot. Then he took off again, running as fast as he could. He was too concerned about the master to notice that Otsugi was not keeping pace.

When he finally reached the rice paddies behind the village and saw the thick smoke rising from the trees around the master's house Kanji felt a surge of panic. Anxiously he looked for his own rooftop through the trees, but it was nowhere in sight, not even when the wind blew the treetops low. All he could see was a thin, menacing column of smoke. Entering the yard he saw before him nothing but a pile of smoldering timbers. Relentlessly the wind swept over the embers, sucking up the ash as soon as it formed. Like red fangs the fire gleamed from countless fissures, devouring the core of the wood. Kanji stood dumbfounded at the sight as the wind buffeted his feet. Then he noticed Yokichi standing nearby, sobbing, and saw with alarm that the boy's cheeks were burned. Uhei was next to him, laid out on a mat that someone had brought. His back was turned and his hand covered the burn on his face.

'What happened?' Kanji demanded.

'The leaves caught fire,' Yokichi sobbed.

'You weren't messing around with 'em, were you?' Kanji thundered.

'I was just there by the fire with Grampa, and then they caught fire,' the boy mumbled as he burst into tears.

Kanji threw his mattock to the ground, its blade digging into the soil near Uhei's head, and ran towards the pile of embers that had once been his house. Feeling the intense heat he drew back and stood by helplessly. The drooping, charred stalks of bamboo at the edge of the forest caught his eye, and then he heard the tumult of voices from next door. Suddenly he remembered why he had come running back from the field. But he could not bring himself to go to the master's aid. Not now. He stood there exhausted, listening to the tumult, and a wave of bitterness swept over him. He wanted to cry. His axe, his rake, all the things he needed to start cleaning up the debris had been consumed by the flames. He was empty-handed. Wearily he picked up his mattock and approached the embers once more. The heat drove him back a few steps. Without a thought to the damage it would do to the blade he thrust the mattock toward one of the few timbers that was still standing and toppled it over.

Panting, Otsugi stepped through the opening in the hedge and saw that her home and the few items of clothing she had managed to accumulate over the years had disappeared. She stood stunned, sweat pouring down her forehead, mourning her loss. Then she saw Yokichi and Uhei laid out on the ground like a corpse. She dropped her rake and ran to Yokichi, gently cradling his burned face in her arms. He was wailing uncontrollably, the sound so pathetic that it made one want to cry. Tears welled up in Otsugi's eyes as she held him to her. She did not ask how it had happened. Holding Yokichi to her, she knelt by Uhei's mat. 'Grampa,' she said softly. In her voice was none of the childish tone she usually used in trying to placate him when he and Kanji were at odds. The word slipped out naturally, filled with the grief she felt. Uhei heard and opened his eyes. He tried to turn his head, but just then dust struck his cheek. He lay back and closed his eyes again.

'Did you get hurt?' Otsugi asked. She lifted his hand and saw the burn on his left cheek. 'Does it sting?' she asked. 'It doesn't look too bad, so you shouldn't worry.' Gently she put her hand on his singed hair. Uhei lay still beneath her touch. For an instant he seemed about to speak, but a gust of wind silenced him.

Otsugi listened to the shouting from next door and a wave of hopelessness engulfed her. Tears streamed down her cheeks onto Uhei's white hair. Eventually she looked up and caught a glimpse of Kanji, sweat pouring from his face, as he moved fitfully back and forth. Suddenly remembering the fire Otsugi picked up her rake and went to her father's aid.

Just then Kanji noticed how hot his mattock had become. When he ran to the well to cool it off he found that the bucket had broken free from its hook and was dangling high in the air above him. He tossed the mattock into the well sink and took up Otsugi's rake.

Suddenly the wind abated and the setting sun appeared at the edge of a low ridge of clouds. For a moment the trees were bathed in flame-colored light. As the sunlight faded and the air grew colder the remains of the fire glowed steadily brighter. Next door the weary firefighters sat down to fill their bellies from the buckets of rice balls that people had brought from near and far.

Afterwards the men from the village began an overnight fire watch, while the men from nearby villages began heading home. A few passersby stopped at Kanji's yard briefly to offer condolences. South Neighbor sent someone over with a basket of rice balls. Later East Neighbor sent over a few of the buckets of rice balls he had received. Other neighbors helped load Uhei onto a cart, which Kanji pulled to the prayer hall. Afterwards he himself went to convey his condolences to East Neighbor, but he was unable to mutter more than a few words before fleeing home.

That night the three of them kept a vigil by the remains of their fire, sitting on the mat that someone had brought for Uhei and not yet come to claim. Kanji was exhausted. He wanted to find out more about how the fire got started, but Yokichi's continued sobbing restrained him.

26

As frost crept forward during the night they kept moving the mat on which they sat closer to the dying embers of the fire. Dressed only in thin work clothes Kanji and Otsugi were keenly aware of the cold behind them and the heat ahead. The night air bit into Yokichi's burns, but the heat only increased the pain. Each time they edged towards the fire he burst into tears. Eventually he grew too tired to cry and began moaning. Somehow they found that even more disconcerting. Neither of them slept at all.

The next morning smoke rose faintly from the fallen beams and pillars. Kanji and Otsugi spent the entire day raking the ashes into piles, with only the cold rice balls in the buckets they had received the night before to sustain them. Kanji piled the charred remains of the beams and pillars by the hedge and splashed water on those that seemed to be smoldering still. From the ashes he gradually uncovered a few pots, pans, and other utensils. Those made of metal had retained their shape although they looked as if they had been thrown away years ago. Kanji piled them carefully off to the side. All the pottery had broken in the heat and not a single cup or plate could be salvaged.

At one point the tip of his sandal struck something small and hard. It was a mass of blackened coins. Kanji quickly looked around, but all he saw was Otsugi intently raking ashes. He picked up the coins and moved into the shadows of the bamboo thicket where he undid his sash and freed his purse from its knot. He dropped the coins into the purse and hastily retied his sash. Nervously he looked around again.

Kanji planned to scatter the ashes over his paddy and dry fields. To keep them dry he covered the piles with the straw and millet stalks some of his neighbors had brought by that morning. South Neighbor's wife came by to give them an old tea kettle and some cups. The water in the kettle was still warm. Eagerly they sat down on their single mat to have a drink and rest.

Meanwhile a large crowd had gathered at East Neighbor's and spent the day clearing up the debris there. Not one of them offered Kanji any help. Their attention focused on the master, less out of gratitude for what he had done for them in the past than out of concern for the future. The night before they had been invisible. In the light of day they knew they would be seen by the master's family and their contributions noted.

Kanji worked in his yard, driving himself on despite his weariness. As he and his children made ready for another night out-of-doors, this time without any embers to keep them warm, someone came and invited them to South Neighbor's house. There Kanji and Otsugi were each able to sink into a hot bath and wash away the sweat, dust and ashes that covered their bodies. They slept soundly at last. Yokichi's cheeks were swollen and covered with blisters the next morning, so South Neighbor's wife smeared his face with sesame oil.

Kanji now set about building a temporary shelter. He used charred beams for the frame and millet stalks as thatch for the roof and walls. To make a simple floor he split some of the charred bamboo from the forest behind him and laid it on the ground. The saw and the axe were borrowed from South Neighbor since the blades of all the tools he had recovered from the ashes had been rendered useless by the fire. It took him two days of constant work to complete the job. Inside the hut were the tea kettle and cups they had received from South Neighbor and the buckets East Neighbor had sent over the night of the fire. There was not a single piece of bedding. Nor was there even a simple hearth dug into the dirt floor by the entrance. To heat water they hung the kettle from a bamboo tripod directly over the fire. The pots and pans they had salvaged were stacked uselessly nearby, still awaiting polishing.

Otsugi, although busy helping Kanji, had not forgotten Uhei. The day after the fire she had sneaked away without a word to her father and visited the prayer hall. Lacking even a single *sen* of her own to buy Uhei something, she had roasted a few of the leftover rice balls in the embers of the fire until they were brown and carried them with her in her apron. Uhei had been alone, curled up in the bedding someone had provided. By his pillow were a small pot and a tray with a tea cup and a soup bowl upside-down on a plate. He was asleep, his pale, wizened face toward the door.

For a moment Otsugi leaned forward, straining to hear his breathing. Then she lifted the lid on the pot. Inside was some rice gruel. When she lifted the bowl she found a little bean paste on the plate. She placed one of the roasted rice balls by his pillow and hurried away. Uhei did not open his eyes. At last he was sleeping deeply.

Once the hut was finished Kanji made the rounds of the neighbors, who gave or loaned him a few old mats and other essential household items. Meanwhile Otsugi set about polishing their burned pots and pans with a whetstone. Parting with some of the coins in his purse Kanji then brought home some bedding and a little rice, barley and bean paste. Life was returning to normal at last.

In a few days the blisters on Yokichi's cheeks broke open. Under the dead skin the flesh was raw and slightly ulcerated. Kanji at last felt sorry for the little boy and began to worry that he might be scarred for life if nothing were done. Without delay he took Yokichi to the doctor across the Kinu River. Smiling all the while the doctor covered the burns with gauze soaked in medicine and wrapped a bandage around the boy's head. He bandaged his hands as well even though the burns on them were less serious. Yokichi was a sight when he returned home, his face swathed in white. Once he had been bandaged the pain subsided and, no longer needing to fear contact with his face or hands, he began roaming the village again at will. The doctor had said that if the bandage dried out it could be removed in five or six days. If it got wetter that meant the burns were getting worse and Yokichi should be brought to see him straight away. Fortunately only a little pus formed, so it seemed he would be all right.

Every so often Otsugi found time to visit Uhei. Still without money to buy him anything she secretly hid some of the rice Kanji had bought in her apron when she set out. It was mixed with barley, of course. She did not expect Uhei to like it, but she thought it might do in a gruel of some sort. As it turned out she need not have gone to the trouble, for Uhei's friends in the prayer group took turns supplying him with decent food.

'Are you feeling any better, Grampa?' she would ask gently every time she visited. 'Has the pain gone?' Oil had been swabbed on his burns. It glowed darkly on the dead cells beneath his broken blisters. Patches of new red tissue were visible here and there. Since even cold air moving over the burns caused him pain, Uhei had to remain on his left side, with his head resting on his arm and his injured cheek facing downward.

'It won't take long to heal up, will it?' Otsugi said, staring at the burns. She spoke as if she were asking about her own wounds.

'I guess not,' Uhei muttered.

Otsugi continued sweetly, 'Now that we've got a little house built we ought to be able to take you home soon.'

That made Uhei smile. 'What sort of house?' he asked.

'What sort? It's just a shack, really, made with burned pillars. The walls aren't even plastered.'

'But there's some straw or thatch, isn't there?'

'Oh yes, but if you brush against it, it makes a lot of noise.' Otsugi had been speaking loudly. Suddenly embarrassed, she knelt low over his pillow and lapsed into silence. Imagining the shack made Uhei recall the damage he and Yokichi had caused. He winced.

'Does it hurt?' Otsugi asked uneasily, catching the change in his expression. The longer she spent with him the more depressed she felt. It was time she got back to work. 'I'll come again,' she whispered as she hurried off. After she had gone the tears welled up in Uhei's eyes. Caught for a moment in the wrinkles on his face, they dropped one by one onto the pillow.

Not once did Kanji visit the prayer hall. After a week he took Yokichi back to the doctor to have the dirty bandages removed. Once again the doctor prepared some medicine. This time he made the paste thicker than before and after applying some of it he put the rest and some extra gauze in a sack. 'You needn't come all this way again,' he told Kanji. 'Just put some of this on from time to time and the burns will heal up fine.'

Yokichi's recovery proceeded rapidly thereafter. Every now and then he stopped by to visit Uhei. The sight of the bandage made the old man sad.

Once when Yokichi went to the prayer hall the slightly built old man from the drinking party was there, applying oil to Uhei's burns. 'Don't let it get you down,' he was saying. 'These burns aren't so bad, and this oil will fix 'em up just fine.' Uhei lay still while the oil was applied.

'No good letting it get to you,' the only man continued, intent on cheering Uhei up. 'That time one of the horses bit my arm, I just bandaged myself up and kept going. Sweat the size of beans was pouring off me, but I didn't give in. As long as you don't give in, wounds will heal up fast. They say old people heal slow, but that's a lot of nonsense.' He spoke less loudly than when he was drunk, but there was still a lot of vigor in his voice. 'It was my fault I got hurt that time. The horses were all excited, and I stuck out my arm to calm 'em down. The one that bit me thought I was just another horse.'

'I got white medicine put on me!' Yokichi declared. He had been staring at Uhei's oil-covered burns for some time.

'Well this stuff here works faster,' the slightly built old man retorted as he put the dish of oil back in its nook on the shrine.

'But the doctor gave me more medicine and told me I didn't have to come back,' Yokichi said after a moment's pause.

'And you think that medicine will cure you?' the old man teased.

Yokichi seemed alarmed. 'Well, I suppose so. Anyway the pain is gone already.'

'You got more of that white medicine?' Uhei asked. His voice was barely audible.

'Uh-huh.'

'And your sister puts it on for you?'

'No, she doesn't.'

'Well, what's it for then?'

'I don't know. Papa keeps it somewhere.' Yokichi leaned against the step and tapped his clogs on the dirt floor below as he answered Uhei's questions.

'Don't you worry about medicine,' the slightly built old man interrupted. 'This oil will fix you up.' In a more vehement tone he said to Yokichi, 'That father of yours, he's a mean one. Taking you to the doctor and spending money on you. But he hasn't come here once! It's for crimes like that that he had his house burned down!'

'But Papa says it was Grampa who burned his house down,' Yokichi muttered.

'He says that?' the old man thundered. 'What did you tell him anyway?'

Yokichi turned pale and did not answer for a moment. 'I said we were there keeping warm, and then the leaves caught fire.'

'It doesn't matter what you said,' Uhei broke in.

'Doesn't it?' the other old man shouted. 'It was an accident! He can't blame you for that.'

'Well, Papa said Grampa wouldn't want to come home after what he did,' Yokichi protested. He was frightened by the old man's shouting, but he was old enough now to try to hold his ground.

'He said that? And does your sister agree?'

'No, she doesn't. She told Papa she came to visit Grampa and then Papa got mad at her. She got mad at Papa, too.' Yokichi felt no compunction about saying all he knew in front of Uhei.

'And your papa doesn't get mad at you for coming here?' The slightly built old man had been taken aback by what Yokichi had said and spoke less forcefully.

'No. If it looks like he's going to, I run away.'

Uhei listened to the exchange with his eyes tightly shut, his face pale. The fire in the hearth had burned out. For a time the three were silent.

'Don't you have anything for me, Grampa?' Yokichi finally asked, a slight quaver in his voice.

'I don't have a *sen* to my name,' Uhei muttered thickly. He cleared his throat and added sadly, 'I had a little money left, but it got burned up along with my tobacco pouch, I suppose.'

'The pouch burned up for sure, but the coins should've turned up when they sifted through the ashes. Maybe somebody stole 'em.' There was a glint in the slightly built old man's eyes as he spoke.

'All I know is Otsugi hasn't said a thing about 'em, and she's been here almost every day. It doesn't matter, though. I don't think I'm ever going to get over these burns.'

'Stop that nonsense,' the slightly built old man grumbled. 'I'm going to ask about those coins. I just bet they turned up.' Looking at Yokichi he yelled, 'You clear out of here now! A big boy like you has no business begging.'

Yokichi retreated, crestfallen. As Uhei watched him go tears welled up in his eyes. He made no attempt to wipe them away.

27

That night the temperature plummeted. Although it was April the cold steadfastly refused to release the land from its grip. Around midnight Uhei got up and lit a fire in the prayer hall hearth. The flames that fluttered up around the base of the tea kettle cast a faint light on his haggard face. He sat gloomily by the hearth, his eyes shut, languidly tossing faggots onto the fire. For a time he seemed to lose consciousness. Just as the flames were about to succumb to the darkness around them he stood up. The festering burn on his cheek was barely visible. Then the fire sizzled out, and his figure disappeared from view. He opened the door and staggered outside. The cold wind hurled icy daggers at him. Uhei shuddered.

That same night Kanji and the children lay huddled beneath their quilts. At one point Kanji became aware that his feet were freezing cold. The icy air rushed into the narrow hut like so many prying pine needles. The trees in the forest moved impatiently. Kanji lay beneath his quilt, fully awake now, listening to a faint rustling on the roof not far above his head. Gradually the sound died away and the cold rushed in anew through the cracks in the wall. From somewhere far off in the distance came the shrill crowing of a cock. Kanji woke Otsugi. As long as dawn was near he decided he had rather get warm by the fire than stay uncomfortably in bed.

When Otsugi stepped outside a moment later she found everything covered in mounds of fresh snow. Huge flakes were still tumbling aslant through the air. She stood transfixed as the north wind gusted about her. Inside Kanji lit a fire in a pile of dried leaves and faggots. The smoke billowed from the eves and then swooped downward, its upward path impeded by the swirling snowflakes. Otsugi picked up the buckets that had been stowed by the doorway. One of them was half full of snow. When she started making her way under the eves the wind whipped at her hair as if it had been waiting for the chance, and snowflakes clustered on the nape of her neck. Both the well bucket and its pole were trimmed in white.

The snow fell lightly on the ground as she filled the well bucket. Just as she turned around a gust of wind hit the bamboo thicket on the other side of the yard and sent snow flying in all directions. Finding it hard to breathe as the wind hit her full in the face she turned to the side. In disbelief she gaped at what she saw beneath the nearby persimmon tree. Letting go of the well bucket she moved forward a· bit, then kicked off her sandals and began running.

'Papa!' she yelled. 'Something awful has happened!'

The agitation in her voice brought Kanji out into the yard. A cold shiver went down his spine. There under the persimmon tree was Uhei, his head leaning against the trunk and snow lying in patches from his chest to his legs. A piece of rope stretched across his body.

'Grampa!' Otsugi cried into his ear, but the old man did not move. The festering burn on his cheek startled Kanji. This was the first time he had seen Uhei since the night of the fire.

'Don't just stand there, Papa!' Otsugi exclaimed as she brushed the snow off Uhei and tried to lift him up. Kanji bent down, his hands trembling, and together they managed to carry Uhei inside and lay him out on a straw mat. In a daze Kanji got to his feet. He stared at the old man's burn, and then all of a sudden he dashed out through the snow to South Neighbor's house.

'Anybody up?' he yelled at the doorway. He caught a glimpse of South Neighbor's wife, dressed in a padded kimono, lighting a fire in the stove, and heard a startled voice nearby. South Neighbor's head poked out from under his quilt.

'Something awful, over at my house,' Kanji gasped. 'Won't you come?' Then he dashed off again through the snow.

South Neighbor got up and hunted for his clogs. He could tell from Kanji's behavior that something out of the ordinary had happened, but he was not about to dash off into a snowstorm without a straw cloak and an umbrella. Not knowing what was in store he set out a few minutes later, plodding awkwardly through the drifts. The entrance to Kanji's hut was so low and narrow that his body blocked the light when he stepped inside. After being out in the snow he found he could not see a thing. He could only hear that Kanji was nearby scolding Yokichi.

When Kanji had returned home Uhei was lying where he had left him. The snow that had remained on him had melted, and his padded kimono was slightly damp. Kanji glanced at his burn again and then at Otsugi, who knelt beside him with her hand against his chest.

'His body's still warm, Papa,' she whispered, 'and he's

breathing.' Kanji felt a wave of relief. He reached over and pulled the quilt off Yokichi, then tugged the boy's arm to wake him up. Yokichi opened his eyes, startled by the rough treatment.

'Hurry up there!' Kanji scolded as the boy hesitated. 'Get your clothes on.'

'That's the best thing,' South Neighbor said as soon as he had heard a brief account of what had happened. 'Get him covered up good. He'll be all right when he warms up. Maybe you should take off his clothes. They're pretty damp.' He picked up Yokichi's quilt and placed it over Uhei. 'This is pretty dirty, isn't it, but it's still warm. You better run over to my house and get him a padded robe to wear while his is drying. This quilt won't be enough.'

The fire had burned out. Carefully keeping his distance, Yokichi tossed leaves on it to get it going again.

'You let Otsū do that!' Kanji commanded as he dashed out the door.

'Bring some more quilts, too, if you can manage 'em!' yelled South Neighbor as Kanji disappeared into the falling snow.

With South Neighbor's help it was no problem to stretch Uhei out on the bedding. Otsugi dried out his clothes by the fire while Kanji kept the blaze going with leaves and faggots. He was too busy even to think how hard it would be to find more fuel now that the forest was blanketed in snow. Slowly Uhei began breathing regularly.

The unusually late snowfall finally ended that afternoon. The sky lay leaden overhead, as if exhausted. When Otsugi stepped out to draw more water from the well she found the bucket heavy with snow and about to break free from its hook. The bamboo at the edge of the forest was bent low towards the ground. As if gasping for breath one of the little leaves would flutter in the breeze, but the snow, heavy with moisture not powdery as in winter, had the stalks firmly in its grasp and refused to let go. Viewed from the north the tall trees had stood like white poles, but now they began slowly to shed the snow from their trunks. Only at the edge of the mulberry field did the thick yellow buds of a few rape stalks that had gone to seed and some withered mugwort rise above the thick blanket of white. Buntings swooped gracefully from the branches of the mulberry trees and hopped about nearby.

The snow had already melted in some of the poorer paddy fields, leaving only the ridges around them starkly white. By evening the ridges too had begun to reemerge, and treetops everywhere had shed their mantles of white. Smoke rose from snow-covered rooftops as the sun set.

Uhei lay asleep, breathing quietly, as melting snow dripped

noisily from the eves overhead. That night South Neighbor's wife delivered two more quilts. She made a second trip later to see how Uhei was getting on. After she left, Yokichi climbed into the bedding at Uhei's feet. Otsugi lay down beside them under one of the borrowed quilts. Kanji spread a mat on the dirt-floored entry and sat down with the other quilt wrapped around him. Leaning back with his feet outstretched he stared into the darkness, the steady dripping outside reverberating in his ears.

The next day dawned brilliantly bright and clear with warm sunlight flooding the entry to the hut. Snow that had survived the night melted in a flurry, and everywhere the soil reasserted its command.

Uhei opened his eyes and looked around uncertainly. It had seemed like the dead of winter to him just before he had lost consciousness, but now he was bathed in the warm light of spring. The sudden change left him bewildered.

He had wept after Yokichi left the prayer hall, deeply hurt by what the boy unwittingly had revealed. He had been too tired to feel anger. Hopelessness swept over him instead. That night as he sat by the languishing fire his mood suddenly changed, and he went outside. As he moved forward in the darkness something caught around his foot. He reached down and picked up a coil of rope. The next thing he knew he was standing in Kanji's yard trying to loop the rope over one of the lower branches of the persimmon tree. It was too dark, his hands too stiff. He tried several times to no avail. Then the north wind had swept down across the rice paddies and through the trees, biting into his flesh. He could hardly move his hands at all now. It began to snow. Exhausted, Uhei sought shelter beneath the persimmon tree. He could feel the snow melting against his neck and trickling down his chest. As his body grew stiffer he felt a slight tingling on his scalp. Far off in the distance he heard a cock crow. Then all was silent, and he dozed off. Had he remained undiscovered for only a short while longer the death he wished for would have overtaken him. But Kanji mistook the white glint of the snow that was visible through the cracks in the wall for daylight and sent Otsugi outside for water. Because of that Uhei was saved.

'You feeling bad, Grampa?' Otsugi murmured when she saw him looking around in bewilderment. 'How about a little something to eat?'

Uhei nodded.

'Are you feeling better, Father?' Kanji added. He was relieved that Uhei had regained consciousness. 'Does your burn still hurt?'

'I still can't sleep on it,' Uhei muttered.

Kanji dashed away and came back a while later with a roll of bleached cotton cloth wrapped up in a newspaper. He plastered a piece of gauze with the rest of the white medicine he had got from the doctor and applied it to Uhei's cheek. Then he cut the cloth into strips and wrapped them around Uhei's head. Uhei lay back and let Kanji do as he wished. Kanji looked at his handiwork with satisfaction. True, the bandage was clumsily tied and would have come loose with the slightest movement. But it covered up the wound he found so unsettling and made him feel he had done his duty. Uhei, too, felt happier, although he could not figure out why.

Overcome with nervousness Kanji went out again. Uhei closed his eyes as the sunlight peeped in through the cracks and played about his feet. When he opened his eyes again he whispered 'Otsū?'

'What is it?' she answered, leaning towards him.

He pulled the right hand out from under the covers and placed it on the top quilt. 'It's so hot. Can't you take one of these off me?'

'It is hot, isn't it. The sun is really sparkling today.' Otsugi removed a quilt and folded it at Uhei's feet. 'This one is really heavy,' she said. 'You'll feel a lot better without it. But it's good you're feeling warm at last. I was really worried yesterday.'

'Can't for the life of me remember weather like this,' Uhei remarked. 'All that snow after the equinox! But from now on it'll just get warmer and warmer. You'll be able to see the barley growing day by day.'

'Our barley's doing just fine already,' Otsugi said with a touch of pride. 'I used to hate all that plowing, but Papa said we had to plow deep or the nightsoil wouldn't be any use.'

'He's right. You have to plow deep for decent yields. In my day that's how we did it, but some farmers nowadays think they know better and plow shallow.'

'At first I got so tired, but now Papa says I dig deeper than he does.'

'We used to say that if you turned farming over to a woman she'd ruin the field in three years, but you seem to be doing just fine.'

'And now that I'm used to it, it doesn't seem like such hard work anymore.'

Uhei rose up a little and pushed the remaining quilt down a bit with his feet. Otsugi caught a glimpse of the burn on his hand.

'You hurt your hand too, Grampa! How about putting some of that medicine on it?' She took the hand in hers and looked at the burn more closely. 'It's not really so bad, though, is it.'

At that moment Kanji came bustling into the hut with several quilts tied to his back. As he put them down he asked, 'Weren't you a little cold last night, Father?'

'He's feeling hot now,' Otsugi broke in. 'We just took one of the quilts off.'

'Ah yes, so you have. Well, we still have to return the ones we borrowed from South Neighbor, so you'll need these anyway.' Kanji inspected Uhei's bandage. 'Has the medicine helped, Father?'

'I can rest easy on the pillow now,' Uhei replied.

Kanji gazed proudly at the bandage. 'I'm thinking of going across the river tomorrow. Anything I can bring you to eat?' he asked, a hint of anxiety in his voice.

'Well now,' Uhei muttered. He swallowed and said, 'I can't think of anything just now.' There was a faint sparkle in his eyes.

'How about some millet jelly, Papa?' Otsugi suggested. 'I'll hide it so Yokichi doesn't get at it. Would you like that, Grampa?'

Uhei nodded.

'And we need another bowl, too. Get a big one that I can use for gruel. You can have 'em fill it up with the jelly.'

'Okay.'

'And as long as you're going, get some medicine. Grampa's hand needs bandaging too.'

'I already thought of the medicine, so you didn't have to mention it,' Kanji protested. His purse had kept them going since the fire, and he still had enough cash left to buy a few more necessities. With the wages he was owed for clearing land that winter he was sure they would get by. But to get even part of that money he would have to go to East Neighbor. The very thought of doing that, when his own fire had burned the master's house down, made him tremble.

28

Kanji went out again that afternoon, a troubled expression on his face as he walked, head bent forward, along the path. The warm sunlight had already begun drying out the soil in the upland fields. Mere specks of white a short while before, the flowers on the magnolia trees that dotted the village had opened fully and seemed to be floating in the blue sky. Green finches darted from the sunshine into the dark bamboo thickets as if oblivious to the difference between winter and spring, but within moments they came hopping back across the ground toward the light. Nothing could resist the warmth.

With his eyes downcast as before Kanji finally passed through the master's gate. All the debris had been cleared away, and only the bare foundation stones of the large house that had stood in the center of the compound remained as testimony to the fire. The trees that surrounded the yard, many of them singed red, seemed taller than before, and the yard itself appeared sunken. Kanji trembled.

The master's family had moved to temporary quarters in part of the gatehouse. To Kanji both the master and the mistress seemed totally at ease, as if no disaster had occurred to them at all. The terror that had gripped him began to subside. When the mistress greeted him sympathetically he finally found the courage to speak.

'There's no one as unlucky as me, Ma'am. No one,' he began in a plaintive tone. It was the first time since the fire that anyone seemed willing to listen to his troubles. 'Maybe it doesn't seem that way to you, what with me having so little to lose.' He was so wrapped up in his own grief that he could think of nothing else. Suddenly he remembered that his own fire had destroyed the master's house as well, and he felt ashamed.

'Well, as they say, one mustn't get too attached to the things of this world,' the mistress responded. 'A house, now that can be rebuilt quickly if we put our minds to it. But not the trees. I feel sorry for them, but nothing can help them now.' As she spoke she gazed at several tall, burned trees nearby. Although they still soared upward it was clear they were fated to wither and die. The rays of the setting sun gleamed through their upper branches. Kanji turned pale and hung his head. He could not speak.

'Oh, I have been thoughtless,' the mistress now said. 'Since you've been burned out too, won't you let me give you a little money?'

'Yes, Ma'am,' Kanji muttered, his head bowed even lower. 'That would be a big help to me, but I didn't know how to ask you for it.' He touched his hand to his tousled hair in a gesture of deference.

'Don't you worry. We can still afford to help you out.'

'But you see, it was a punishment. That's the only way I can figure it.' Kanji hesitated a moment. 'A punishment for making my wife die.' He lowered his voice. 'I have to build some sort of house, Ma'am, and then I want to settle things for my family. Please keep looking after me, Ma'am. My boy will be old enough to work in a few years, and then I'll take him out of school and start training him in farming.'

'I see,' the mistress murmured consolingly.

'I want to ask you something else, Ma'am. About what's called being unfilial to parents. If a parent doesn't make a complaint to the police the police can't do anything, can they?'

'Well, I have the impression the police don't act rashly in such matters,' the mistress replied, a little surprised by the question.

'You see, I'm thinking about looking after Grampa from now on. You don't think it's too late, do you?'

'Oh no, not at all! Old people are always grateful when they're treated kindly. You be good to him. You know, he doesn't have much time left.'

'Him and me, we had a nice talk yesterday, and he looked pleased. I put some of the burn medicine I got for my boy on him. It ran out, so I've got to go to the doctor again. But it's too late for that today. I'll go tomorrow, and Otsū told me to buy some millet jelly for him too, as long as I was over there.'

'Yes, I heard he'd got burned. So that's why you brought him back home.'

'Uh, yes,' Kanji muttered sheepishly. At the same time he was relieved to find that the mistress somehow had not heard about what had happened at dawn the day before.

'And another thing, Okamisan,' he said abruptly, looking anxious. 'If someone got a hold of another person's money, he'd end up being punished for it, wouldn't he?'

'Well now.' The mistress was startled by the change of topic and had no idea what Kanji was driving at.

He took no notice of her puzzlement but went on compulsively, expressing his pent-up fear. 'But if he didn't spend it on himself, that'd be all right, wouldn't it?'

'I don't know what sort of money you're talking about, but I'd say it would be wrong to spend it.'

'But Okamisan, if someone lost it and you didn't let on at first you'd found it, then it'd look funny giving it back later, wouldn't it? Like you stole it even. It'd be better to give the person something instead. That's it. That way there'd be no trouble at all.'

'Oh no, if you find someone's money the right thing is to give it back.' The mistress spoke softly but emphatically.

Kanji winced and glanced up at her dejectedly. 'So maybe if he gave it back and then did something for the person who'd lost it everything would be all right.'

'I suppose so,' the mistress replied. She had remembered now about the trouble Kanji used to get into stealing, but she did not feel inclined to probe any further into what it was he was so agitated about. Instead she reached for some coins and laid them on the mat beside her. 'Now then, about settling things for your family. Just what did you have in mind?' she asked gently.

'Ah yes, Ma'am,' Kanji mumbled, his head bowed so low the words were scarcely audible. 'I . . . well . . .' He was too upset to say more. He felt as if he were fainting. Someone seemed to be calling him from a distance, and then he came to. It had been the mistress's voice.

'Why don't you put this money away?' she was asking. She could do nothing more for him and wanted the conversation to end.

'Thank you very much, Okamisan,' Kanji responded formally. When he withdrew his purse from his sash he noticed how thin it felt. He peered inside for an instant and reached in to withdraw a coin from the bottom. The charred crust that had covered it when he had picked it up from the ashes had fallen away in places, revealing the bright copper underneath. Kanji brought the coin closer to his eyes and stared at it intently. Suddenly he became aware of what he was doing. With a flustered glance towards the mistress he dropped the coin back into his purse.

Translator's Note

As mentioned in the introduction, the main characters in *The Soil* were drawn from life. With the exception of 'Oshina', who died in 1903 at the age of 38, all of them outlived the author.

'The Master' died in 1921 at the age of 64.

'Kanji' died in 1936 at the age of 71.

'Uhei' died in 1942 at the age of 94.

'The Mistress' died in 1944 at the age of 81.

'Yokichi' died in 1972 at the age of 73.

'Otsugi' died in 1978 at the age of 91. Her husband of many years died the following day, and a joint burial service was held for the two of them.

Glossary of Japanese Terms

bu unit of weight; one-tenth of a *momme*; 37.4 centigrams
furoshiki square cloth for wrapping packages and bundles
hakama a long, divided skirt for men's formal wear
haori a short formal coat
kanpyō dried gourd shavings
kiriboshi dried strips of radish
konnyaku devil's tongue (an edible plant)
mo old unit of coinage; one-tenth of a *rin*
momme unit of weight; 3.75 grams
nenbutsu a Buddhist invocation
okamisan an honorific term of address for another's wife;
    madam
ominaeshi a flowering plant (patrinia scabiosaefolia)
rin old unit of coinage; one-tenth of a *sen*
sakaki an evergreen shrub belonging to the camellia family;
    used in Shinto rituals
sen old unit of coinage; hundredth part of a yen
shu old unit of coinage; of less value than a *mo*
tabi cloth socks
toda a perennial wild grain, similar in appearance to rice
udo a perennial shrub with edible leaves
umeboshi pickled plum
yukata an unlined cotton garment for summer wear; similar
    in style to a kimono